15,000

Spanish Verbs

fully conjugated in all the tenses
using pattern verbs

by Stephen Thompson, Ph.D.

The Center for Innovative Language Learning
Washington, DC

R
468.2421
T3778f
1998

Address all inquiries to:
The Center for Innovative Language Learning
320 Independence Avenue, Southeast
Washington, DC 20003   USA

Library of Congress Catalog Card Number (LCCN): 97-91633

International Standard Book Number (ISBN): 0965141810

Publisher's Cataloging-in-Publication Data

Thompson, Stephen J.
    15,000 Spanish verbs fully conjugated in all the tenses using pattern verbs/ by Stephen J. Thompson.
    p.   cm.
ISBN: 0965141810
1. Spanish language-Verb-Tables. I. Title.
PC4271.T46 1998
468.2'421

Printed in Canada

20 19 18 17 16 15 14 13 12 11 10 9 8 7 6 5 4 3 2 1

*I hope this book makes your study and use
of Spanish easier and more enjoyable.*

To my parents, family, and friends, with love and gratitude.

*For helpful suggestions, I wish to especially thank Mark Churchwell,
Gilbert Galván, William Hermann, William Jennings,
Lee-Alison Sibley, and Anton Trinidad.*

*My thanks to David Rabasca, without whose encouragement this book
would not have come to fruition, and to Mark Churchwell
for proofreading the final manuscript.*

*I wish to gratefully acknowledge Lee-Alison Sibley and her 150 7th and 8th grade
students of Spanish in the public school system of Fairfax County, Virginia, who, for an
entire school year, used and successfully classroom-tested
an earlier version of this book.*

Introduction

This self-teaching book lets you   see at a glance which conjugations are irregular, and which <u>part</u> of a conjugation is irregular. The book does that by showing the irregular part of a conjugation in red. Omitted letters are indicated by showing the next letter in red. Showing the irregular part of a conjugation in red helps you find and learn irregular conjugations. No other book does that.

This book is easy to use. Just follow the two steps of instruction on the back cover. Four examples on the back cover illustrate the instructions.

Sections of the book are easy to locate. Hold the book with the back cover facing you. Slightly bend the book with your right hand, exposing the page markers in the book. Line up a page marker in the table of contents on the back cover with a page marker in the book. That is the page where a section begins. Open the book to that page.

Spanish is a verb-rich language because descriptive, precise verbs are used more commonly than in English. This book makes learning Spanish more fun and relevant to your own life by helping you use verbs related to your own academic studies, hobbies, friendships, personal interests, job, and leisure activities. It does this by not restricting you to a particular, smaller set of verbs that may have been selected for inclusion in other conjugation books because the verbs are more general and less descriptive. Similarly, this book will take you further than other books, because it:

 ◆ has more verb patterns;
 ◆ has more verbs keyed to those verb patterns; and
 ◆ describes in words what each pattern verb illustrates.

In addition, this book helps you learn and use the subjunctive mood. It does that by placing the subjunctive next to its counterpart indicative mood. If you are not ready to learn and use the subjunctive, you can easily ignore it. The feature is important because in Spanish the subjunctive is used much more frequently than in English. It is used to express emotions, to indicate uncertainty (such as a future event), to signal doubt, and to make requests. So, when you want to speak and write more authentic Spanish, and when you want to more fully understand Spanish speakers and writers, this book can help you more than other Spanish verb conjugation books.

The small size and light weight of this book make it a convenient traveling companion that you can easily slip into your pocket, purse, briefcase, or backpack.

This book makes a welcome gift -- to pre-teens and up, to beginning students of Spanish and fluent users of the language, including teachers, translators, travelers and those who use Spanish at home, work or with friends.

The subject and reflexive pronouns are on the page facing pattern 1 for easy reference. The subject pronouns are omitted from the non-reflexive conjugations in order to emphasize the verb forms.

On April 27, 1994, the Spanish language academies eliminated ch and ll as separate letters of the Spanish alphabet. So, ch and ll, at any place in a word, are now alphabetized the same as in English.

Pattern Verbs

in alphabetical order

Subject Pronouns for Non-reflexive Verbs

<u>Singular</u>

yo
tú
usted (Ud.), él, ella, ello

<u>Plural</u>

nosotros, nosotras
vosotros, vosotras
ustedes (Uds.), ellos, ellas

Reflexive Pronouns

<u>Singular</u>

me
te
se

<u>Plural</u>

nos
os
se

Pattern 1: regular "ar" verbs.
No example verb is needed. Add the verb stem you want.
Present participle: -ando   Past participle: -ado

Singular		Plural	
Indicativo	*Subjunctivo*	*Indicativo*	*Subjunctivo*
Presente	*Presente*	*Presente*	*Presente*
-o	-e	-amos	-emos
-as	-es	-áis	-éis
-a	-e	-an	-en
Imperfecto	*Imperfecto*	*Imperfecto*	*Imperfecto*
-aba	-ara OR -ase	-ábamos	-áramos OR -ásemos
-abas	-aras OR -ases	-abais	-arais OR -aseis
-aba	-ara OR -ase	-aban	-aran OR -asen
Pretérito		*Pretérito*	
-é		-amos	
-aste		-asteis	
-ó		-aron	
Futuro	*Futuro*	*Futuro*	*Futuro*
-aré	-are	-aremos	-áremos
-arás	-ares	-aréis	-areis
-ará	-are	-arán	-aren
Potencial		*Potencial*	
-aría		-aríamos	
-arías		-aríais	
-aría		-arían	

Imperativo	
Singular	Plural
(not used); no (not used)	-emos; no -emos
-a; no -es	-ad; no -éis
-e; no -e	-en; no -en

Conjugate reflexive verbs the same as above, use a reflexive pronoun as shown on page 80, and make the changes for imperatives and present participles shown there in red.
Make compound tenses by adding a past participle on page 83 or 84.
Translation possibilities are on page 88. Conjugation tips are on page 89.

2
regular "er" verbs

Pattern 2: regular "er" verbs.
No example verb is needed. Add the verb stem you want.
Present participle: -iendo   Past participle: -ido

Singular		Plural	
Indicativo	*Subjunctivo*	*Indicativo*	*Subjunctivo*
Presente	*Presente*	*Presente*	*Presente*
-o	-a	-emos	-amos
-es	-as	-éis	-áis
-e	-a	-en	-an
Imperfecto	*Imperfecto*	*Imperfecto*	*Imperfecto*
-ía	-iera	-íamos	-iéramos
	OR		OR
	-iese		-iésemos
-ías	-ieras	-íais	-ierais
	OR		OR
	-ieses		-ieseis
-ía	-iera	-ían	-ieran
	OR		OR
	-iese		-iesen
Pretérito		*Pretérito*	
-í		-imos	
-iste		-isteis	
-ió		-ieron	
Futuro	*Futuro*	*Futuro*	*Futuro*
-eré	-iere	-eremos	-iéremos
-erás	-ieres	-eréis	-iereis
-erá	-iere	-erán	-ieren
Potencial		*Potencial*	
-ería		-eríamos	
-erías		-eríais	
-ería		-erían	

Imperativo	
Singular	*Plural*
(not used); no (not used)	-amos; no -amos
-e; no -as	-ed; no -áis
-a; no -a	-an; no -an

Conjugate reflexive verbs the same as above, use a reflexive pronoun as shown on page 81, and make the changes for imperatives and present participles shown there in red.
Make compound tenses by adding a past participle on page 83 or 84.
Translation possibilities are on page 88. Conjugation tips are on page 90.

Pattern 3: regular "ir" verbs.
No example verb is needed. Add the verb stem you want.
Present participle: -iendo   Past participle: -ido

Singular		Plural	
Indicativo	*Subjunctivo*	*Indicativo*	*Subjunctivo*
Presente	*Presente*	*Presente*	*Presente*
-o	-a	-imos	-amos
-es	-as	-ís	-áis
-e	-a	-en	-an
Imperfecto	*Imperfecto*	*Imperfecto*	*Imperfecto*
-ía	-iera	-íamos	-iéramos
	OR		OR
	-iese		-iésemos
-ías	-ieras	-íais	-ierais
	OR		OR
	-ieses		-ieseis
-ía	-iera	-ían	-ieran
	OR		OR
	-iese		-iesen
Pretérito		*Pretérito*	
-í		-imos	
-iste		-isteis	
-ió		-ieron	
Futuro	*Futuro*	*Futuro*	*Futuro*
-iré	-iere	-iremos	-iéremos
-irás	-ieres	-iréis	-iereis
-irá	-iere	-irán	-ieren
Potencial		*Potencial*	
-iría		-iríamos	
-irías		-iríais	
-iría		-irían	

Imperativo	
Singular	Plural
(not used); no (not used)	-amos; no -amos
-e; no -as	-id; no -áis
-a; no -a	-an; no -an

Conjugate reflexive verbs the same as above, use a reflexive pronoun as shown on page
   82, and make the changes for imperatives and present participles shown there in red.
Make compound tenses by adding a past participle on page 83 or 84.
Translation possibilities are on page 88. Conjugation tips are on page 91.

4
abolir

Pattern 4: Some conjugations customarily are not used.
Abolir (abol-ir) (to abolish, annul) is the pattern verb.
Present participle: abol-iendo   Past participle: abol-ido

Singular		Plural	
Indicativo	*Subjunctivo*	*Indicativo*	*Subjunctivo*
Presente	*Presente*	*Presente*	*Presente*
(not used)	(not used)	abol-imos	(not used)
(not used)	(not used)	abol-ís	(not used)
(not used)	(not used)	(not used)	(not used)
Imperfecto	*Imperfecto*	*Imperfecto*	*Imperfecto*
abol-ía	abol-iera	abol-íamos	abol-iéramos
	OR		OR
	abol-iese		abol-iésemos
abol-ías	abol-ieras	abol-íais	abol-ierais
	OR		OR
	abol-ieses		abol-ieseis
abol-ía	abol-iera	abol-ían	abol-ieran
	OR		OR
	abol-iese		abol-iesen
Pretérito		*Pretérito*	
abol-í		abol-imos	
abol-iste		abol-isteis	
abol-ió		abol-ieron	
Futuro	*Futuro*	*Futuro*	*Futuro*
abol-iré	abol-iere	abol-iremos	abol-iéremos
abol-irás	abol-ieres	abol-iréis	abol-iereis
abol-irá	abol-iere	abol-irán	abol-ieren
Potencial		*Potencial*	
abol-iría		abol-iríamos	
abol-irías		abol-iríais	
abol-iría		abol-irían	

Imperativo	
Singular	Plural
(not used); no (not used)	(not used); no (not used)
(not used); no (not used)	abol-id; no abol-áis
(not used); no (not used)	(not used); no (not used)

Conjugate reflexive verbs the same as above, use a reflexive pronoun as shown on page 82, and make the changes for imperatives and present participles shown there in red.
Make compound tenses by adding a past participle on page 83 or 84.
Translation possibilities are on page 88. Conjugation tips are on page 91.

Pattern 5: i in stem ⟹ ie when stressed.
Adquirir (adquir-ir) (to acquire) is the pattern verb.
Present participle: adquir-iendo   Past participle: adquir-ido

Singular		Plural	
Indicativo	*Subjunctivo*	*Indicativo*	*Subjunctivo*

Presente	*Presente*	*Presente*	*Presente*
adquier-o	adquier-a	adquir-imos	adquier-amos
adquier-es	adquier-as	adquir-ís	adquir-áis
adquier-e	adquier-a	adquier-en	adquier-an

Imperfecto	*Imperfecto*	*Imperfecto*	*Imperfecto*
adquir-ía	adquir-iera OR adquir-iese	adquir-íamos	adquir-iéramos OR adquir-iésemos
adquir-ías	adquir-ieras OR adquir-ieses	adquir-íais	adquir-ierais OR adquir-ieseis
adquir-ía	adquir-iera OR adquir-iese	adquir-ían	adquir-ieran OR adquir-iesen

Pretérito		*Pretérito*	
adquir-í		adquir-imos	
adquir-iste		adquir-isteis	
adquir-ió		adquir-ieron	

Futuro	*Futuro*	*Futuro*	*Futuro*
adquir-iré	adquir-iere	adquir-iremos	adquir-iéremos
adquir-irás	adquir-ieres	adquir-iréis	adquir-iereis
adquir-irá	adquir-iere	adquir-irán	adquir-ieren

Potencial		*Potencial*	
adquir-iría		adquir-iríamos	
adquir-irías		adquir-iríais	
adquir-iría		adquir-irían	

Imperativo	
Singular	Plural
(not used); no (not used)	adquir-amos; no adquir-amos
adquier-e; no adquier-as	adquir-id; no adquir-áis
adquier-a; no adquier-a	adquier-an; no adquier-an

Conjugate reflexive verbs the same as above, use a reflexive pronoun as shown on page 82, and make the changes for imperatives and present participles shown there in red.
Make compound tenses by adding a past participle on page 83 or 84.
Translation possibilities are on page 88. Conjugation tips are on page 91.

6
agorar

Agorar (agor-ar) (to predict) is the pattern verb.
Present participle: agor-ando Past participle: agor-ado

Singular		Plural	
Indicativo	*Subjunctivo*	*Indicativo*	*Subjunctivo*
Presente	*Presente*	*Presente*	*Presente*
agüer-o	agüer-e	agor-amos	agor-emos
agüer-as	agüer-es	agor-áis	agor-éis
agüer-a	agüer-e	agüer-an	agüer-en
Imperfecto	*Imperfecto*	*Imperfecto*	*Imperfecto*
agor-aba	agor-ara	agor-ábamos	agor-áramos
	OR		OR
	agor-ase		agor-ásemos
agor-abas	agor-aras	agor-abais	agor-arais
	OR		OR
	agor-ases		agor-aseis
agor-aba	agor-ara	agor-aban	agor-aran
	OR		OR
	agor-ase		agor-asen
Pretérito		*Pretérito*	
agor-é		agor-amos	
agor-aste		agor-asteis	
agor-ó		agor-aron	
Futuro	*Futuro*	*Futuro*	*Futuro*
agor-aré	agor-are	agor-aremos	agor-áremos
agor-arás	agor-ares	agor-aréis	agor-areis
agor-ará	agor-are	agor-arán	agor-aren
Potencial		*Potencial*	
agor-aría		agor-aríamos	
agor-arías		agor-aríais	
agor-aría		agor-arían	

Imperativo	
Singular	Plural
(not used); no (not used)	agor-emos; no agor-emos
agüer-a; no agüer-es	agor-ad; no agor-éis
agüer-e; no agüer-e	agüer-en; no agüer-en

Conjugate reflexive verbs the same as above, use a reflexive pronoun as shown on page 80, and make the changes for imperatives and present participles shown there in red.
Make compound tenses by adding a past participle on page 83 or 84.
Translation possibilities are on page 88. Conjugation tips are on page 89.

Pattern 7: gu ➧ gü before e to retain the gw sound.
Aguar (agu-ar) (to water, dilute, spoil, mar) is the pattern verb.
Present participle: agu-ando   Past participle: agu-ado

Singular		Plural	
Indicativo	*Subjunctivo*	*Indicativo*	*Subjunctivo*
Presente	*Presente*	*Presente*	*Presente*
agu-o	agü-e	agu-amos	agü-emos
agu-as	agü-es	agu-áis	agü-éis
agu-a	agü-e	agu-an	agü-en
Imperfecto	*Imperfecto*	*Imperfecto*	*Imperfecto*
agu-aba	agu-ara OR agu-ase	agu-ábamos	agu-áramos OR agu-ásemos
agu-abas	agu-aras OR agu-ases	agu-abais	agu-arais OR agu-aseis
agu-aba	agu-ara OR agu-ase	agu-aban	agu-aran OR agu-asen
Pretérito		*Pretérito*	
agü-é		agu-amos	
agu-aste		agu-asteis	
agu-ó		agu-aron	
Futuro	*Futuro*	*Futuro*	*Futuro*
agu-aré	agu-are	agu-aremos	agu-áremos
agu-arás	agu-ares	agu-aréis	agu-areis
agu-ará	agu-are	agu-arán	agu-aren
Potencial		*Potencial*	
agu-aría		agu-aríamos	
agu-arías		agu-aríais	
agu-aría		agu-arían	

Imperativo	
Singular	Plural
(not used); no (not used)	agü-emos; no agü-emos
agu-a; no agü-es	agu-ad; no agü-éis
agü-e; no agü-e	agü-en; no agü-en

Conjugate reflexive verbs the same as above, use a reflexive pronoun as shown on page
80, and make the changes for imperatives and present participles shown there in red.
Make compound tenses by adding a past participle on page 83 or 84.
Translation possibilities are on page 88. Conjugation tips are on page 89.

8
ahincar

Pattern 8: i ➡ í when stressed, c ➡ qu before e.
Ahincar (ahinc-ar) (to urge, press) is the pattern verb.
Present participle: ahinc-ando   Past participle: ahinc-ado

Singular		Plural	
Indicativo	*Subjunctivo*	*Indicativo*	*Subjunctivo*
Presente	*Presente*	*Presente*	*Presente*
ahínc-o	ahínqu-e	ahinc-amos	ahinqu-emos
ahínc-as	ahínqu-es	ahinc-áis	ahinqu-éis
ahínc-a	ahínqu-e	ahínc-an	ahínqu-en
Imperfecto	*Imperfecto*	*Imperfecto*	*Imperfecto*
ahinc-aba	ahinc-ara OR ahinc-ase	ahinc-ábamos	ahinc-áramos OR ahinc-ásemos
ahinc-abas	ahinc-aras OR ahinc-ases	ahinc-abais	ahinc-arais OR ahinc-aseis
ahinc-aba	ahinc-ara OR ahinc-ase	ahinc-aban	ahinc-aran OR ahinc-asen
Pretérito		*Pretérito*	
ahinqu-é		ahinc-amos	
ahinc-aste		ahinc-asteis	
ahinc-ó		ahinc-aron	
Futuro	*Futuro*	*Futuro*	*Futuro*
ahinc-aré	ahinc-are	ahinc-aremos	ahinc-áremos
ahinc-arás	ahinc-ares	ahinc-aréis	ahinc-areis
ahinc-ará	ahinc-are	ahinc-arán	ahinc-aren
Potencial		*Potencial*	
ahinc-aría		ahinc-aríamos	
ahinc-arías		ahinc-aríais	
ahinc-aría		ahinc-arían	

Imperativo	
Singular	Plural
(not used); no (not used)	ahinqu-emos; no ahinqu-emos
ahínc-a; no ahínqu-es	ahinc-ad; no ahinqu-éis
ahínqu-e; no ahínqu-e	ahínqu-en; no ahínqu-en

Conjugate reflexive verbs the same as above, use a reflexive pronoun as shown on page 80, and make the changes for imperatives and present participles shown there in red.
Make compound tenses by adding a past participle on page 83 or 84.
Translation possibilities are on page 88. Conjugation tips are on page 89.

8

Pattern 9: i ⟹ í, (u ⟹ ú in verbs like actuar). I.e., the weak vowel i or u is stressed. **9**
Airar (air-ar) (to anger, irritate) is the pattern verb.
Present participle: air-ando   Past participle: air-ado   **airar**

Singular		Plural	
Indicativo	*Subjunctivo*	*Indicativo*	*Subjunctivo*
Presente	*Presente*	*Presente*	*Presente*
aír-o	aír-e	air-amos	air-emos
aír-as	aír-es	air-áis	air-éis
aír-a	aír-e	aír-an	aír-en
Imperfecto	*Imperfecto*	*Imperfecto*	*Imperfecto*
air-aba	air-ara	air-ábamos	air-áramos
	OR		OR
	air-ase		air-ásemos
air-abas	air-aras	air-abais	air-arais
	OR		OR
	air-ases		air-aseis
air-aba	air-ara	air-aban	air-aran
	OR		OR
	air-ase		air-asen
Pretérito		*Pretérito*	
air-é		air-amos	
air-aste		air-asteis	
air-ó		air-aron	
Futuro	*Futuro*	*Futuro*	*Futuro*
air-aré	air-are	air-aremos	air-áremos
air-arás	air-ares	air-aréis	air-areis
air-ará	air-are	air-arán	air-aren
Potencial		*Potencial*	
air-aría		air-aríamos	
air-arías		air-aríais	
air-aría		air-arían	

Imperativo	
Singular	*Plural*
(not used); no (not used)	air-emos; no air-emos
aír-a; no aír-es	air-ad; no air-éis
aír-e; no aír-e	aír-en; no aír-en

Conjugate reflexive verbs the same as above, use a reflexive pronoun as shown on page
  80, and make the changes for imperatives and present participles shown there in red.
Make compound tenses by adding a past participle on page 83 or 84.
Translation possibilities are on page 88. Conjugation tips are on page 89.

10
andar

Pattern 10: a ➡ i or ie, é ➡ e, ó ➡ o, uv is added.
Andar (and-ar) (to walk) is the pattern verb.
Present participle: and-ando   Past participle: and-ado

Singular		Plural	
Indicativo	*Subjunctivo*	*Indicativo*	*Subjunctivo*
Presente	*Presente*	*Presente*	*Presente*
and-o	and-e	and-amos	and-emos
and-as	and-es	and-áis	and-éis
and-a	and-e	and-an	and-en
Imperfecto	*Imperfecto*	*Imperfecto*	*Imperfecto*
and-aba	anduv-iera	and-ábamos	anduv-iéramos
	OR		OR
	anduv-iese		anduv-iésemos
and-abas	anduv-ieras	and-abais	anduv-ierais
	OR		OR
	anduv-ieses		anduv-ieseis
and-aba	anduv-iera	and-aban	anduv-ieran
	OR		OR
	anduv-iese		anduv-iesen
Pretérito		*Pretérito*	
anduv-e		anduv-imos	
anduv-iste		anduv-isteis	
anduv-o		anduv-ieron	
Futuro	*Futuro*	*Futuro*	*Futuro*
and-aré	anduv-iere	and-aremos	anduv-iéremos
and-arás	anduv-ieres	and-aréis	anduv-iereis
and-ará	anduv-iere	and-arán	anduv-ieren
Potencial		*Potencial*	
and-aría		and-aríamos	
and-arías		and-aríais	
and-aría		and-arían	

Imperativo	
Singular	*Plural*
(not used); no (not used)	and-emos; no and-emos
and-a; no and-es	and-ad; no and-éis
and-e; no and-e	and-en; no and-en

Conjugate reflexive verbs the same as above, use a reflexive pronoun as shown on page 80, and make the changes for imperatives and present participles shown there in red.
Make compound tenses by adding a past participle on page 83 or 84.
Translation possibilities are on page 88. Conjugation tips are on page 89.

Pattern 11: Some conjugations customarily are not used.
Aplacer (aplac-er) (to please, to satisfy) is the pattern verb.
Present participle: aplac-iendo   Past participle: aplac-ido

Singular		Plural	
Indicativo	*Subjunctivo*	*Indicativo*	*Subjunctivo*
Presente	*Presente*	*Presente*	*Presente*
(not used)	(not used)	(not used)	(not used)
(not used)	(not used)	(not used)	(not used)
aplac-e	(not used)	aplac-en	(not used)
Imperfecto	*Imperfecto*	*Imperfecto*	*Imperfecto*
(not used)	(not used)	(not used)	(not used)
	OR		OR
	(not used)		(not used)
(not used)	(not used)	(not used)	(not used)
	OR		OR
	(not used)		(not used)
aplac-ía	(not used)	aplac-ían	(not used)
	OR		OR
	(not used)		(not used)
Pretérito		*Pretérito*	
(not used)		(not used)	
(not used)		(not used)	
(not used)		(not used)	
Futuro	*Futuro*	*Futuro*	*Futuro*
(not used)	(not used)	(not used)	(not used)
(not used)	(not used)	(not used)	(not used)
(not used)	(not used)	(not used)	(not used)
Potencial		*Potencial*	
(not used)		(not used)	
(not used)		(not used)	
(not used)		(not used)	

Imperativo	
Singular	Plural
(not used); no (not used)	(not used); no (not used)
(not used); no (not used)	(not used); no (not used)
(not used); no (not used)	(not used); no (not used)

Conjugate reflexive verbs the same as above, use a reflexive pronoun as shown on page 81, and make the changes for imperatives and present participles shown there in red.
Make compound tenses by adding a past participle on page 83 or 84.
Translation possibilities are on page 88. Conjugation tips are on page 90.

12
argüir

Pattern 12: i ⟹ y, y is added, ü ⟹ u before y.
Argüir (argü-ir) (to argue) is the pattern verb.
Present participle: argu-yendo   Past participle: argü-ido

Singular		Plural	
Indicativo	*Subjunctivo*	*Indicativo*	*Subjunctivo*
Presente	*Presente*	*Presente*	*Presente*
arguy-o	arguy-a	argü-imos	arguy-amos
arguy-es	arguy-as	argü-ís	arguy-áis
arguy-e	arguy-a	arguy-en	arguy-an
Imperfecto	*Imperfecto*	*Imperfecto*	*Imperfecto*
argü-ía	argu-yera	argü-íamos	argu-yéramos
	OR		OR
	argu-yese		argu-yésemos
argü-ías	argu-yeras	argü-íais	argu-yerais
	OR		OR
	argu-yeses		argu-yeseis
argü-ía	argu-yera	argü-ían	argu-yeran
	OR		OR
	argu-yese		argu-yesen
Pretérito		*Pretérito*	
argü-í		argü-imos	
argü-iste		argü-isteis	
argu-yó		argu-yeron	
Futuro	*Futuro*	*Futuro*	*Futuro*
argü-iré	argu-yere	argü-iremos	argu-yéremos
argü-irás	argu-yeres	argü-iréis	argu-yereis
argü-irá	argu-yere	argü-irán	argu-yeren
Potencial		*Potencial*	
argü-iría		argü-iríamos	
argü-irías		argü-iríais	
argü-iría		argü-irían	

Imperativo	
Singular	*Plural*
(not used); no (not used)	arguy-amos; no arguy-amos
arguy-e; no arguy-as	argü-id; no arguy-áis
arguy-a; no arguy-a	arguy-an; no arguy-an

Conjugate reflexive verbs the same as above, use a reflexive pronoun as shown on page 82, and make the changes for imperatives and present participles shown there in red.
Make compound tenses by adding a past participle on page 83 or 84.
Translation possibilities are on page 88. Conjugation tips are on page 91.

Pattern 13: g is added.
Asir (as-ir) (to grasp) is the pattern verb.
Present participle: as-iendo   Past participle: as-ido

Singular		Plural	
Indicativo	*Subjunctivo*	*Indicativo*	*Subjunctivo*
Presente	*Presente*	*Presente*	*Presente*
asg-o	asg-a	as-imos	asg-amos
as-es	asg-as	as-ís	asg-áis
as-e	asg-a	as-en	asg-an
Imperfecto	*Imperfecto*	*Imperfecto*	*Imperfecto*
as-ía	as-iera	as-íamos	as-iéramos
	OR		OR
	as-iese		as-iésemos
as-ías	as-ieras	as-íais	as-ierais
	OR		OR
	as-ieses		as-ieseis
as-ía	as-iera	as-ían	as-ieran
	OR		OR
	as-iese		as-iesen
Pretérito		*Pretérito*	
as-í		as-imos	
as-iste		as-isteis	
as-ió		as-ieron	
Futuro	*Futuro*	*Futuro*	*Futuro*
as-iré	as-iere	as-iremos	as-iéremos
as-irás	as-ieres	as-iréis	as-iereis
as-irá	as-iere	as-irán	as-ieren
Potencial		*Potencial*	
as-iría		as-iríamos	
as-irías		as-iríais	
as-iría		as-irían	

Imperativo	
Singular	Plural
(not used); no (not used)	asg-amos; no asg-amos
as-e; no asg-as	as-id; no asg-áis
asg-a; no asg-a	asg-an; no asg-an

Conjugate reflexive verbs the same as above, use a reflexive pronoun as shown on page 82, and make the changes for imperatives and present participles shown there in red.
Make compound tenses by adding a past participle on page 83 or 84.
Translation possibilities are on page 88. Conjugation tips are on page 91.

14
atañer

Pattern 14: Some conjugations customarily are not used.
Atañer (atañ-er) (to concern) is the pattern verb.
Present participle: atañ-endo   Past participle: atañ-ido

Singular		Plural	
Indicativo	*Subjunctivo*	*Indicativo*	*Subjunctivo*
Presente	*Presente*	*Presente*	*Presente*
(not used)	(not used)	(not used)	(not used)
(not used)	(not used)	(not used)	(not used)
atañ-e	atañ-a	atañ-en	atañ-an
Imperfecto	*Imperfecto*	*Imperfecto*	*Imperfecto*
(not used)	(not used)	(not used)	(not used)
	OR		OR
	(not used)		(not used)
(not used)	(not used)	(not used)	(not used)
	OR		OR
	(not used)		(not used)
atañ-ía	atañ-era	atañ-ían	atañ-eran
	OR		OR
	atañ-ese		atañ-esen
Pretérito		*Pretérito*	
(not used)		(not used)	
(not used)		(not used)	
atañ-ó		atañ-eron	
Futuro	*Futuro*	*Futuro*	*Futuro*
(not used)	(not used)	(not used)	(not used)
(not used)	(not used)	(not used)	(not used)
atañ-erá	atañ-ere	atañ-erán	atañ-eren
Potencial		*Potencial*	
(not used)		(not used)	
(not used)		(not used)	
atañ-ería		atañ-erían	

Imperativo	
Singular	Plural
(not used); no (not used)	(not used); no (not used)
(not used); no (not used)	(not used); no (not used)
atañ-a; no atañ-a	atañ-an; no atañ-an

Conjugate reflexive verbs the same as above, use a reflexive pronoun as shown on page 81, and make the changes for imperatives and present participles shown there in red.
Make compound tenses by adding a past participle on page 83 or 84.
Translation possibilities are on page 88. Conjugation tips are on page 90.

Pattern 15: o ➡ üe when stressed, z ➡ c before e.
Avergonzar (avergonz-ar) (to shame) is the pattern verb.
Present participle: avergonz-ando   Past participle: avergonz-ado

Singular		Plural	
Indicativo	*Subjunctivo*	*Indicativo*	*Subjunctivo*
Presente	*Presente*	*Presente*	*Presente*
averg üenz-o	averg üen c-e	avergonz-amos	avergon c-emos
averg üenz-as	averg üen c-es	avergonz-áis	avergon c-éis
averg üenz-a	averg üen c-e	averg üenz-an	averg üen c-en
Imperfecto	*Imperfecto*	*Imperfecto*	*Imperfecto*
avergonz-aba	avergonz-ara OR avergonz-ase	avergonz-ábamos	avergonz-áramos OR avergonz-ásemos
avergonz-abas	avergonz-aras OR avergonz-ases	avergonz-abais	avergonz-arais OR avergonz-aseis
avergonz-aba	avergonz-ara OR avergonz-ase	avergonz-aban	avergonz-aran OR avergonz-asen
Pretérito		*Pretérito*	
avergon c-é		avergonz-amos	
avergonz-aste		avergonz-asteis	
avergonz-ó		avergonz-aron	
Futuro	*Futuro*	*Futuro*	*Futuro*
avergonz-aré	avergonz-are	avergonz-aremos	avergonz-áremos
avergonz-arás	avergonz-ares	avergonz-aréis	avergonz-areis
avergonz-ará	avergonz-are	avergonz-arán	avergonz-aren
Potencial		*Potencial*	
avergonz-aría		avergonz-aríamos	
avergonz-arías		avergonz-aríais	
avergonz-aría		avergonz-arían	

Imperativo	
Singular	Plural
(not used); no (not used)	avergon c-emos; no avergon c-emos
averg üenz-a; no averg üen c-es	avergonz-ad; no avergon c-éis
averg üen c-e; no averg üen c-e	averg üen c-en; no averg üen c-en

Conjugate reflexive verbs the same as above, use a reflexive pronoun as shown on page
   80, and make the changes for imperatives and present participles shown there in red.
Make compound tenses by adding a past participle on page 83 or 84.
Translation possibilities are on page 88. Conjugation tips are on page 89.

16
balbucir

Pattern 16: Some conjugations customarily are not used.
Balbucir (balbuc-ir) (to stammer) is the pattern verb.
Present participle: balbuc-iendo   Past participle: balbuc-ido

Singular		Plural	
Indicativo	*Subjunctivo*	*Indicativo*	*Subjunctivo*
Presente	*Presente*	*Presente*	*Presente*
(not used)	(not used)	balbuc-imos	(not used)
(not used)	(not used)	balbuc-ís	(not used)
(not used)	(not used)	(not used)	(not used)
Imperfecto	*Imperfecto*	*Imperfecto*	*Imperfecto*
balbuc-ía	balbuc-iera OR balbuc-iese	balbuc-íamos	balbuc-iéramos OR balbuc-iésemos
balbuc-ías	balbuc-ieras OR balbuc-ieses	balbuc-íais	balbuc-ierais OR balbuc-ieseis
balbuc-ía	balbuc-iera OR balbuc-iese	balbuc-ían	balbuc-ieran OR balbuc-iesen
Pretérito		*Pretérito*	
balbuc-í		balbuc-imos	
balbuc-iste		balbuc-isteis	
balbuc-ió		balbuc-ieron	
Futuro	*Futuro*	*Futuro*	*Futuro*
balbuc-iré	balbuc-iere	balbuc-iremos	balbuc-iéremos
balbuc-irás	balbuc-ieres	balbuc-iréis	balbuc-iereis
balbuc-irá	balbuc-iere	balbuc-irán	balbuc-ieren
Potencial		*Potencial*	
balbuc-iría		balbuc-iríamos	
balbuc-irías		balbuc-iríais	
balbuc-iría		balbuc-irían	

Imperativo	
Singular	*Plural*
(not used); no (not used)	(not used); no (not used)
(not used); no balbuz-as	(not used); no balbuz-áis
(not used); no (not used)	(not used); no (not used)

Conjugate reflexive verbs the same as above, use a reflexive pronoun as shown on page 82, and make the changes for imperatives and present participles shown there in red.
Make compound tenses by adding a past participle on page 83 or 84.
Translation possibilities are on page 88. Conjugation tips are on page 91.

Pattern 17: i is deleted before e or o.
Bruñir (bruñ-ir) (to polish) is the pattern verb.
Present participle: bruñ-endo   Past participle: bruñ-ido

	Singular			*Plural*	
	Indicativo	*Subjunctivo*		*Indicativo*	*Subjunctivo*
Presente	*Presente*		*Presente*	*Presente*	
	bruñ-o	bruñ-a		bruñ-imos	bruñ-amos
	bruñ-es	bruñ-as		bruñ-ís	bruñ-áis
	bruñ-e	bruñ-a		bruñ-en	bruñ-an
Imperfecto	*Imperfecto*		*Imperfecto*	*Imperfecto*	
	bruñ-ía	bruñ-era		bruñ-íamos	bruñ-éramos
		OR			OR
		bruñ-ese			bruñ-ésemos
	bruñ-ías	bruñ-eras		bruñ-íais	bruñ-erais
		OR			OR
		bruñ-eses			bruñ-eseis
	bruñ-ía	bruñ-era		bruñ-ían	bruñ-eran
		OR			OR
		bruñ-ese			bruñ-esen
Pretérito			*Pretérito*		
	bruñ-í			bruñ-imos	
	bruñ-iste			bruñ-isteis	
	bruñ-ó			bruñ-eron	
Futuro	*Futuro*		*Futuro*	*Futuro*	
	bruñ-iré	bruñ-ere		bruñ-iremos	bruñ-éremos
	bruñ-irás	bruñ-eres		bruñ-iréis	bruñ-ereis
	bruñ-irá	bruñ-ere		bruñ-irán	bruñ-eren
Potencial			*Potencial*		
	bruñ-iría			bruñ-iríamos	
	bruñ-irías			bruñ-iríais	
	bruñ-iría			bruñ-irían	

Imperativo	
Singular	*Plural*
(not used); no (not used)	bruñ-amos; no bruñ-amos
bruñ-e; no bruñ-as	bruñ-id; no bruñ-áis
bruñ-a; no bruñ-a	bruñ-an; no bruñ-an

Conjugate reflexive verbs the same as above, use a reflexive pronoun as shown on page
  82, and make the changes for imperatives and present participles shown there in red.
Make compound tenses by adding a past participle on page 83 or 84.
Translation possibilities are on page 88. Conjugation tips are on page 91.

18
caber

Pattern 18: a ➡ u or e, b ➡ p, c ➡ qu before e.
Caber (cab-er) (to fit, to fit into) is the pattern verb.
Present participle: cab-iendo   Past participle: cab-ido

Singular		Plural	
Indicativo	*Subjunctivo*	*Indicativo*	*Subjunctivo*
Presente	*Presente*	*Presente*	*Presente*
quep-o	quep-a	cab-emos	quep-amos
cab-es	quep-as	cab-éis	quep-áis
cab-e	quep-a	cab-en	quep-an
Imperfecto	*Imperfecto*	*Imperfecto*	*Imperfecto*
cab-ía	cup-iera	cab-íamos	cup-iéramos
	OR		OR
	cup-iese		cup-iésemos
cab-ías	cup-ieras	cab-íais	cup-ierais
	OR		OR
	cup-ieses		cup-ieseis
cab-ía	cup-iera	cab-ían	cup-ieran
	OR		OR
	cup-iese		cup-iesen
Pretérito		*Pretérito*	
cup-e		cup-imos	
cup-iste		cup-isteis	
cup-o		cup-ieron	
Futuro	*Futuro*	*Futuro*	*Futuro*
cab-ré	cup-iere	cab-remos	cup-iéremos
cab-rás	cup-ieres	cab-réis	cup-iereis
cab-rá	cup-iere	cab-rán	cup-ieren
Potencial		*Potencial*	
cab-ría		cab-ríamos	
cab-rías		cab-ríais	
cab-ría		cab-rían	

Imperativo	
Singular	Plural
(not used); no (not used)	quep-amos; no quep-amos
cab-e; no quep-as	cab-ed; no quep-áis
quep-a; no quep-a	quep-an; no quep-an

Conjugate reflexive verbs the same as above, use a reflexive pronoun as shown on page
81, and make the changes for imperatives and present participles shown there in red.
Make compound tenses by adding a past participle on page 83 or 84.
Translation possibilities are on page 88. Conjugation tips are on page 90.

18

Pattern 19: i ➡ í when stressed, g ➡ gu before e.
Cabrahigar (cabrahig-ar) (to pollinate, e.g., fruit trees) is the pattern verb.
Present participle: cabrahig-ando   Past participle: cabrahig-ado

19

cabrahigar

Singular		Plural	
Indicativo	*Subjunctivo*	*Indicativo*	*Subjunctivo*
Presente	*Presente*	*Presente*	*Presente*
cabrahíg-o	cabrahígu-e	cabrahíg-amos	cabrahigu-emos
cabrahíg-as	cabrahígu-es	cabrahíg-áis	cabrahigu-éis
cabrahíg-a	cabrahígu-e	cabrahíg-an	cabrahígu-en
Imperfecto	*Imperfecto*	*Imperfecto*	*Imperfecto*
cabrahig-aba	cabrahig-ara OR cabrahig-ase	cabrahig-ábamos	cabrahig-áramos OR cabrahig-ásemos
cabrahig-abas	cabrahig-aras OR cabrahig-ases	cabrahig-abais	cabrahig-arais OR cabrahig-aseis
cabrahig-aba	cabrahig-ara OR cabrahig-ase	cabrahig-aban	cabrahig-aran OR cabrahig-asen
Pretérito		*Pretérito*	
cabrahigu-é		cabrahig-amos	
cabrahig-aste		cabrahig-asteis	
cabrahig-ó		cabrahig-aron	
Futuro	*Futuro*	*Futuro*	*Futuro*
cabrahig-aré	cabrahig-are	cabrahig-aremos	cabrahig-áremos
cabrahig-arás	cabrahig-ares	cabrahig-aréis	cabrahig-areis
cabrahig-ará	cabrahig-are	cabrahig-arán	cabrahig-aren
Potencial		*Potencial*	
cabrahig-aría		cabrahig-aríamos	
cabrahig-arías		cabrahig-aríais	
cabrahig-aría		cabrahig-arían	

Imperativo	
Singular	Plural
(not used); no (not used)	cabrahigu-emos; no cabrahigu-emos
cabrahíg-a; no cabrahígu-es	cabrahig-ad; no cabrahigu-éis
cabrahígu-e; no cabrahígu-e	cabrahígu-en; no cabrahígu-en

Conjugate reflexive verbs the same as above, use a reflexive pronoun as shown on page 80, and make the changes for imperatives and present participles shown there in red.
Make compound tenses by adding a past participle on page 83 or 84.
Translation possibilities are on page 88. Conjugation tips are on page 89.

20

caer

Pattern 20: add ig, i ➡ í or y. Similar to oír.
Caer (ca-er) (to fall, to decline) is the pattern verb.
Present participle: ca-yendo   Past participle: ca-ído

	Singular			Plural	
	Indicativo	*Subjunctivo*		*Indicativo*	*Subjunctivo*
Presente	*Presente*		*Presente*		*Presente*
	caig-o	caig-a		ca-emos	caig-amos
	ca-es	caig-as		ca-éis	caig-áis
	ca-e	caig-a		ca-en	caig-an
Imperfecto	*Imperfecto*		*Imperfecto*		*Imperfecto*
	ca-ía	ca-yera		ca-íamos	ca-yéramos
		OR			OR
		ca-yese			ca-yésemos
	ca-ías	ca-yeras		ca-íais	ca-yerais
		OR			OR
		ca-yeses			ca-yeseis
	ca-ía	ca-yera		ca-ían	ca-yeran
		OR			OR
		ca-yese			ca-yesen
Pretérito			*Pretérito*		
	ca-í			ca-ímos	
	ca-íste			ca-ísteis	
	ca-yó			ca-yeron	
Futuro	*Futuro*		*Futuro*		*Futuro*
	ca-eré	ca-yere		ca-eremos	ca-yéremos
	ca-erás	ca-yeres		ca-eréis	ca-yereis
	ca-erá	ca-yere		ca-erán	ca-yeren
Potencial			*Potencial*		
	ca-ería			ca-eríamos	
	ca-erías			ca-eríais	
	ca-ería			ca-erían	

	Imperativo	
Singular		Plural
(not used); no (not used)		caig-amos; no caig-amos
ca-e; no caig-as		ca-ed; no caig-áis
caig-a; no caig-a		caig-an; no caig-an

Conjugate reflexive verbs the same as above, use a reflexive pronoun as shown on page
81, and make the changes for imperatives and present participles shown there in red.
Make compound tenses by adding a past participle on page 83 or 84.
Translation possibilities are on page 88. Conjugation tips are on page 90.

20

Pattern 21: z ➡ c before e to retain the s or th sound.
Cazar (caz-ar) (to hunt) is the pattern verb.
Present participle: caz-ando   Past participle: caz-ado

Singular		Plural	
Indicativo	*Subjunctivo*	*Indicativo*	*Subjunctivo*
Presente	*Presente*	*Presente*	*Presente*
caz-o	cac-e	caz-amos	cac-emos
caz-as	cac-es	caz-áis	cac-éis
caz-a	cac-e	caz-an	cac-en
Imperfecto	*Imperfecto*	*Imperfecto*	*Imperfecto*
caz-aba	caz-ara OR caz-ase	caz-ábamos	caz-áramos OR caz-ásemos
caz-abas	caz-aras OR caz-ases	caz-abais	caz-arais OR caz-aseis
caz-aba	caz-ara OR caz-ase	caz-aban	caz-aran OR caz-asen
Pretérito		*Pretérito*	
cac-é		caz-amos	
caz-aste		caz-asteis	
caz-ó		caz-aron	
Futuro	*Futuro*	*Futuro*	*Futuro*
caz-aré	caz-are	caz-aremos	caz-áremos
caz-arás	caz-ares	caz-aréis	caz-areis
caz-ará	caz-are	caz-arán	caz-aren
Potencial		*Potencial*	
caz-aría		caz-aríamos	
caz-arías		caz-aríais	
caz-aría		caz-arían	

Imperativo	
Singular	Plural
(not used); no (not used)	cac-emos; no cac-emos
caz-a; no cac-es	caz-ad; no cac-éis
cac-e; no cac-e	cac-en; no cac-en

Conjugate reflexive verbs the same as above, use a reflexive pronoun as shown on page
   80, and make the changes for imperatives and present participles shown there in red.
Make compound tenses by adding a past participle on page 83 or 84.
Translation possibilities are on page 88. Conjugation tips are on page 89.

22
cocer

Pattern 22: o ➡ ue when stressed, c ➡ z before a or o.
Cocer (coc-er) (to cook, boil) is the pattern verb.
Present participle: coc-iendo   Past participle: coc-ido

Singular		Plural	
Indicativo	Subjunctivo	Indicativo	Subjunctivo
Presente	*Presente*	*Presente*	*Presente*
cuez-o	cuez-a	coc-emos	coz-amos
cuec-es	cuez-as	coc-éis	coz-áis
cuec-e	cuez-a	cuec-en	cuez-an
Imperfecto	*Imperfecto*	*Imperfecto*	*Imperfecto*
coc-ía	coc-iera	coc-íamos	coc-iéramos
	OR		OR
	coc-iese		coc-iésemos
coc-ías	coc-ieras	coc-íais	coc-ierais
	OR		OR
	coc-ieses		coc-ieseis
coc-ía	coc-iera	coc-ían	coc-ieran
	OR		OR
	coc-iese		coc-iesen
Pretérito		*Pretérito*	
coc-í		coc-imos	
coc-iste		coc-isteis	
coc-ió		coc-ieron	
Futuro	*Futuro*	*Futuro*	*Futuro*
coc-eré	coc-iere	coc-eremos	coc-iéremos
coc-erás	coc-ieres	coc-eréis	coc-iereis
coc-erá	coc-iere	coc-erán	coc-ieren
Potencial		*Potencial*	
coc-ería		coc-eríamos	
coc-erías		coc-eríais	
coc-ería		coc-erían	

Imperativo	
Singular	Plural
(not used); no (not used)	coz-amos; no coz-amos
cuec-e; no cuez-as	coc-ed; no coz-áis
cuez-a; no cuez-a	cuez-an; no cuez-an

Conjugate reflexive verbs the same as above, use a reflexive pronoun as shown on page
  81, and make the changes for imperatives and present participles shown there in red.
Make compound tenses by adding a past participle on page 83 or 84.
Translation possibilities are on page 88. Conjugation tips are on page 90.

Pattern 23: g ➡ j before a or o to retain the ha sound.
Coger (cog-er) (to catch, gather, collect) is the pattern verb.
Present participle: cog-iendo   Past participle: cog-ido

Singular		Plural	
Indicativo	*Subjunctivo*	*Indicativo*	*Subjunctivo*
Presente	*Presente*	*Presente*	*Presente*
coj-o	coj-a	cog-emos	coj-amos
cog-es	coj-as	cog-éis	coj-áis
cog-e	coj-a	cog-en	coj-an
Imperfecto	*Imperfecto*	*Imperfecto*	*Imperfecto*
cog-ía	cog-iera	cog-íamos	cog-iéramos
	OR		OR
	cog-iese		cog-iésemos
cog-ías	cog-ieras	cog-íais	cog-ierais
	OR		OR
	cog-ieses		cog-ieseis
cog-ía	cog-iera	cog-ían	cog-ieran
	OR		OR
	cog-iese		cog-iesen
Pretérito		*Pretérito*	
cog-í		cog-imos	
cog-iste		cog-isteis	
cog-ió		cog-ieron	
Futuro	*Futuro*	*Futuro*	*Futuro*
cog-eré	cog-iere	cog-eremos	cog-iéremos
cog-erás	cog-ieres	cog-eréis	cog-iereis
cog-erá	cog-iere	cog-erán	cog-ieren
Potencial		*Potencial*	
cog-ería		cog-eríamos	
cog-erías		cog-eríais	
cog-ería		cog-erían	

Imperativo	
Singular	Plural
(not used); no (not used)	coj-amos; no coj-amos
cog-e; no coj-as	cog-ed; no coj-áis
coj-a; no coj-a	coj-an; no coj-an

Conjugate reflexive verbs the same as above, use a reflexive pronoun as shown on page
    81, and make the changes for imperatives and present participles shown there in red.
Make compound tenses by adding a past participle on page 83 or 84.
Translation possibilities are on page 88. Conjugation tips are on page 90.

24
colgar

Pattern 24: o ⟹ ue when stressed, g ⟹ gu before e.
Colgar (colg-ar) (to hang, to drape) is the pattern verb.
Present participle: colg-ando   Past participle: colg-ado

Singular		Plural	
Indicativo	*Subjunctivo*	*Indicativo*	*Subjunctivo*
Presente	*Presente*	*Presente*	*Presente*
cuelg-o	cuelgu-e	colg-amos	colgu-emos
cuelg-as	cuelgu-es	colg-áis	colgu-éis
cuelg-a	cuelgu-e	cuelg-an	cuelgu-en
Imperfecto	*Imperfecto*	*Imperfecto*	*Imperfecto*
colg-aba	colg-ara OR colg-ase	colg-ábamos	colg-áramos OR colg-ásemos
colg-abas	colg-aras OR colg-ases	colg-abais	colg-arais OR colg-aseis
colg-aba	colg-ara OR colg-ase	colg-aban	colg-aran OR colg-asen
Pretérito		*Pretérito*	
colgu-é		colg-amos	
colg-aste		colg-asteis	
colg-ó		colg-aron	
Futuro	*Futuro*	*Futuro*	*Futuro*
colg-aré	colg-are	colg-aremos	colg-áremos
colg-arás	colg-ares	colg-aréis	colg-areis
colg-ará	colg-are	colg-arán	colg-aren
Potencial		*Potencial*	
colg-aría		colg-aríamos	
colg-arías		colg-aríais	
colg-aría		colg-arían	

Imperativo	
Singular	Plural
(not used); no (not used)	colgu-emos; no colgu-emos
cuelg-a; no cuelgu-es	colg-ad; no colgu-éis
cuelgu-e; no cuelgu-e	cuelgu-en; no cuelgu-en

Conjugate reflexive verbs the same as above, use a reflexive pronoun as shown on page 80, and make the changes for imperatives and present participles shown there in red.
Make compound tenses by adding a past participle on page 83 or 84.
Translation possibilities are on page 88.   Conjugation tips are on page 89.

Pattern 25: o ⟹ ue when stressed.
Contar (cont-ar) (to count) is the pattern verb.
Present participle: cont-ando   Past participle: cont-ado

Singular		Plural	
Indicativo	*Subjunctivo*	*Indicativo*	*Subjunctivo*
Presente	*Presente*	*Presente*	*Presente*
cuent-o	cuent-e	cont-amos	cont-emos
cuent-as	cuent-es	cont-áis	cont-éis
cuent-a	cuent-e	cuent-an	cuent-en
Imperfecto	*Imperfecto*	*Imperfecto*	*Imperfecto*
cont-aba	cont-ara OR cont-ase	cont-ábamos	cont-áramos OR cont-ásemos
cont-abas	cont-aras OR cont-ases	cont-abais	cont-arais OR cont-aseis
cont-aba	cont-ara OR cont-ase	cont-aban	cont-aran OR cont-asen
Pretérito		*Pretérito*	
cont-é		cont-amos	
cont-aste		cont-asteis	
cont-ó		cont-aron	
Futuro	*Futuro*	*Futuro*	*Futuro*
cont-aré	cont-are	cont-aremos	cont-áremos
cont-arás	cont-ares	cont-aréis	cont-areis
cont-ará	cont-are	cont-arán	cont-aren
Potencial		*Potencial*	
cont-aría		cont-aríamos	
cont-arías		cont-aríais	
cont-aría		cont-arían	

Imperativo	
Singular	Plural
(not used); no (not used)	cont-emos; no cont-emos
cuent-a; no cuent-es	cont-ad; no cont-éis
cuent-e; no cuent-e	cuent-en; no cuent-en

Conjugate reflexive verbs the same as above, use a reflexive pronoun as shown on page 80, and make the changes for imperatives and present participles shown there in red.
Make compound tenses by adding a past participle on page 83 or 84.
Translation possibilities are on page 88. Conjugation tips are on page 89.

Pattern 26: i ➡ y or í.
Creer (cre-er) (to believe) is the pattern verb.
Present participle: cre-yendo   Past participle: cre-ído

Singular		Plural	
Indicativo	*Subjunctivo*	*Indicativo*	*Subjunctivo*
Presente	*Presente*	*Presente*	*Presente*
cre-o	cre-a	cre-emos	cre-amos
cre-es	cre-as	cre-éis	cre-áis
cre-e	cre-a	cre-en	cre-an
Imperfecto	*Imperfecto*	*Imperfecto*	*Imperfecto*
cre-ía	cre-yera	cre-íamos	cre-yéramos
	OR		OR
	cre-yese		cre-yésemos
cre-ías	cre-yeras	cre-íais	cre-yerais
	OR		OR
	cre-yeses		cre-yeseis
cre-ía	cre-yera	cre-ían	cre-yeran
	OR		OR
	cre-yese		cre-yesen
Pretérito		*Pretérito*	
cre-í		cre-ímos	
cre-íste		cre-ísteis	
cre-yó		cre-yeron	
Futuro	*Futuro*	*Futuro*	*Futuro*
cre-eré	cre-yere	cre-eremos	cre-yéremos
cre-erás	cre-yeres	cre-eréis	cre-yereis
cre-erá	cre-yere	cre-erán	cre-yeren
Potencial		*Potencial*	
cre-ería		cre-eríamos	
cre-erías		cre-eríais	
cre-ería		cre-erían	

Imperativo	
Singular	Plural
(not used); no (not used)	cre-amos; no cre-amos
cre-e; no cre-as	cre-ed; no cre-áis
cre-a; no cre-a	cre-an; no cre-an

Conjugate reflexive verbs the same as above, use a reflexive pronoun as shown on page 81, and make the changes for imperatives and present participles shown there in red.
Make compound tenses by adding a past participle on page 83 or 84.
Translation possibilities are on page 88. Conjugation tips are on page 90.

Pattern 27: a ➡ i or ie, á ➡ a, e ➡ é, é ➡ e or í, ó ➡ io, y is added.
Dar (d-ar) (to give, cause, yield) is the pattern verb.
Present participle: d-ando   Past participle: d-ado

Singular		Plural	
Indicativo	*Subjunctivo*	*Indicativo*	*Subjunctivo*
Presente	*Presente*	*Presente*	*Presente*
d-oy	d-é	d-amos	d-emos
d-as	d-es	d-ais	d-eis
d-a	d-é	d-an	d-en
Imperfecto	*Imperfecto*	*Imperfecto*	*Imperfecto*
d-aba	d-iera	d-ábamos	d-iéramos
	OR		OR
	d-iese		d-iésemos
d-abas	d-ieras	d-abais	d-ierais
	OR		OR
	d-ieses		d-ieseis
d-aba	d-iera	d-aban	d-ieran
	OR		OR
	d-iese		d-iesen
Pretérito		*Pretérito*	
d-í		d-imos	
d-iste		d-isteis	
d-io		d-ieron	
Futuro	*Futuro*	*Futuro*	*Futuro*
d-aré	d-iere	d-aremos	d-iéremos
d-arás	d-ieres	d-aréis	d-iereis
d-ará	d-iere	d-arán	d-ieren
Potencial		*Potencial*	
d-aría		d-aríamos	
d-arías		d-aríais	
d-aría		d-arían	

Imperativo	
Singular	Plural
(not used); no (not used)	d-emos; no d-emos
d-a; no d-es	d-ad; no d-eis
d-é; no d-é	d-en; no d-en

Conjugate reflexive verbs the same as above, use a reflexive pronoun as shown on page 80, and make the changes for imperatives and present participles shown there in red.
Make compound tenses by adding a past participle on page 83 or 84.
Translation possibilities are on page 88. Conjugation tips are on page 89.

28
decir

Pattern 28: e ⟹ i, c ⟹ g or j, plus other changes.
Decir (dec-ir) (to say, tell, talk) is the pattern verb.
Present participle: dic-iendo   Past participle: dic-ho

Singular		Plural	
Indicativo	*Subjunctivo*	*Indicativo*	*Subjunctivo*
Presente	*Presente*	*Presente*	*Presente*
dig-o	dig-a	dec-imos	dig-amos
dic-es	dig-as	dec-ís	dig-áis
dic-e	dig-a	dic-en	dig-an
Imperfecto	*Imperfecto*	*Imperfecto*	*Imperfecto*
dec-ía	dij-era	dec-íamos	dij-éramos
	OR		OR
	dij-ese		dij-ésemos
dec-ías	dij-eras	dec-íais	dij-erais
	OR		OR
	dij-eses		dij-eseis
dec-ía	dij-era	dec-ían	dij-eran
	OR		OR
	dij-ese		dij-esen
Pretérito		*Pretérito*	
dij-e		dij-imos	
dij-iste		dij-isteis	
dij-o		dij-eron	
Futuro	*Futuro*	*Futuro*	*Futuro*
d-iré	dij-ere	d-iremos	dij-éremos
d-irás	dij-eres	d-iréis	dij-ereis
d-irá	dij-ere	d-irán	dij-eren
Potencial		*Potencial*	
d-iría		d-iríamos	
d-irías		d-iríais	
d-iría		d-irían	

Imperativo

Singular	Plural
(not used); no (not used)	dig-amos; no dig-amos
d-i; no dig-as	dec-id; no dig-áis
dig-a; no dig-a	dig-an; no dig-an

Conjugate reflexive verbs the same as above, use a reflexive pronoun as shown on page 82, and make the changes for imperatives and present participles shown there in red.
Make compound tenses by adding a past participle on page 83 or 84.
Translation possibilities are on page 88. Conjugation tips are on page 91.

Pattern 29: qu ➡ c before a or o to retain the k sound.
Delinquir (delinqu-ir) (to be delinquent) is the pattern verb.
Present participle: delinqu-iendo   Past participle: delinqu-ido

Singular		Plural	
Indicativo	*Subjunctivo*	*Indicativo*	*Subjunctivo*
Presente	*Presente*	*Presente*	*Presente*
delinc-o	delinc-a	delinqu-imos	delinc-amos
delinqu-es	delinc-as	delinqu-ís	delinc-áis
delinqu-e	delinc-a	delinqu-en	delinc-an
Imperfecto	*Imperfecto*	*Imperfecto*	*Imperfecto*
delinqu-ía	delinqu-iera	delinqu-íamos	delinqu-iéramos
	OR		OR
	delinqu-iese		delinqu-iésemos
delinqu-ías	delinqu-ieras	delinqu-íais	delinqu-ierais
	OR		OR
	delinqu-ieses		delinqu-ieseis
delinqu-ía	delinqu-iera	delinqu-ían	delinqu-ieran
	OR		OR
	delinqu-iese		delinqu-iesen
Pretérito		*Pretérito*	
delinqu-í		delinqu-imos	
delinqu-iste		delinqu-isteis	
delinqu-ió		delinqu-ieron	
Futuro	*Futuro*	*Futuro*	*Futuro*
delinqu-iré	delinqu-iere	delinqu-iremos	delinqu-iéremos
delinqu-irás	delinqu-ieres	delinqu-iréis	delinqu-iereis
delinqu-irá	delinqu-iere	delinqu-irán	delinqu-ieren
Potencial		*Potencial*	
delinqu-iría		delinqu-iríamos	
delinqu-irías		delinqu-iríais	
delinqu-iría		delinqu-irían	

Imperativo	
Singular	Plural
(not used); no (not used)	delinc-amos; no delinc-amos
delinqu-e; no delinc-as	delinqu-id; no delinc-áis
delinc-a; no delinc-a	delinc-an; no delinc-an

Conjugate reflexive verbs the same as above, use a reflexive pronoun as shown on page 82, and make the changes for imperatives and present participles shown there in red.
Make compound tenses by adding a past participle on page 83 or 84.
Translation possibilities are on page 88. Conjugation tips are on page 91.

distinguir

Pattern 30: gu ➡ g before a or o to retain the hard g sound.
Distinguir (distingu-ir) (to distinguish) is the pattern verb.
Present participle: distingu-iendo   Past participle: distingu-ido

Singular		Plural	
Indicativo	*Subjunctivo*	*Indicativo*	*Subjunctivo*
Presente	*Presente*	*Presente*	*Presente*
disting-o	disting-a	distingu-imos	disting-amos
distingu-es	disting-as	distingu-ís	disting-áis
distingu-e	disting-a	distingu-en	disting-an
Imperfecto	*Imperfecto*	*Imperfecto*	*Imperfecto*
distingu-ía	distingu-iera	distingu-íamos	distingu-iéramos
	OR		OR
	distingu-iese		distingu-iésemos
distingu-ías	distingu-ieras	distingu-íais	distingu-ierais
	OR		OR
	distingu-ieses		distingu-ieseis
distingu-ía	distingu-iera	distingu-ían	distingu-ieran
	OR		OR
	distingu-iese		distingu-iesen
Pretérito		*Pretérito*	
distingu-í		distingu-imos	
distingu-iste		distingu-isteis	
distingu-ió		distingu-ieron	
Futuro	*Futuro*	*Futuro*	*Futuro*
distingu-iré	distingu-iere	distingu-iremos	distingu-iéremos
distingu-irás	distingu-ieres	distingu-iréis	distingu-iereis
distingu-irá	distingu-iere	distingu-irán	distingu-ieren
Potencial		*Potencial*	
distingu-iría		distingu-iríamos	
distingu-irías		distingu-iríais	
distingu-iría		distingu-irían	

Imperativo	
Singular	*Plural*
(not used); no (not used)	disting-amos; no disting-amos
distingu-e; no disting-as	distingu-id; no disting-áis
disting-a; no disting-a	disting-an; no disting-an

Conjugate reflexive verbs the same as above, use a reflexive pronoun as shown on page 82, and make the changes for imperatives and present participles shown there in red.
Make compound tenses by adding a past participle on page 83 or 84.
Translation possibilities are on page 88. Conjugation tips are on page 91.

Pattern 31: o ➡ ue or u.
Dormir (dorm-ir) (to sleep) is the pattern verb.
Present participle: durm-iendo   Past participle: dorm-ido

Singular		Plural	
Indicativo	*Subjunctivo*	*Indicativo*	*Subjunctivo*
Presente	*Presente*	*Presente*	*Presente*
duerm-o	duerm-a	dorm-imos	durm-amos
duerm-es	duerm-as	dorm-ís	durm-áis
duerm-e	duerm-a	duerm-en	duerm-an
Imperfecto	*Imperfecto*	*Imperfecto*	*Imperfecto*
dorm-ía	durm-iera	dorm-íamos	durm-iéramos
	OR		OR
	durm-iese		durm-iésemos
dorm-ías	durm-ieras	dorm-íais	durm-ierais
	OR		OR
	durm-ieses		durm-ieseis
dorm-ía	durm-iera	dorm-ían	durm-ieran
	OR		OR
	durm-iese		durm-iesen
Pretérito		*Pretérito*	
dorm-í		dorm-imos	
dorm-iste		dom-isteis	
durm-ió		durm-ieron	
Futuro	*Futuro*	*Futuro*	*Futuro*
dorm-iré	durm-iere	dorm-iremos	durm-iéremos
dorm-irás	durm-ieres	dorm-iréis	durm-iereis
dorm-irá	durm-iere	dorm-irán	durm-ieren
Potencial		*Potencial*	
dorm-iría		dorm-iríamos	
dorm-irías		dorm-iríais	
dorm-iría		dorm-irían	

Imperativo	
Singular	Plural
(not used); no (not used)	durm-amos; no durm-amos
duerm-e; no duerm-as	dorm-id; no durm-áis
duerm-a; no duerm-a	duerm-an; no duerm-an

Conjugate reflexive verbs the same as above, use a reflexive pronoun as shown on page
   82, and make the changes for imperatives and present participles shown there in red.
Make compound tenses by adding a past participle on page 83 or 84.
Translation possibilities are on page 88. Conjugation tips are on page 91.

32
elegir

Pattern 32: e ➡ i, g ➡ j, plus past participle electo.
Elegir (eleg-ir) (to elect) is the pattern verb.
Present participle: elig-iendo Past participle: eleg-ido

Singular		Plural	
Indicativo	*Subjunctivo*	*Indicativo*	*Subjunctivo*
Presente	*Presente*	*Presente*	*Presente*
elij-o	elij-a	eleg-imos	elij-amos
elig-es	elij-as	eleg-ís	elij-áis
elig-e	elij-a	elig-en	elij-an
Imperfecto	*Imperfecto*	*Imperfecto*	*Imperfecto*
eleg-ía	elig-iera OR elig-iese	eleg-íamos	elig-iéramos OR elig-iésemos
eleg-ías	elig-ieras OR elig-ieses	eleg-íais	elig-ierais OR elig-ieseis
eleg-ía	elig-iera OR elig-iese	eleg-ían	elig-ieran OR elig-iesen
Pretérito		*Pretérito*	
eleg-í		eleg-imos	
eleg-iste		eleg-isteis	
elig-ió		elig-ieron	
Futuro	*Futuro*	*Futuro*	*Futuro*
eleg-iré	elig-iere	eleg-iremos	elig-iéremos
eleg-irás	elig-ieres	eleg-iréis	elig-iereis
eleg-irá	elig-iere	eleg-irán	elig-ieren
Potencial		*Potencial*	
eleg-iría		eleg-iríamos	
eleg-irías		eleg-iríais	
eleg-iría		eleg-irían	

Imperativo	
Singular	Plural
(not used); no (not used)	elij-amos; no elij-amos
elig-e; no elij-as	eleg-id; no elij-áis
elij-a; no elij-a	elij-an; no elij-an

Conjugate reflexive verbs the same as above, use a reflexive pronoun as shown on page 82, and make the changes for imperatives and present participles shown there in red.
Make compound tenses by adding a past participle on page 83 or 84.
Translation possibilities are on page 88. Conjugation tips are on page 91.

Pattern 33: Some conjugations customarily are not used.
Embaír (emba-ír) (to deceive, trick) is the pattern verb.
Present participle: emba-yendo   Past participle: emba-ído

Singular		Plural	
Indicativo	*Subjunctivo*	*Indicativo*	*Subjunctivo*
Presente	*Presente*	*Presente*	*Presente*
(not used)	(not used)	emba-ímos	(not used)
(not used)	(not used)	emba-ís	(not used)
(not used)	(not used)	(not used)	(not used)
Imperfecto	*Imperfecto*	*Imperfecto*	*Imperfecto*
emba-ía	emba-yera OR emba-yese	emba-íamos	emba-yéramos OR emba-yésemos
emba-ías	emba-yeras OR emba-yeses	emba-íais	emba-yerais OR emba-yeseis
emba-ía	emba-yera OR emba-yese	emba-ían	emba-yeran OR emba-yesen
Pretérito		*Pretérito*	
emba-í		emba-ímos	
emba-íste		emba-ísteis	
emba-yó		emba-yeron	
Futuro	*Futuro*	*Futuro*	*Futuro*
emba-iré	emba-yere	emba-iremos	emba-yéremos
emba-irás	emba-yeres	emba-iréis	emba-yereis
emba-irá	emba-yere	emba-irán	emba-yeren
Potencial		*Potencial*	
emba-iría		emba-iríamos	
emba-irías		emba-iríais	
emba-iría		emba-irían	

Imperativo	
Singular	Plural
(not used); no (not used)	(not used); no (not used)
(not used); no (not used)	emba-id; no (not used)
(not used); no (not used)	(not used); no (not used)

Conjugate reflexive verbs the same as above, use a reflexive pronoun as shown on page
  82, and make the changes for imperatives and present participles shown there in red.
Make compound tenses by adding a past participle on page 83 or 84.
Translation possibilities are on page 88. Conjugation tips are on page 91.

34
empezar

Pattern 34: e in stem ➡ ie when stressed, z ➡ c before e.
Empezar (empez-ar) (to begin) is the pattern verb.
Present participle: empez-ando   Past participle: empez-ado

Singular		Plural	
Indicativo	*Subjunctivo*	*Indicativo*	*Subjunctivo*
Presente	*Presente*	*Presente*	*Presente*
empiez-o	empiec-e	empez-amos	empec-emos
empiez-as	empiec-es	empez-áis	empec-éis
empiez-a	empiec-e	empiez-an	empiec-en
Imperfecto	*Imperfecto*	*Imperfecto*	*Imperfecto*
empez-aba	empez-ara	empez-ábamos	empez-áramos
	OR		OR
	empez-ase		empez-ásemos
empez-abas	empez-aras	empez-abais	empez-arais
	OR		OR
	empez-ases		empez-aseis
empez-aba	empez-ara	empez-aban	empez-aran
	OR		OR
	empez-ase		empez-asen
Pretérito		*Pretérito*	
empec-é		empez-amos	
empez-aste		empez-asteis	
empez-ó		empez-aron	
Futuro	*Futuro*	*Futuro*	*Futuro*
empez-aré	empez-are	empez-aremos	empez-áremos
empez-arás	empez-ares	empez-aréis	empez-areis
empez-ará	empez-are	empez-arán	empez-aren
Potencial		*Potencial*	
empez-aría		empez-aríamos	
empez-arías		empez-aríais	
empez-aría		empez-arían	

Imperativo	
Singular	Plural
(not used); no (not used)	empec-emos; no empec-emos
empiez-a; no empiec-es	empez-ad; no empec-éis
empiec-e; no empice-e	empiec-en; no empiec-en

Conjugate reflexive verbs the same as above, use a reflexive pronoun as shown on page 80, and make the changes for imperatives and present participles shown there in red.
Make compound tenses by adding a past participle on page 83 or 84.
Translation possibilities are on page 88. Conjugation tips are on page 89.

Pattern 35: i ➡ í when stressed, z ➡ c before e.
Enraizar (enraiz-ar) (to grow roots, take root) is the pattern verb.
Present participle: enraiz-ando   Past participle: enraiz-ado

Singular		Plural	
Indicativo	*Subjunctivo*	*Indicativo*	*Subjunctivo*
Presente	*Presente*	*Presente*	*Presente*
enraíz-o	enraíc-e	enraiz-amos	enraic-emos
enraíz-as	enraíc-es	enraiz-áis	enraic-éis
enraíz-a	enraíc-e	enraíz-an	enraíc-en
Imperfecto	*Imperfecto*	*Imperfecto*	*Imperfecto*
enraiz-aba	enraiz-ara	enraiz-ábamos	enraiz-áramos
	OR		OR
	enraiz-ase		enraiz-ásemos
enraiz-abas	enraiz-aras	enraiz-abais	enraiz-arais
	OR		OR
	enraiz-ases		enraiz-aseis
enraiz-aba	enraiz-ara	enraiz-aban	enraiz-aran
	OR		OR
	enraiz-ase		enraiz-asen
Pretérito		*Pretérito*	
enraic-é		enraiz-amos	
enraiz-aste		enraiz-asteis	
enraiz-ó		enraiz-aron	
Futuro	*Futuro*	*Futuro*	*Futuro*
enraiz-aré	enraiz-are	enraiz-aremos	enraiz-áremos
enraiz-arás	enraiz-ares	enraiz-aréis	enraiz-areis
enraiz-ará	enraiz-are	enraiz-arán	enraiz-aren
Potencial		*Potencial*	
enraiz-aría		enraiz-aríamos	
enraiz-arías		enraiz-aríais	
enraiz-aría		enraiz-arían	

Imperativo	
Singular	Plural
(not used); no (not used)	enraic-emos; no enraic-emos
enraíz-a; no enraíc-es	enraiz-ad; no enraic-éis
enraíc-e; no enraíc-e	enraíc-en; no enraíc-en

Conjugate reflexive verbs the same as above, use a reflexive pronoun as shown on page 80, and make the changes for imperatives and present participles shown there in red.
Make compound tenses by adding a past participle on page 83 or 84.
Translation possibilities are on page 88. Conjugation tips are on page 89.

36
erguir

Pattern 36: e ⟶ i, gu ⟶ g, y is added.
Erguir (ergu-ir) (to be erect) is the pattern verb.
Present participle: irgu-iendo   Past participle: ergu-ido

Singular		Plural	
Indicativo	*Subjunctivo*	*Indicativo*	*Subjunctivo*
Presente	*Presente*	*Presente*	*Presente*
irg-o, yerg-o	irg-a, yerg-a	ergu-imos	irg-amos, yerg-amos
irgu-es, yergu-es	irg-as, yerg-as	ergu-ís	irg-áis, yerg-áis
irgu-e, yergu-e	irg-a, yerg-a	irgu-en, yergu-en	irg-an, yerg-an
Imperfecto	*Imperfecto*	*Imperfecto*	*Imperfecto*
ergu-ía	irgu-iera OR irgu-iese	ergu-íamos	irgu-iéramos OR irgu-iésemos
ergu-ías	irgu-ieras OR irgu-ieses	ergu-íais	irgu-ierais OR irgu-ieseis
ergu-ía	irgu-iera OR irgu-iese	ergu-ían	irgu-ieran OR irgu-iesen
Pretérito		*Pretérito*	
ergu-í		ergu-imos	
ergu-iste		ergu-isteis	
irgu-ió		irgu-ieron	
Futuro	*Futuro*	*Futuro*	*Futuro*
ergu-iré	irgu-iere	ergu-iremos	irgu-iéremos
ergu-irás	irgu-ieres	ergu-iréis	irgu-iereis
ergu-irá	irgu-iere	ergu-irán	irgu-ieren
Potencial		*Potencial*	
ergu-iría		ergu-iríamos	
ergu-irías		ergu-iríais	
ergu-iría		ergu-irían	

Imperativo

Singular	Plural
(not used); no (not used)	irg-amos, yerg-amos; no irg-amos, no yerg-amos
irgu-e, yergu-e; no irg-as, no yerg-as	ergu-id; no irg-áis, no yerg-áis
irg-a, yerg-a; no irg-a, no yerg-a	irg-an, yerg-an; no irg-an, no yerg-an

Conjugate reflexive verbs the same as above, use a reflexive pronoun as shown on page 82, and make the changes for imperatives and present participles shown there in red.
Make compound tenses by adding a past participle on page 83 or 84.
Translation possibilities are on page 88. Conjugation tips are on page 91.

Pattern 37: y is added before e in stem when e is stressed.
Errar (err-ar) (to be wrong or mistaken) is the pattern verb.
Present participle: err-ando   Past participle: err-ado

	Singular		Plural	
	Indicativo	*Subjunctivo*	*Indicativo*	*Subjunctivo*
Presente	*Presente*	*Presente*	*Presente*	*Presente*
	yerr-o	yerr-e	err-amos	err-emos
	yerr-as	yerr-es	err-áis	err-éis
	yerr-a	yerr-e	yerr-an	yerr-en
Imperfecto	*Imperfecto*	*Imperfecto*	*Imperfecto*	*Imperfecto*
	err-aba	err-ara OR err-ase	err-ábamos	err-áramos OR err-ásemos
	err-abas	err-aras OR err-ases	err-abais	err-arais OR err-aseis
	err-aba	err-ara OR err-ase	err-aban	err-aran OR err-asen
Pretérito		*Pretérito*		
	err-é		err-amos	
	err-aste		err-asteis	
	err-ó		err-aron	
Futuro	*Futuro*	*Futuro*	*Futuro*	*Futuro*
	err-aré	err-are	err-aremos	err-áremos
	err-arás	err-ares	err-aréis	err-areis
	err-ará	err-are	err-arán	err-aren
Potencial		*Potencial*		
	err-aría		err-aríamos	
	err-arías		err-aríais	
	err-aría		err-arían	

Imperativo	
Singular	Plural
(not used); no (not used)	err-emos; no err-emos
yerr-a; no yerr-es	err-ad; no err-éis
yerr-e; no yerr-e	yerr-en; no yerr-en

Conjugate reflexive verbs the same as above, use a reflexive pronoun as shown on page 80, and make the changes for imperatives and present participles shown there in red.
Make compound tenses by adding a past participle on page 83 or 84.
Translation possibilities are on page 88. Conjugation tips are on page 89.

38

estar

Pattern 38: a ➠ i or ie, é ➠ e, ó ➠ o, add y, add uv, + accents.
Estar (est-ar) (to be, to stand) (an auxiliary verb) is the pattern verb.
Present participle: est-ando   Past participle: est-ado

Singular		Plural	
Indicativo	*Subjunctivo*	*Indicativo*	*Subjunctivo*
Presente	*Presente*	*Presente*	*Presente*
est-oy	est-é	est-amos	est-emos
est-ás	est-és	est-áis	est-éis
est-á	est-é	est-án	est-én
Imperfecto	*Imperfecto*	*Imperfecto*	*Imperfecto*
est-aba	estuv-iera	est-ábamos	estuv-iéramos
	OR		OR
	estuv-iese		estuv-iésemos
est-abas	estuv-ieras	est-abais	estuv-ierais
	OR		OR
	estuv-ieses		estuv-ieseis
est-aba	estuv-iera	est-aban	estuv-ieran
	OR		OR
	estuv-iese		estuv-iesen
Pretérito		*Pretérito*	
estuv-e		estuv-imos	
estuv-iste		estuv-isteis	
estuv-o		estuv-ieron	
Futuro	*Futuro*	*Futuro*	*Futuro*
est-aré	estuv-iere	est-aremos	estuv-iéremos
est-arás	estuv-ieres	est-aréis	estuv-iereis
est-ará	estuv-iere	est-arán	estuv-ieren
Potencial		*Potencial*	
est-aría		est-aríamos	
est-arías		est-aríais	
est-aría		est-arían	

Imperativo	
Singular	Plural
(not used); no (not used)	est-emos; no est-emos
est-á; no est-és	est-ad; no est-éis
est-é; no est-é	est-én; no est-én

Conjugate reflexive verbs the same as above, use a reflexive pronoun as shown on page 80, and make the changes for imperatives and present participles shown there in red.
Make compound tenses by adding a past participle on page 83 or 84.
Translation possibilities are on page 88. Conjugation tips are on page 89.

Pattern 39: o ⟹ ue when stressed, z ⟹ c before e.
Forzar (forz-ar) (to force) is the pattern verb.
Present participle: forz-ando   Past participle: forz-ado

Singular		Plural	
Indicativo	*Subjunctivo*	*Indicativo*	*Subjunctivo*
Presente	*Presente*	*Presente*	*Presente*
fuerz-o	fuerc-e	forz-amos	forc-emos
fuerz-as	fuerc-es	forz-áis	forc-éis
fuerz-a	fuerc-e	fuerz-an	fuerc-en
Imperfecto	*Imperfecto*	*Imperfecto*	*Imperfecto*
forz-aba	forz-ara	forz-ábamos	forz-áramos
	OR		OR
	forz-ase		forz-ásemos
forz-abas	forz-aras	forz-abais	forz-arais
	OR		OR
	forz-ases		forz-aseis
forz-aba	forz-ara	forz-aban	forz-aran
	OR		OR
	forz-ase		forz-asen
Pretérito		*Pretérito*	
forc-é		forz-amos	
forz-aste		forz-asteis	
forz-ó		forz-aron	
Futuro	*Futuro*	*Futuro*	*Futuro*
forz-aré	forz-are	forz-aremos	forz-áremos
forz-arás	forz-ares	forz-aréis	forz-areis
forz-ará	forz-are	forz-arán	forz-aren
Potencial		*Potencial*	
forz-aría		forz-aríamos	
forz-arías		forz-aríais	
forz-aría		forz-arían	

Imperativo	
Singular	Plural
(not used); no (not used)	forc-emos; no forc-emos
fuerz-a; no fuerc-es	forz-ad; no forc-éis
fuerc-e; no fuerc-e	fuerc-en; no fuerc-en

Conjugate reflexive verbs the same as above, use a reflexive pronoun as shown on page
80, and make the changes for imperatives and present participles shown there in red.
Make compound tenses by adding a past participle on page 83 or 84.
Translation possibilities are on page 88. Conjugation tips are on page 89.

40
haber

Pattern 40: a ⟹ e or u, e ⟹ a, o ⟹ e, b ⟹ y, delete a, e and b.
Haber (hab-er) (to have) (an auxilary verb) is the pattern verb.
Present participle: hab-iendo   Past participle: hab-ido

Singular		Plural	
Indicativo	*Subjunctivo*	*Indicativo*	*Subjunctivo*
Presente	*Presente*	*Presente*	*Presente*
h-e	hay-a	h-emos	hay-amos
h-as	hay-as	hab-éis	hay-áis
h-a, ha-y[1]	hay-a	ha-n	hay-an
Imperfecto	*Imperfecto*	*Imperfecto*	*Imperfecto*
hab-ía	hub-iera	hab-íamos	hub-iéramos
	OR		OR
	hub-iese		hub-iésemos
hab-ías	hub-ieras	hab-íais	hub-ierais
	OR		OR
	hub-ieses		hub-ieseis
hab-ía	hub-iera	hab-ían	hub-ieran
	OR		OR
	hub-iese		hub-iesen
Pretérito		*Pretérito*	
hub-e		hub-imos	
hub-iste		hub-isteis	
hub-o		hub-ieron	
Futuro	*Futuro*	*Futuro*	*Futuro*
hab-ré	hub-iere	hab-remos	hub-iéremos
hab-rás	hub-ieres	hab-réis	hub-iereis
hab-rá	hub-iere	hab-rán	hub-ieren
Potencial		*Potencial*	
hab-ría		hab-ríamos	
hab-rías		hab-ríais	
hab-ría		hab-rían	

Imperativo

Singular	Plural
(not used); no (not used)	hay-amos; no hay-amos
h-é or h-e; no hay-as	hab-ed; no hay-áis
hay-a; no hay-a	hay-an; no hay-an

Conjugate reflexive verbs the same as above, use a reflexive pronoun as shown on page
   81, and make the changes for imperatives and present participles shown there in red.
Make compound tenses by adding a past participle on page 83 or 84.
Translation possibilities are on page 88. Conjugation tips are on page 90.
[1]When using the impersonal, the third person singular form is hay.

Pattern 41: a ➡ i, c ➡ g or z, delete c or e, irregular past participle.
Hacer (hac-er) (to make, to do) is the pattern verb.
Present participle: hac-iendo   Past participle: hec-ho

Singular		Plural	
Indicativo	*Subjunctivo*	*Indicativo*	*Subjunctivo*
Presente	*Presente*	*Presente*	*Presente*
hag-o	hag-a	hac-emos	hag-amos
hac-es	hag-as	hac-éis	hag-áis
hac-e	hag-a	hac-en	hag-an
Imperfecto	*Imperfecto*	*Imperfecto*	*Imperfecto*
hac-ía	hic-iera	hac-íamos	hic-iéramos
	OR		OR
	hic-iese		hic-iésemos
hac-ías	hic-ieras	hac-íais	hic-ierais
	OR		OR
	hic-ieses		hic-ieseis
hac-ía	hic-iera	hac-ían	hic-ieran
	OR		OR
	hic-iese		hic-iesen
Pretérito		*Pretérito*	
hic-e		hic-imos	
hic-iste		hic-isteis	
hiz-o		hic-ieron	
Futuro	*Futuro*	*Futuro*	*Futuro*
ha-ré	hic-iere	ha-remos	hic-iéremos
ha-rás	hic-ieres	ha-réis	hic-iereis
ha-rá	hic-iere	ha-rán	hic-ieren
Potencial		*Potencial*	
ha-ría		ha-ríamos	
ha-rías		ha-ríais	
ha-ría		ha-rían	

Imperativo	
Singular	Plural
(not used); no (not used)	hag-amos; no hag-amos
haz; no hag-as	hac-ed; no hag-áis
hag-a; no hag-a	hag-an; no hag-an

Conjugate reflexive verbs the same as above, use a reflexive pronoun as shown on page
81, and make the changes for imperatives and present participles shown there in red.
Make compound tenses by adding a past participle on page 83 or 84.
Translation possibilities are on page 88. Conjugation tips are on page 90.

Pattern 42: i ➡ y, y is added.
Huir (hu-ir) (to flee, avoid, shun) is the pattern verb.
Present participle: hu-yendo   Past participle: hu-ido

Singular		Plural	
Indicativo	*Subjunctivo*	*Indicativo*	*Subjunctivo*
Presente	*Presente*	*Presente*	*Presente*
huy-o	huy-a	hu-imos	huy-amos
huy-es	huy-as	hu-ís	huy-áis
huy-e	huy-a	huy-en	huy-an
Imperfecto	*Imperfecto*	*Imperfecto*	*Imperfecto*
hu-ía	hu-yera	hu-íamos	hu-yéramos
	OR		OR
	hu-yese		hu-yésemos
hu-ías	hu-yeras	hu-íais	hu-yerais
	OR		OR
	hu-yeses		hu-yeseis
hu-ía	hu-yera	hu-ían	hu-yeran
	OR		OR
	hu-yese		hu-yesen
Pretérito		*Pretérito*	
hu-í		hu-imos	
hu-iste		hu-isteis	
hu-yó		hu-yeron	
Futuro	*Futuro*	*Futuro*	*Futuro*
hu-iré	hu-yere	hu-iremos	hu-yéremos
hu-irás	hu-yeres	hu-iréis	hu-yereis
hu-irá	hu-yere	hu-irán	hu-yeren
Potencial		*Potencial*	
hu-iría		hu-iríamos	
hu-irías		hu-iríais	
hu-iría		hu-irían	

Imperativo	
Singular	Plural
(not used); no (not used)	huy-amos; no huy-amos
huy-e; no huy-as	hu-id; no huy-áis
huy-a; no huy-a	huy-an; no huy-an

Conjugate reflexive verbs the same as above, use a reflexive pronoun as shown on page 82, and make the changes for imperatives and present participles shown there in red.
Make compound tenses by adding a past participle on page 83 or 84.
Translation possibilities are on page 88. Conjugation tips are on page 91.

Pattern 43: v, va, vay, ib, and fu are roots, plus other changes.
Ir (ir) (to go) is the pattern verb.
Present participle: yendo   Past participle: ido

Singular		Plural	
Indicativo	*Subjunctivo*	*Indicativo*	*Subjunctivo*
Presente	*Presente*	*Presente*	*Presente*
v-oy	vay-a	va-mos	vay-amos
v-as	vay-as	va-is	vay-áis
v-a	vay-a	va-n	vay-an
Imperfecto	*Imperfecto*	*Imperfecto*	*Imperfecto*
ib-a	fu-era	íb-amos	fu-éramos
	OR		OR
	fu-ese		fu-ésemos
ib-as	fu-eras	ib-ais	fu-erais
	OR		OR
	fu-eses		fu-eseis
ib-a	fu-era	ib-an	fu-eran
	OR		OR
	fu-ese		fu-esen
Pretérito		*Pretérito*	
fu-i		fu-imos	
fu-iste		fu-isteis	
fu-e		fu-eron	
Futuro	*Futuro*	*Futuro*	*Futuro*
iré	fu-ere	iremos	fu-éremos
irás	fu-eres	iréis	fu-ereis
irá	fu-ere	irán	fu-eren
Potencial		*Potencial*	
iría		iríamos	
irías		iríais	
iría		irían	

Imperativo	
Singular	Plural
(not used); no (not used)	v-amos or vay-amos; no vay-amos
v-e; no vay-as	id; no vay-áis
vay-a; no vay-a	vay-an; no vay-an

Conjugate reflexive verbs the same as above, use a reflexive pronoun as shown on page
82, and make the changes for imperatives and present participles shown there in red.
Make compound tenses by adding a past participle on page 83 or 84.
Translation possibilities are on page 88. Conjugation tips are on page 91.

44
jugar

Pattern 44: u ➡ ue when stressed, g ➡ gu before e.
Jugar (jug-ar) (to play, gamble, risk) is the pattern verb.
Present participle: jug-ando   Past participle: jug-ado

Singular		Plural	
Indicativo	*Subjunctivo*	*Indicativo*	*Subjunctivo*
Presente	*Presente*	*Presente*	*Presente*
jueg-o	juegu-e	jug-amos	jugu-emos
jueg-as	juegu-es	jug-áis	jugu-éis
jueg-a	juegu-e	jueg-an	juegu-en
Imperfecto	*Imperfecto*	*Imperfecto*	*Imperfecto*
jug-aba	jug-ara	jug-ábamos	jug-áramos
	OR		OR
	jug-ase		jug-ásemos
jug-abas	jug-aras	jug-abais	jug-arais
	OR		OR
	jug-ases		jug-aseis
jug-aba	jug-ara	jug-aban	jug-aran
	OR		OR
	jug-ase		jug-asen
Pretérito		*Pretérito*	
jugu-é		jug-amos	
jug-aste		jug-asteis	
jug-ó		jug-aron	
Futuro	*Futuro*	*Futuro*	*Futuro*
jug-aré	jug-are	jug-aremos	jug-áremos
jug-arás	jug-ares	jug-aréis	jug-areis
jug-ará	jug-are	jug-arán	jug-aren
Potencial		*Potencial*	
jug-aría		jug-aríamos	
jug-arías		jug-aríais	
jug-aría		jug-arían	

Imperativo	
Singular	Plural
(not used); no (not used)	jugu-emos; no jugu-emos
jueg-a; no juegu-es	jug-ad; no jugu-éis
juegu-e; no juegu-e	juegu-en; no juegu-en

Conjugate reflexive verbs the same as above, use a reflexive pronoun as shown on page
   80, and make the changes for imperatives and present participles shown there in red.
Make compound tenses by adding a past participle on page 83 or 84.
Translation possibilities are on page 88. Conjugation tips are on page 89.

Pattern 45: Some conjugations customarily are not used.
Llover (llov-er) (to rain, leak) is the pattern verb.
Present participle: llov-iendo   Past participle: llov-ido

Singular		Plural	
Indicativo	*Subjunctivo*	*Indicativo*	*Subjunctivo*
Presente	*Presente*	*Presente*	*Presente*
(not used)	(not used)	(not used)	(not used)
(not used)	(not used)	(not used)	(not used)
lluev-e (or está lloviendo) lluev-a		(not used)	(not used)
Imperfecto	*Imperfecto*	*Imperfecto*	*Imperfecto*
(not used)	(not used)	(not used)	(not used)
	OR		OR
	(not used)		(not used)
(not used)	(not used)	(not used)	(not used)
	OR		OR
	(not used)		(not used)
llov-ía (or estaba lloviendo) llov-iera		(not used)	(not used)
	OR		OR
	llov-iese		(not used)
Pretérito		*Pretérito*	
(not used)		(not used)	
(not used)		(not used)	
llov-ió		(not used)	
Futuro	*Futuro*	*Futuro*	*Futuro*
(not used)	(not used)	(not used)	(not used)
(not used)	(not used)	(not used)	(not used)
llov-erá	(not used)	(not used)	(not used)
Potencial		*Potencial*	
(not used)		(not used)	
(not used)		(not used)	
llov-ería		(not used)	

Imperativo	
Singular	Plural
(not used); no (not used)	(not used); no (not used)
(not used); no (not used)	(not used); no (not used)
¡Que lluev-a! (Let it rain!); no (not used)	(not used); no (not used)

Conjugate reflexive verbs the same as above, use a reflexive pronoun as shown on page 81, and make the changes for imperatives and present participles shown there in red.
Make compound tenses by adding a past participle on page 83 or 84.
Translation possibilities are on page 88. Conjugation tips are on page 90.

46

mecer

Pattern 46: c ⟹ z before a or o to retain the s or th sound.
Mecer (mec-er) (to rock, swing, stir) is the pattern verb.
Present participle: mec-iendo   Past participle: mec-ido

Singular		Plural	
Indicativo	*Subjunctivo*	*Indicativo*	*Subjunctivo*
Presente	*Presente*	*Presente*	*Presente*
mez-o	mez-a	mec-emos	mez-amos
mec-es	mez-as	mec-éis	mez-áis
mec-e	mez-a	mec-en	mez-an
Imperfecto	*Imperfecto*	*Imperfecto*	*Imperfecto*
mec-ía	mec-iera	mec-íamos	mec-iéramos
	OR		OR
	mec-iese		mec-iésemos
mec-ías	mec-ieras	mec-íais	mec-ierais
	OR		OR
	mec-ieses		mec-ieseis
mec-ía	mec-iera	mec-ían	mec-ieran
	OR		OR
	mec-iese		mec-iesen
Pretérito		*Pretérito*	
mec-í		mec-imos	
mec-iste		mec-isteis	
mec-ió		mec-ieron	
Futuro	*Futuro*	*Futuro*	*Futuro*
mec-eré	mec-iere	mec-eremos	mec-iéremos
mec-erás	mec-ieres	mec-eréis	mec-iereis
mec-erá	mec-iere	mec-erán	mec-ieren
Potencial		*Potencial*	
mec-ería		mec-eríamos	
mec-erías		mec-eríais	
mec-ería		mec-erían	

Imperativo	
Singular	Plural
(not used); no (not used)	mez-amos; no mez-amos
mec-e; no mez-as	mec-ed; no mez-áis
mez-a; no mez-a	mez-an; no mez-an

Conjugate reflexive verbs the same as above, use a reflexive pronoun as shown on page 81, and make the changes for imperatives and present participles shown there in red.
Make compound tenses by adding a past participle on page 83 or 84.
Translation possibilities are on page 88.   Conjugation tips are on page 90.

Pattern 47: o ⟹ ue when stressed.
Mover (mov-er) (to move, stir, sway, use, abort) is the pattern verb.
Present participle: mov-iendo   Past participle: mov-ido

Singular		Plural	
Indicativo	*Subjunctivo*	*Indicativo*	*Subjunctivo*
Presente	*Presente*	*Presente*	*Presente*
muev-o	muev-a	mov-emos	mov-amos
muev-es	muev-as	mov-éis	mov-áis
muev-e	muev-a	muev-en	muev-an
Imperfecto	*Imperfecto*	*Imperfecto*	*Imperfecto*
mov-ía	mov-iera	mov-íamos	mov-iéramos
	OR		OR
	mov-iese		mov-iésemos
mov-ías	mov-ieras	mov-íais	mov-ierais
	OR		OR
	mov-ieses		mov-ieseis
mov-ía	mov-iera	mov-ían	mov-ieran
	OR		OR
	mov-iese		mov-iesen
Pretérito		*Pretérito*	
mov-í		mov-imos	
mov-iste		mov-isteis	
mov-ió		mov-ieron	
Futuro	*Futuro*	*Futuro*	*Futuro*
mov-eré	mov-iere	mov-eremos	mov-iéremos
mov-erás	mov-ieres	mov-eréis	mov-iereis
mov-erá	mov-iere	mov-erán	mov-ieren
Potencial		*Potencial*	
mov-ería		mov-eríamos	
mov-erías		mov-eríais	
mov-ería		mov-erían	

Imperativo	
Singular	Plural
(not used); no (not used)	mov-amos; no mov-amos
muev-e; no muev-as	mov-ed; no mov-áis
muev-a; no muev-a	muev-an; no muev-an

Conjugate reflexive verbs the same as above, use a reflexive pronoun as shown on page 81, and make the changes for imperatives and present participles shown there in red.
Make compound tenses by adding a past participle on page 83 or 84.
Translation possibilities are on page 88. Conjugation tips are on page 90.

Pattern 48: c ⟹ zc before a or o.
Nacer (nac-er) (to be born, to bud) is the pattern verb.
Present participle: nac-iendo   Past participle: nac-ido

Singular		Plural	
Indicativo	*Subjunctivo*	*Indicativo*	*Subjunctivo*
Presente	*Presente*	*Presente*	*Presente*
nazc-o	nazc-a	nac-emos	nazc-amos
nac-es	nazc-as	nac-éis	nazc-áis
nac-e	nazc-a	nac-en	nazc-an
Imperfecto	*Imperfecto*	*Imperfecto*	*Imperfecto*
nac-ía	nac-iera	nac-íamos	nac-iéramos
	OR		OR
	nac-iese		nac-iésemos
nac-ías	nac-ieras	nac-íais	nac-ierais
	OR		OR
	nac-ieses		nac-ieseis
nac-ía	nac-iera	nac-ían	nac-ieran
	OR		OR
	nac-iese		nac-iesen
Pretérito		*Pretérito*	
nac-í		nac-imos	
nac-iste		nac-isteis	
nac-ió		nac-ieron	
Futuro	*Futuro*	*Futuro*	*Futuro*
nac-eré	nac-iere	nac-eremos	nac-iéremos
nac-erás	nac-ieres	nac-eréis	nac-iereis
nac-erá	nac-iere	nac-erán	nac-ieren
Potencial		*Potencial*	
nac-ería		nac-eríamos	
nac-erías		nac-eríais	
nac-ería		nac-erían	

Imperativo	
Singular	Plural
(not used); no (not used)	nazc-amos; no nazc-amos
nac-e; no nazc-as	nac-ed; no nazc-áis
nazc-a; no nazc-a	nazc-an; no nazc-an

Conjugate reflexive verbs the same as above, use a reflexive pronoun as shown on page
81, and make the changes for imperatives and present participles shown there in red.
Make compound tenses by adding a past participle on page 83 or 84.
Translation possibilities are on page 88. Conjugation tips are on page 90.

Pattern 49: add ig or y, i ➡ í or y. Similar to caer.
Oír (o-ir) (to hear, listen to) is the pattern verb.
Present participle: o-yendo   Past participle: o-ído

	Singular		Plural	
	Indicativo	*Subjunctivo*	*Indicativo*	*Subjunctivo*
Presente	*Presente*	*Presente*	*Presente*	*Presente*
	oig-o	oig-a	o-ímos	oig-amos
	oy-es	oig-as	o-ís	oig-áis
	oy-e	oig-a	oy-en	oig-an
Imperfecto	*Imperfecto*	*Imperfecto*	*Imperfecto*	*Imperfecto*
	o-ía	o-yera	o-íamos	o-yéramos
		OR		OR
		o-yese		o-yésemos
	o-ías	o-yeras	o-íais	o-yerais
		OR		OR
		o-yeses		o-yeseis
	o-ía	o-yera	o-ían	o-yeran
		OR		OR
		o-yese		o-yesen
Pretérito			*Pretérito*	
	o-í		o-ímos	
	o-iste		o-ísteis	
	o-yó		o-yeron	
Futuro	*Futuro*		*Futuro*	*Futuro*
	o-iré	o-yere	o-iremos	o-yéremos
	o-irás	o-yeres	o-iréis	o-yereis
	o-irá	o-yere	o-irán	o-yeren
Potencial			*Potencial*	
	o-iría		o-iríamos	
	o-irías		o-iríais	
	o-iría		o-irían	

Imperativo	
Singular	Plural
(not used); no (not used)	oig-amos; no oig-amos
oy-e; no oig-as	o-íd; no oig-áis
oig-a; no oig-a	oig-an; no oig-an

Conjugate reflexive verbs the same as above, use a reflexive pronoun as shown on page 82, and make the changes for imperatives and present participles shown there in red.
Make compound tenses by adding a past participle on page 83 or 84.
Translation possibilities are on page 88. Conjugation tips are on page 91.

50

oler

Pattern 50: o ➠ hue when stressed.
Oler (ol-er) (to smell, look into) is the pattern verb.
Present participle: ol-iendo   Past participle: ol-ido

Singular		Plural	
Indicativo	*Subjunctivo*	*Indicativo*	*Subjunctivo*
Presente	*Presente*	*Presente*	*Presente*
huel-o	huel-a	ol-emos	ol-amos
huel-es	huel-as	ol-éis	ol-áis
huel-e	huel-a	huel-en	huel-an
Imperfecto	*Imperfecto*	*Imperfecto*	*Imperfecto*
ol-ía	ol-iera	ol-íamos	ol-iéramos
	OR		OR
	ol-iese		ol-iésemos
ol-ías	ol-ieras	ol-íais	ol-ierais
	OR		OR
	ol-ieses		ol-ieseis
ol-ía	ol-iera	ol-ían	ol-ieran
	OR		OR
	ol-iese		ol-iesen
Pretérito		*Pretérito*	
ol-í		ol-imos	
ol-iste		ol-isteis	
ol-ió		ol-ieron	
Futuro	*Futuro*	*Futuro*	*Futuro*
ol-eré	ol-iere	ol-eremos	ol-iéremos
ol-erás	ol-ieres	ol-eréis	ol-iereis
ol-erá	ol-iere	ol-erán	ol-ieren
Potencial		*Potencial*	
ol-ería		ol-eríamos	
ol-erías		ol-eríais	
ol-ería		ol-erían	

Imperativo	
Singular	Plural
(not used); no (not used)	ol-amos; no ol-amos
huel-e; no huel-as	ol-ed; no ol-áis
huel-a; no huel-a	huel-an; no huel-an

Conjugate reflexive verbs the same as above, use a reflexive pronoun as shown on page
  81, and make the changes for imperatives and present participles shown there in red.
Make compound tenses by adding a past participle on page 83 or 84.
Translation possibilities are on page 88. Conjugation tips are on page 90.

Pattern 51: g ➡ gu before e to retain the hard g sound.
Pagar (pag-ar) (to pay, pay for) is the pattern verb.
Present participle: pag-ando   Past participle: pag-ado

Singular		Plural	
Indicativo	*Subjunctivo*	*Indicativo*	*Subjunctivo*
Presente	*Presente*	*Presente*	*Presente*
pag-o	pagu-e	pag-amos	pagu-emos
pag-as	pagu-es	pag-áis	pagu-éis
pag-a	pagu-e	pag-an	pagu-en
Imperfecto	*Imperfecto*	*Imperfecto*	*Imperfecto*
pag-aba	pag-ara OR pag-ase	pag-ábamos	pag-áramos OR pag-ásemos
pag-abas	pag-aras OR pag-ases	pag-abais	pag-arais OR pag-aseis
pag-aba	pag-ara OR pag-ase	pag-aban	pag-aran OR pag-asen
Pretérito		*Pretérito*	
pagu-é		pag-amos	
pag-aste		pag-asteis	
pag-ó		pag-aron	
Futuro	*Futuro*	*Futuro*	*Futuro*
pag-aré	pag-are	pag-aremos	pag-áremos
pag-arás	pag-ares	pag-aréis	pag-areis
pag-ará	pag-are	pag-arán	pag-aren
Potencial		*Potencial*	
pag-aría		pag-aríamos	
pag-arías		pag-aríais	
pag-aría		pag-arían	

Imperativo	
Singular	Plural
(not used); no (not used)	pagu-emos; no pagu-emos
pag-a; no pagu-es	pag-ad; no pagu-éis
pagu-e; no pagu-e	pagu-en; no pagu-en

Conjugate reflexive verbs the same as above, use a reflexive pronoun as shown on page
  80, and make the changes for imperatives and present participles shown there in red.
Make compound tenses by adding a past participle on page 83 or 84.
Translation possibilities are on page 88. Conjugation tips are on page 89.

52
pedir

Pattern 52: e ⟹ i.
Pedir (ped-ir) (to ask, ask for, request) is the pattern verb.
Present participle: pid-iendo   Past participle: ped-ido

Singular		Plural	
Indicativo	*Subjunctivo*	*Indicativo*	*Subjunctivo*
Presente	*Presente*	*Presente*	*Presente*
pid-o	pid-a	ped-imos	pid-amos
pid-es	pid-as	ped-ís	pid-áis
pid-e	pid-a	pid-en	pid-an
Imperfecto	*Imperfecto*	*Imperfecto*	*Imperfecto*
ped-ía	pid-iera	ped-íamos	pid-iéramos
	OR		OR
	pid-iese		pid-iésemos
ped-ías	pid-ieras	ped-íais	pid-ierais
	OR		OR
	pid-ieses		pid-ieseis
ped-ía	pid-iera	ped-ían	pid-ieran
	OR		OR
	pid-iese		pid-iesen
Pretérito		*Pretérito*	
ped-í		ped-imos	
ped-iste		ped-isteis	
pid-ió		pid-ieron	
Futuro	*Futuro*	*Futuro*	*Futuro*
ped-iré	pid-iere	ped-iremos	pid-iéremos
ped-irás	pid-ieres	ped-iréis	pid-iereis
ped-irá	pid-iere	ped-irán	pid-ieren
Potencial		*Potencial*	
ped-iría		ped-iríamos	
ped-irías		ped-iríais	
ped-iría		ped-irían	

Imperativo	
Singular	Plural
(not used); no (not used)	pid-amos; no pid-amos
pid-e; no pid-as	ped-id; no pid-áis
pid-a; no pid-a	pid-an; no pid-an

Conjugate reflexive verbs the same as above, use a reflexive pronoun as shown on page 82, and make the changes for imperatives and present participles shown there in red.
Make compound tenses by adding a past participle on page 83 or 84.
Translation possibilities are on page 88. Conjugation tips are on page 91.

Pattern 53: e in stem ➡ ie when stressed.
Pensar (pens-ar) (to think, think over) is the pattern verb.
Present participle: pens-ando   Past participle: pens-ado

Singular		Plural	
Indicativo	*Subjunctivo*	*Indicativo*	*Subjunctivo*
Presente	*Presente*	*Presente*	*Presente*
piens-o	piens-e	pens-amos	pens-emos
piens-as	piens-es	pens-áis	pens-éis
piens-a	piens-e	piens-an	piens-en
Imperfecto	*Imperfecto*	*Imperfecto*	*Imperfecto*
pens-aba	pens-ara	pens-ábamos	pens-áramos
	OR		OR
	pens-ase		pens-ásemos
pens-abas	pens-aras	pens-abais	pens-arais
	OR		OR
	pens-ases		pens-aseis
pens-aba	pens-ara	pens-aban	pens-aran
	OR		OR
	pens-ase		pens-asen
Pretérito		*Pretérito*	
pens-é		pens-amos	
pens-aste		pens-asteis	
pens-ó		pens-aron	
Futuro	*Futuro*	*Futuro*	*Futuro*
pens-aré	pens-are	pens-aremos	pens-áremos
pens-arás	pens-ares	pens-aréis	pens-areis
pens-ará	pens-are	pens-arán	pens-aren
Potencial		*Potencial*	
pens-aría		pens-aríamos	
pens-arías		pens-aríais	
pens-aría		pens-arían	

Imperativo	
Singular	Plural
(not used); no (not used)	pens-emos; no pens-emos
piens-a; no piens-es	pens-ad; no pens-éis
piens-e; no piens-e	piens-en; no piens-en

Conjugate reflexive verbs the same as above, use a reflexive pronoun as shown on page
   80, and make the changes for imperatives and present participles shown there in red.
Make compound tenses by adding a past participle on page 83 or 84.
Translation possibilities are on page 88. Conjugation tips are on page 89.

54
placer

Pattern 54: c ⟶ zc before a or o, pleg and plug are roots.
Placer (plac-er) (to please) is the pattern verb.
Present participle: plac-iendo   Past participle: plac-ido

Singular		Plural	
Indicativo	*Subjunctivo*	*Indicativo*	*Subjunctivo*
Presente	*Presente*	*Presente*	*Presente*
plazc-o	plazc-a	plac-emos	plazc-amos
plac-es	plazc-as	plac-éis	plazc-áis
plac-e	plazc-a, plegu-e	plac-en	plazc-an
Imperfecto	*Imperfecto*	*Imperfecto*	*Imperfecto*
plac-ía	plac-iera	plac-íamos	plac-iéramos
	OR		OR
	plac-iese		plac-iésemos
plac-ías	plac-ieras	plac-íais	plac-ierais
	OR		OR
	plac-ieses		plac-ieseis
plac-ía	plac-iera, plugu-iera	plac-ían	plac-ieran
	OR		OR
	plac-iese, plugu-iese		plac-iesen
Pretérito		*Pretérito*	
plac-í		plac-imos	
plac-iste		plac-isteis	
plac-ió, plug-o		plac-ieron, plugu-ieron	
Futuro	*Futuro*	*Futuro*	*Futuro*
plac-eré	plac-iere	plac-eremos	plac-iéremos
plac-erás	plac-ieres	plac-eréis	plac-iereis
plac-erá	plac-iere, plug-iere	plac-erán	plac-ieren
Potencial		*Potencial*	
plac-ería		plac-eríamos	
plac-erías		plac-eríais	
plac-ería		plac-erían	

Imperativo	
Singular	Plural
(not used); no (not used)	plazc-amos; no plazc-amos
plac-e; no plazc-as	plac-ed; no plazc-áis
plazc-a; no plazc-a	plazc-an; no plazc-an

Conjugate reflexive verbs the same as above, use a reflexive pronoun as shown on page 81, and make the changes for imperatives and present participles shown there in red.
Make compound tenses by adding a past participle on page 83 or 84.
Translation possibilities are on page 88. Conjugation tips are on page 90.

Pattern 55: e is deleted, é ⟹ e, o ⟹ u or ue, ó ⟹ o.
Poder (pod-er) (to be able, to be possible) is the pattern verb.
Present participle: pud-iendo   Past participle: pod-ido

Singular		Plural	
Indicativo	*Subjunctivo*	*Indicativo*	*Subjunctivo*

Presente	*Presente*	*Presente*	*Presente*
pued-o	pued-a	pod-emos	pod-amos
pued-es	pued-as	pod-éis	pod-áis
pued-e	pued-a	pued-en	pued-an
Imperfecto	*Imperfecto*	*Imperfecto*	*Imperfecto*
pod-ía	pud-iera	pod-íamos	pud-iéramos
	OR		OR
	pud-iese		pud-iésemos
pod-ías	pud-ieras	pod-íais	pud-ierais
	OR		OR
	pud-ieses		pud-ieseis
pod-ía	pud-iera	pod-ían	pud-ieran
	OR		OR
	pud-iese		pud-iesen
Pretérito		*Pretérito*	
pud-e		pud-imos	
pud-iste		pud-isteis	
pud-o		pud-ieron	
Futuro	*Futuro*	*Futuro*	*Futuro*
pod-ré	pud-iere	pod-remos	pud-iéremos
pod-rás	pud-ieres	pod-réis	pud-iereis
pod-rá	pud-iere	pod-rán	pud-ieren
Potencial		*Potencial*	
pod-ría		pod-ríamos	
pod-rías		pod-ríais	
pod-ría		pod-rían	

Imperativo	
Singular	Plural
(not used); no (not used)	pod-amos; no pod-amos
pued-e; no pued-as	pod-ed; no pod-áis
pued-a; no pued-a	pued-an; no pued-an

Conjugate reflexive verbs the same as above, use a reflexive pronoun as shown on page
81, and make the changes for imperatives and present participles shown there in red.
Make compound tenses by adding a past participle on page 83 or 84.
Translation possibilities are on page 88.   Conjugation tips are on page 90.

56

podrir (and pudrir)

Pattern 56: podr and pudr are roots, plus o ➡ u.
Podrir (podr-ir) (to rot, putrefy) is the pattern verb.
Present participle: pudr-iendo   Past participle: podr-ido

Singular		Plural	
Indicativo	*Subjunctivo*	*Indicativo*	*Subjunctivo*
Presente	*Presente*	*Presente*	*Presente*
pudr-o	pudr-a	pudr-imos	pudr-amos
pudr-es	pudr-as	pudr-ís	pudr-áis
pudr-e	pudr-a	pudr-en	pudr-an
Imperfecto	*Imperfecto*	*Imperfecto*	*Imperfecto*
pudr-ía	pudr-iera	pudr-íamos	pudr-iéramos
	OR		OR
	pudr-iese		pudr-iésemos
pudr-ías	pudr-ieras	pudr-íais	pudr-ierais
	OR		OR
	pudr-ieses		pudr-ieseis
pudr-ía	pudr-iera	pudr-ían	pudr-ieran
	OR		OR
	pudr-iese		pudr-iesen
Pretérito		*Pretérito*	
pudr-í, podr-í		pudr-imos	
pudr-iste		pudr-isteis	
pudr-ió		pudr-ieron	
Futuro	*Futuro*	*Futuro*	*Futuro*
pudr-iré, podr-iré	pudr-iere	pudr-iremos	pudr-iéremos
pudr-irás	pudr-ieres	pudr-iréis	pudr-iereis
pudr-irá	pudr-iere	pudr-irán	pudr-ieren
Potencial		*Potencial*	
pudr-iría, podr-iría		pudr-iríamos	
pudr-irías		pudr-iríais	
pudr-iría		pudr-irían	

Imperativo	
Singular	Plural
(not used); no (not used)	pudr-amos; no pudr-amos
pudr-e; no pudr-as	pudr-id; no pudr-áis
pudr-a; no pudr-a	pudr-an; no pudr-an

Conjugate reflexive verbs the same as above, use a reflexive pronoun as shown on page 82, and make the changes for imperatives and present participles shown there in red.
Make compound tenses by adding a past participle on page 83 or 84.
Translation possibilities are on page 88. Conjugation tips are on page 91.

Pattern 57: e is deleted, o ➡ u, add d or g, n ➡ s, plus other changes. **57**
Poner (pon-er) (to put, set, lay, place) is the pattern verb.
Present participle: pon-iendo   Past participle: pu-esto **poner**

	Singular		Plural	
	Indicativo	*Subjunctivo*	*Indicativo*	*Subjunctivo*
Presente	*Presente*		*Presente*	*Presente*
	pong-o	pong-a	pon-emos	pong-amos
	pon-es	pong-as	pon-éis	pong-áis
	pon-e	pong-a	pon-en	pong-an
Imperfecto	*Imperfecto*		*Imperfecto*	*Imperfecto*
	pon-ía	pus-iera	pon-íamos	pus-iéramos
		OR		OR
		pus-iese		pus-iésemos
	pon-ías	pus-ieras	pon-íais	pus-ierais
		OR		OR
		pus-ieses		pus-ieseis
	pon-ía	pus-iera	pon-ían	pus-ieran
		OR		OR
		pus-iese		pus-iesen
Pretérito			*Pretérito*	
	pus-e		pus-imos	
	pus-iste		pus-isteis	
	pus-o		pus-ieron	
Futuro	*Futuro*		*Futuro*	*Futuro*
	pond-ré	pus-iere	pond-remos	pus-iéremos
	pond-rás	pus-ieres	pond-réis	pus-iereis
	pond-rá	pus-iere	pond-rán	pus-ieren
Potencial			*Potencial*	
	pond-ría		pond-ríamos	
	pond-rías		pond-ríais	
	pond-ría		pond-rían	

Imperativo	
Singular	Plural
(not used); no (not used)	pong-amos; no pong-amos
pon; no pong-as	pon-ed; no pong-áis
pong-a; no pong-a	pong-an; no pong-an

Conjugate reflexive verbs the same as above, use a reflexive pronoun as shown on page
81, and make the changes for imperatives and present participles shown there in red.
Make compound tenses by adding a past participle on page 83 or 84.
Translation possibilities are on page 88. Conjugation tips are on page 90.

58
predecir

Pattern 58: e ➠ i, c ➠ g or j, plus other changes.
Predecir (predec-ir) (to predict) is the pattern verb.
Present participle: predic-iendo Past participle: predic-ho

Singular		Plural	
Indicativo	*Subjunctivo*	*Indicativo*	*Subjunctivo*

Presente	*Presente*	*Presente*	*Presente*
predig-o	predig-a	predec-imos	predig-amos
predic-es	predig-as	predec-ís	predig-áis
predic-e	predig-a	predic-en	predig-an

Imperfecto	*Imperfecto*	*Imperfecto*	*Imperfecto*
predec-ía	predij-era OR predij-ese	predec-íamos	predij-éramos OR predij-ésemos
predec-ías	predij-eras OR predij-eses	predec-íais	predij-erais OR predij-eseis
predec-ía	predij-era OR predij-ese	predec-ían	predij-eran OR predij-esen

Pretérito		*Pretérito*	
predij-e		predij-imos	
predij-iste		predij-isteis	
predij-o		predij-eron	

Futuro	*Futuro*	*Futuro*	*Futuro*
predec-iré	predij-ere	predec-iremos	predij-éremos
predec-irás	predij-eres	predec-iréis	predij-ereis
predec-irá	predij-ere	predec-irán	predij-eren

Potencial		*Potencial*	
predec-iría		predec-iríamos	
predec-irías		predec-iríais	
predec-iría		predec-irían	

Imperativo	
Singular	Plural
(not used); no (not used)	predig-amos; no predig-amos
predic-e; no predig-as	predec-id; no predig-áis
predig-a; no predig-a	predig-an; no predig-an

Conjugate reflexive verbs the same as above, use a reflexive pronoun as shown on page 82, and make the changes for imperatives and present participles shown there in red.
Make compound tenses by adding a past participle on page 83 or 84.
Translation possibilities are on page 88. Conjugation tips are on page 91.

Pattern 59: c ⟶ zc or j, i is deleted.
Producir (produc-ir) (to produce, yield, beat) is the pattern verb.
Present participle: produc-iendo   Past participle: produc-ido

59
producir

Singular		Plural	
Indicativo	*Subjunctivo*	*Indicativo*	*Subjunctivo*
Presente	*Presente*	*Presente*	*Presente*
produzc-o	produzc-a	produc-imos	produzc-amos
produc-es	produzc-as	produc-ís	produzc-áis
produc-e	produzc-a	produc-en	produzc-an
Imperfecto	*Imperfecto*	*Imperfecto*	*Imperfecto*
produc-ía	produj-era	produc-íamos	peoduj-éramos
	OR		OR
	produj-ese		produj-ésemos
produc-ías	produj-eras	produc-íais	produj-erais
	OR		OR
	produj-eses		produj-eseis
produc-ía	produj-era	produc-ían	produj-eran
	OR		OR
	produj-ese		produj-esen
Pretérito		*Pretérito*	
produj-e		produj-imos	
produj-iste		produj-isteis	
produj-o		produj-eron	
Futuro	*Futuro*	*Futuro*	*Futuro*
produc-iré	produj-ere	produc-iremos	produj-éremos
produc-irás	produj-eres	produc-iréis	produj-ereis
produc-irá	produj-ere	produc-irán	produj-eren
Potencial		*Potencial*	
produc-iría		produc-iríamos	
produc-irías		produc-iríais	
produc-iría		produc-irían	

Imperativo	
Singular	Plural
(not used); no (not used)	produzc-amos; no produzc-amos
produc-e; no produzc-as	produc-id; no produzc-áis
produzc-a; no produzc-a	produzc-an; no produzc-an

Conjugate reflexive verbs the same as above, use a reflexive pronoun as shown on page
   82, and make the changes for imperatives and present participles shown there in red.
Make compound tenses by adding a past participle on page 83 or 84.
Translation possibilities are on page 88.   Conjugation tips are on page 91.

60

querer

Pattern 60: e ➡ ie or i, delete e, plus other changes.
Querer (quer-er) (to wish, want, desire) is the pattern verb.
Present participle: quer-iendo   Past participle: quer-ido

Singular		Plural	
Indicativo	*Subjunctivo*	*Indicativo*	*Subjunctivo*
Presente	*Presente*	*Presente*	*Presente*
quier-o	quier-a	quer-emos	quer-amos
quier-es	quier-as	quer-éis	quer-áis
quier-e	quier-a	quier-en	quier-an
Imperfecto	*Imperfecto*	*Imperfecto*	*Imperfecto*
quer-ía	quis-iera	quer-íamos	quis-iéramos
	OR		OR
	quis-iese		quis-iésemos
quer-ías	quis-ieras	quer-íais	quis-ierais
	OR		OR
	quis-ieses		quis-ieseis
quer-ía	quis-iera	quer-ían	quis-ieran
	OR		OR
	quis-iese		quis-iesen
Pretérito		*Pretérito*	
quis-e		quis-imos	
quis-iste		quis-isteis	
quis-o		quis-ieron	
Futuro	*Futuro*	*Futuro*	*Futuro*
quer-ré	quis-iere	quer-remos	quis-iéremos
quer-rás	quis-ieres	quer-réis	quis-iereis
quer-rá	quis-iere	quer-rán	quis-ieren
Potencial		*Potencial*	
quer-ría		quer-ríamos	
quer-rías		quer-ríais	
quer-ría		quer-rían	

Imperativo	
Singular	Plural
(not used); no (not used)	quer-amos; no quer-amos
quier-e; no quier-as	quer-ed; no quer-áis
quier-a; no quier-a	quier-an; no quier-an

Conjugate reflexive verbs the same as above, use a reflexive pronoun as shown on page 81, and make the changes for imperatives and present participles shown there in red.
Make compound tenses by adding a past participle on page 83 or 84.
Translation possibilities are on page 88. Conjugation tips are on page 90.

Pattern 61: raig and ray are roots, plus i ➡ í or y.
Raer (ra-er) (to scrape, scratch) is the pattern verb.
Present participle: ra-yendo   Past participle: ra-ído

Singular		Plural	
Indicativo	*Subjunctivo*	*Indicativo*	*Subjunctivo*
Presente	*Presente*	*Presente*	*Presente*
ra-o, raig-o, ray-o	raig-a, ray-a	ra-emos	raig-amos, ray-amos
ra-es	raig-as, ray-as	ra-éis	raig-áis, ray-áis
ra-e	raig-a, ray-a	ra-en	raig-an, ray-an
Imperfecto	*Imperfecto*	*Imperfecto*	*Imperfecto*
ra-ía	ra-yera	ra-íamos	ra-yéramos
	OR		OR
	ra-yese		ra-yésemos
ra-ías	ra-yeras	ra-íais	ra-yerais
	OR		OR
	ra-yeses		ra-yeseis
ra-ía	ra-yera	ra-ían	ra-yeran
	OR		OR
	ra-yese		ra-yesen
Pretérito		*Pretérito*	
ra-í		ra-ímos	
ra-íste		ra-ísteis	
ra-yó		ra-yeron	
Futuro	*Futuro*	*Futuro*	*Futuro*
ra-eré	ra-yere	ra-eremos	ra-yéremos
ra-erás	ra-yeres	ra-eréis	ra-yereis
ra-erá	ra-yere	ra-erán	ra-yeren
Potencial		*Potencial*	
ra-ería		ra-eríamos	
ra-erías		ra-eríais	
ra-ería		ra-erían	

Imperativo	
Singular	Plural
(not used); no (not used)	raig-amos, ray-amos; no raig-amos, no ray-amos
ra-e; no raig-as, no ray-as	ra-ed; no raig-áis, no ray-áis
raig-a, ray-a; no raig-a, no ray-a	raig-an, ray-an; no raig-an, no ray-an

Conjugate reflexive verbs the same as above, use a reflexive pronoun as shown on page
  81, and make the changes for imperatives and present participles shown there in red.
Make compound tenses by adding a past participle on page 83 or 84.
Translation possibilities are on page 88. Conjugation tips are on page 90.

61

62

regar

Pattern 62: e ➡ ie when stressed, g ➡ gu before e.
Regar (reg-ar) (to water, irrigate) is the pattern verb.
Present participle: reg-ando   Past participle: reg-ado

Singular		Plural	
Indicativo	*Subjunctivo*	*Indicativo*	*Subjunctivo*
Presente	*Presente*	*Presente*	*Presente*
rieg-o	riegu-e	reg-amos	regu-emos
rieg-as	riegu-es	reg-áis	regu-éis
rieg-a	riegu-e	rieg-an	riegu-en
Imperfecto	*Imperfecto*	*Imperfecto*	*Imperfecto*
reg-aba	reg-ara	reg-ábamos	reg-áramos
	OR		OR
	reg-ase		reg-ásemos
reg-abas	reg-aras	reg-abais	reg-arais
	OR		OR
	reg-ases		reg-aseis
reg-aba	reg-ara	reg-aban	reg-aran
	OR		OR
	reg-ase		reg-asen
Pretérito		*Pretérito*	
regu-é		reg-amos	
reg-aste		reg-asteis	
reg-ó		reg-aron	
Futuro	*Futuro*	*Futuro*	*Futuro*
reg-aré	reg-are	reg-aremos	reg-áremos
reg-arás	reg-ares	reg-aréis	reg-areis
reg-ará	reg-are	reg-arán	reg-aren
Potencial		*Potencial*	
reg-aría		reg-aríamos	
reg-arías		reg-aríais	
reg-aría		reg-arían	

Imperativo	
Singular	Plural
(not used); no (not used)	regu-emos; no regu-emos
rieg-a; no riegu-es	reg-ad; no regu-éis
riegu-e; no riegu-e	riegu-en; no riegu-en

Conjugate reflexive verbs the same as above, use a reflexive pronoun as shown on page
  80, and make the changes for imperatives and present participles shown there in red.
Make compound tenses by adding a past participle on page 83 or 84.
Translation possibilities are on page 88. Conjugation tips are on page 89.

Pattern 63: e ➠ i or í, e is deleted, i ➠ í.
Reír (re-ír) (to laugh, laugh at) is the pattern verb.
Present participle: r-iendo   Past participle: re-ído

Singular		Plural	
Indicativo	*Subjunctivo*	*Indicativo*	*Subjunctivo*
Presente	*Presente*	*Presente*	*Presente*
rí-o	rí-a	re-ímos	ri-amos
rí-es	rí-as	re-ís	ri-áis
rí-e	rí-a	rí-en	ri-an
Imperfecto	*Imperfecto*	*Imperfecto*	*Imperfecto*
re-ía	r-iera	re-íamos	r-iéramos
	OR		OR
	r-iese		r-iésemos
re-ías	r-ieras	re-íais	r-ierais
	OR		OR
	r-ieses		r-ieseis
re-ía	r-iera	re-ían	r-ieran
	OR		OR
	r-iese		r-iesen
Pretérito		*Pretérito*	
re-í		re-ímos	
re-íste		re-ísteis	
r-ió		r-ieron	
Futuro	*Futuro*	*Futuro*	*Futuro*
re-iré	r-iere	re-iremos	r-iéremos
re-irás	r-ieres	re-iréis	r-iereis
re-irá	r-iere	re-irán	r-ieren
Potencial		*Potencial*	
re-iría		re-iríamos	
re-irías		re-iríais	
re-iría		re-irían	

Imperativo	
Singular	Plural
(not used); no (not used)	ri-amos; no ri-amos
rí-e; no rí-as	re-íd; no ri-áis
rí-a; no rí-a	rí-an; no rí-an

Conjugate reflexive verbs the same as above, use a reflexive pronoun as shown on page
 82, and make the changes for imperatives and present participles shown there in red.
Make compound tenses by adding a past participle on page 83 or 84.
Translation possibilities are on page 88. Conjugation tips are on page 91.

64
reñir

Pattern 64: e ⟶ i, i is deleted.
Reñir (reñ-ir) (to fight, scold) is the pattern verb.
Present participle: riñ-endo   Past participle: reñ-ido

Singular		Plural	
Indicativo	*Subjunctivo*	*Indicativo*	*Subjunctivo*
Presente	*Presente*	*Presente*	*Presente*
riñ-o	riñ-a	reñ-imos	riñ-amos
riñ-es	riñ-as	reñ-ís	riñ-áis
riñ-e	riñ-a	riñ-en	riñ-an
Imperfecto	*Imperfecto*	*Imperfecto*	*Imperfecto*
reñ-ía	riñ-era	reñ-íamos	riñ-éramos
	OR		OR
	riñ-ese		riñ-ésemos
reñ-ías	riñ-eras	reñ-íais	riñ-erais
	OR		OR
	riñ-eses		riñ-eseis
reñ-ía	riñ-era	reñ-ían	riñ-eran
	OR		OR
	riñ-ese		riñ-esen
Pretérito		*Pretérito*	
reñ-í		reñ-imos	
reñ-iste		reñ-isteis	
riñ-ó		riñ-eron	
Futuro	*Futuro*	*Futuro*	*Futuro*
reñ-iré	riñ-ere	reñ-iremos	riñ-éremos
reñ-irás	riñ-eres	reñ-iréis	riñ-ereis
reñ-irá	riñ-ere	reñ-irán	riñ-eren
Potencial		*Potencial*	
reñ-iría		reñ-iríamos	
reñ-irías		reñ-iríais	
reñ-iría		reñ-irían	

Imperativo	
Singular	*Plural*
(not used); no (not used)	riñ-amos; no riñ-amos
riñ-e; no riñ-as	reñ-id; no riñ-áis
riñ-a; no riñ-a	riñ-an; no riñ-an

Conjugate reflexive verbs the same as above, use a reflexive pronoun as shown on page 82, and make the changes for imperatives and present participles shown there in red.
Make compound tenses by adding a past participle on page 83 or 84.
Translation possibilities are on page 88. Conjugation tips are on page 91.

Pattern 65: roig and roy are roots, plus i ➡ í or y.
Roer (ro-er) (to nibble [at], gnaw) is the pattern verb.
Present participle: ro-yendo   Past participle: ro-ído

	Singular		Plural
Indicativo	*Subjunctivo*	*Indicativo*	*Subjunctivo*
Presente	*Presente*	*Presente*	*Presente*
ro-o, roig-o, roy-o	ro-a, roig-a, roy-o	ro-emo^5	ro-amos, roig-amos, roy-amos
ro-es	ro-as, roig-as, roy-as	ro-éis	ro-áis, roig-áis, roy-áis
ro-e	ro-a, roig-a, roy-a	ro-en	ro-an, roig-an, roy-an
Imperfecto	*Imperfecto*	*Imperfecto*	*Imperfecto*
ro-ía	ro-yera OR ro-yese	ro-íamos	ro-yéramos OR ro-yésemos
ro-ías	ro-yeras OR ro-yeses	ro-íais	ro-yerais OR ro-yeseis
ro-ía	ro-yera OR ro-yese	ro-ían	ro-yeran OR ro-yesen
Pretérito		*Pretérito*	
ro-í		ro-ímos	
ro-íste		ro-ísteis	
ro-yó		ro-yeron	
Futuro	*Futuro*	*Futuro*	*Futuro*
ro-eré	ro-yere	ro-eremos	ro-yéremos
ro-erás	ro-yeres	ro-eréis	ro-yereis
ro-erá	ro-yere	ro-erán	ro-yeren
Potencial		*Potencial*	
ro-ería		ro-eríamos	
ro-erías		ro-eríais	
ro-ería		ro-erían	

Imperativo	
Singular	Plural
(not used); no (not used)	ro-amos, roig-amos, roy-amos; no ro-amos, no roig-amos, no roy-amos
ro-e; no ro-as, no roig-as, no roy-as	ro-ed; no ro-áis, no roig-áis, no roy-áis
ro-a, roig-a, roy-a; no ro-a, no roig-a, no roy-a	ro-an, roig-an, roy-an; no ro-an, no roig-an, no roy-an

Conjugate reflexive verbs the same as above, use a reflexive pronoun as shown on page
81, and make the changes for imperatives and present participles shown there in red.
Make compound tenses by adding a past participle on page 83 or 84.
Translation possibilities are on page 88. Conjugation tips are on page 90.

66
saber

Pattern 66: a ⟹ e or u, e is deleted, b ⟹ p.
Saber (sab-er) (to know, find out) is the pattern verb.
Present participle: sab-iendo   Past participle: sab-ido

Singular		Plural	
Indicativo	*Subjunctivo*	*Indicativo*	*Subjunctivo*
Presente	*Presente*	*Presente*	*Presente*
s-é	sep-a	sab-emos	sep-amos
sab-es	sep-as	sab-éis	sep-áis
sab-e	sep-a	sab-en	sep-an
Imperfecto	*Imperfecto*	*Imperfecto*	*Imperfecto*
sab-ía	sup-iera	sab-íamos	sup-iéramos
	OR		OR
	sup-iese		sup-iésemos
sab-ías	sup-ieras	sab-íais	sup-ierais
	OR		OR
	sup-ieses		sup-ieseis
sab-ía	sup-iera	sab-ían	sup-ieran
	OR		OR
	sup-iese		sup-iesen
Pretérito		*Pretérito*	
sup-e		sup-imos	
sup-iste		sup-isteis	
sup-o		sup-ieron	
Futuro	*Futuro*	*Futuro*	*Futuro*
sab-ré	sup-iere	sab-remos	sup-iéremos
sab-rás	sup-ieres	sab-réis	sup-iereis
sab-rá	sup-iere	sab-rán	sup-ieren
Potencial		*Potencial*	
sab-ría		sab-ríamos	
sab-rías		sab-ríais	
sab-ría		sab-rían	

Imperativo	
Singular	Plural
(not used); no (not used)	sep-amos; no sep-amos
sab-e; no sep-as	sab-ed; no sep-áis
sep-a; no sep-a	sep-an; no sep-an

Conjugate reflexive verbs the same as above, use a reflexive pronoun as shown on page
81, and make the changes for imperatives and present participles shown there in red.
Make compound tenses by adding a past participle on page 83 or 84.
Translation possibilities are on page 88. Conjugation tips are on page 90.

Pattern 67: c ➡ qu before e to retain the k sound.
Sacar (sac-ar) (to take out, get out) is the pattern verb.
Present participle: sac-ando   Past participle: sac-ado

Singular		Plural	
Indicativo	*Subjunctivo*	*Indicativo*	*Subjunctivo*
Presente	*Presente*	*Presente*	*Presente*
sac-o	saqu-e	sac-amos	saqu-emos
sac-as	saqu-es	sac-áis	saqu-éis
sac-a	saqu-e	sac-an	saqu-en
Imperfecto	*Imperfecto*	*Imperfecto*	*Imperfecto*
sac-aba	sac-ara	sac-ábamos	sac-áramos
	OR		OR
	sac-ase		sac-ásemos
sac-abas	sac-aras	sac-abais	sac-arais
	OR		OR
	sac-ases		sac-aseis
sac-aba	sac-ara	sac-aban	sac-aran
	OR		OR
	sac-ase		sac-asen
Pretérito		*Pretérito*	
saqu-é		sac-amos	
sac-aste		sac-asteis	
sac-ó		sac-aron	
Futuro	*Futuro*	*Futuro*	*Futuro*
sac-aré	sac-are	sac-aremos	sac-áremos
sac-arás	sac-ares	sac-aréis	sac-areis
sac-ará	sac-are	sac-arán	sac-aren
Potencial		*Potencial*	
sac-aría		sac-aríamos	
sac-arías		sac-aríais	
sac-aría		sac-arían	

Imperativo	
Singular	Plural
(not used); no (not used)	saqu-emos; no saqu-emos
sac-a; no saqu-es	sac-ad; no saqu-éis
saqu-e; no saqu-e	saqu-en; no saqu-en

Conjugate reflexive verbs the same as above, use a reflexive pronoun as shown on page
  80, and make the changes for imperatives and present participles shown there in red.
Make compound tenses by adding a past participle on page 83 or 84.
Translation possibilities are on page 88. Conjugation tips are on page 89.

68
salir

Pattern 68: i is deleted, add d or g.
Salir (sal-ir) (to leave, to go out) is the pattern verb.
Present participle: sal-iendo   Past participle: sal-ido

Singular		Plural	
Indicativo	*Subjunctivo*	*Indicativo*	*Subjunctivo*
Presente	*Presente*	*Presente*	*Presente*
salg-o	salg-a	sal-imos	salg-amos
sal-es	salg-as	sal-ís	salg-áis
sal-e	salg-a	sal-en	salg-an
Imperfecto	*Imperfecto*	*Imperfecto*	*Imperfecto*
sal-ía	sal-iera	sal-íamos	sal-iéramos
	OR		OR
	sal-iese		sal-iésemos
sal-ías	sal-ieras	sal-íais	sal-ierais
	OR		OR
	sal-ieses		sal-ieseis
sal-ía	sal-iera	sal-ían	sal-ieran
	OR		OR
	sal-iese		sal-iesen
Pretérito		*Pretérito*	
sal-í		sal-imos	
sal-iste		sal-isteis	
sal-ió		sal-ieron	
Futuro	*Futuro*	*Futuro*	*Futuro*
sald-ré	sal-iere	sald-remos	sal-iéremos
sald-rás	sal-ieres	sald-réis	sal-iereis
sald-rá	sal-iere	sald-rán	sal-ieren
Potencial		*Potencial*	
sald-ría		sald-ríamos	
sald-rías		sald-ríais	
sald-ria		sald-rían	

Imperativo	
Singular	Plural
(not used); no (not used)	salg-amos; no salg-amos
sal; no salg-as	sal-id; no salg-áis
salg-a; no salg-a	salg-an; no salg-an

Conjugate reflexive verbs the same as above, use a reflexive pronoun as shown on page 82, and make the changes for imperatives and present participles shown there in red.
Make compound tenses by adding a past participle on page 83 or 84.
Translation possibilities are on page 88. Conjugation tips are on page 91.

Pattern 69: a ⟹ i, etc. as in hacer, plus a tú imperative.
Satisfacer (satisfac-er) (to satisfy) is the pattern verb.
Present participle: satisfac-iendo   Past participle: satisfec-ho

Singular		Plural	
Indicativo	*Subjunctivo*	*Indicativo*	*Subjunctivo*
Presente	*Presente*	*Presente*	*Presente*
satisfag-o	satisfag-a	satisfac-emos	satisfag-amos
satisfac-es	satisfag-as	satisfac-éis	satisfag-áis
satisfac-e	satisfag-a	satisfac-en	satisfag-an
Imperfecto	*Imperfecto*	*Imperfecto*	*Imperfecto*
satisfac-ía	satisfic-iera	satisfac-íamos	satisfic-iéramos
	OR		OR
	satisfic-iese		satisfic-iésemos
satisfac-ías	satisfic-ieras	satisfac-íais	satisfic-ierais
	OR		OR
	satisfic-ieses		satisfic-ieseis
satisfac-ía	satisfic-iera	satisfac-ían	satisfic-ieran
	OR		OR
	satisfic-iese		satisfic-iesen
Pretérito		*Pretérito*	
satisfic-e		satisfic-imos	
satisfic-iste		satisfic-isteis	
satisfiz-o		satisfic-ieron	
Futuro	*Futuro*	*Futuro*	*Futuro*
satisfa-ré	satisfic-iere	satisfa-remos	satisfic-iéremos
satisfa-rás	satisfic-ieres	satisfa-réis	satisfic-iereis
satisfa-rá	satisfic-iere	satisfa-rán	satisfic-ieren
Potencial		*Potencial*	
satisfa-ría		satisfa-ríamos	
satisfa-rías		satisfa-ríais	
satisfa-ría		satisfa-rían	

Imperativo	
Singular	Plural
(not used); no (not used)	satisfag-amos; no satisfag-amos
satisfaz, satisfac-e; no satisfag-as	satisfac-ed; no satisfag-áis
satisfag-a; no satisfag-a	satisfag-an; no satisfag-an

Conjugate reflexive verbs the same as above, use a reflexive pronoun as shown on page
    81, and make the changes for imperatives and present participles shown there in red.
Make compound tenses by adding a past participle on page 83 or 84.
Translation possibilities are on page 88. Conjugation tips are on page 90.

70
seguir

Pattern 70: e ➡ i, gu ➡ g before a or o.
Seguir (segu-ir) (to follow, pursue) is the pattern verb.
Present participle: sigu-iendo   Past participle: segu-ido

Singular		Plural	
Indicativo	*Subjunctivo*	*Indicativo*	*Subjunctivo*
Presente	*Presente*	*Presente*	*Presente*
sig-o	sig-a	segu-imos	sig-amos
sigu-es	sig-as	segu-ís	sig-áis
sigu-e	sig-a	sigu-en	sig-an
Imperfecto	*Imperfecto*	*Imperfecto*	*Imperfecto*
segu-ía	sigu-iera OR sigu-iese	segu-íamos	sigu-iéramos OR sigu-iésemos
segu-ías	sigu-ieras OR sigu-ieses	segu-íais	sigu-ierais OR sigu-ieseis
segu-ía	sigu-iera OR sigu-iese	segu-ían	sigu-ieran OR sigu-iesen
Pretérito		*Pretérito*	
segu-í		segu-imos	
segu-iste		segu-isteis	
sigu-ió		sigu-ieron	
Futuro	*Futuro*	*Futuro*	*Futuro*
segu-iré	sigu-iere	segu-iremos	sigu-iéremos
segu-irás	sigu-ieres	segu-iréis	sigu-iereis
segu-irá	sigu-iere	segu-irán	sigu-ieren
Potencial		*Potencial*	
segu-iría		segu-iríamos	
segu-irías		segu-iríais	
segu-iría		segu-irían	

Imperativo	
Singular	Plural
(not used); no (not used)	sig-amos; no sig-amos
sigu-e; no sig-as	segu-id; no sig-áis
sig-a; no sig-a	sig-an; no sig-an

Conjugate reflexive verbs the same as above, use a reflexive pronoun as shown on page
   82, and make the changes for imperatives and present participles shown there in red.
Make compound tenses by adding a past participle on page 83 or 84.
Translation possibilities are on page 88. Conjugation tips are on page 91.

Pattern 71: e ➠ ie when stressed, e ➠ i.
Sentir (sent-ir) (to feel, sense, regret) is the pattern verb.
Present participle: sint-iendo   Past participle: sent-ido

Singular		Plural	
Indicativo	*Subjunctivo*	*Indicativo*	*Subjunctivo*
Presente	*Presente*	*Presente*	*Presente*
sient-o	sient-a	sent-imos	sint-amos
sient-es	sient-as	sent-ís	sint-áis
sient-e	sient-a	sient-en	sint-an
Imperfecto	*Imperfecto*	*Imperfecto*	*Imperfecto*
sent-ía	sint-iera	sent-íamos	sint-iéramos
	OR		OR
	sint-iese		sint-iésemos
sent-ías	sint-ieras	sent-íais	sint-ierais
	OR		OR
	sint-ieses		sint-ieseis
sent-ía	sint-iera	sent-ían	sint-ieran
	OR		OR
	sint-iese		sint-iesen
Pretérito		*Pretérito*	
sent-í		sent-imos	
sent-iste		sent-isteis	
sint-ió		sint-ieron	
Futuro	*Futuro*	*Futuro*	*Futuro*
sent-iré	sint-iere	sent-iremos	sint-iéremos
sent-irás	sint-ieres	sent-iréis	sint-iereis
sent-irá	sint-iere	sent-irán	sint-ieren
Potencial		*Potencial*	
sent-iría		sent-iríamos	
sent-irías		sent-iríais	
sent-iría		sent-irían	

Imperativo	
Singular	Plural
(not used); no (not used)	sint-amos; no sint-amos
sient-e; no sient-as	sent-id; no sint-áis
sient-a; no sient-a	sient-an; no sient-an

Conjugate reflexive verbs the same as above, use a reflexive pronoun as shown on page
82, and make the changes for imperatives and present participles shown there in red.
Make compound tenses by adding a past participle on page 83 or 84.
Translation possibilities are on page 88. Conjugation tips are on page 91.

72

ser

Pattern 72: er, fu and se are roots, plus other changes.
Ser (s-er) (to be) (an auxiliary verb) is the pattern verb.
Present participle: s-iendo   Past participle: s-ido

Singular		Plural	
Indicativo	*Subjunctivo*	*Indicativo*	*Subjunctivo*
Presente	*Presente*	*Presente*	*Presente*
s-oy	se-a	s-omos	se-amos
er-es	se-as	s-ois	se-áis
es	se-a	s-on	se-an
Imperfecto	*Imperfecto*	*Imperfecto*	*Imperfecto*
er-a	fu-era	ér-amos	fu-éramos
	OR		OR
	fu-ese		fu-ésemos
er-as	fu-eras	er-ais	fu-erais
	OR		OR
	fu-eses		fu-eseis
er-a	fu-era	er-an	fu-eran
	OR		OR
	fu-ese		fu-esen
Pretérito		*Pretérito*	
fu-i		fu-imos	
fu-iste		fu-isteis	
fu-e		fu-eron	
Futuro	*Futuro*	*Futuro*	*Futuro*
s-eré	fu-ere	s-eremos	fu-éremos
s-erás	fu-eres	s-eréis	fu-ereis
s-erá	fu-ere	s-erán	fu-eren
Potencial		*Potencial*	
s-ería		s-eríamos	
s-erías		s-eríais	
s-ería		s-erían	

Imperativo	
Singular	Plural
(not used); no (not used)	se-amos; no se-amos
s-é; no se-as	s-ed; no se-áis
se-a; no se-a	se-an; no se-an

Conjugate reflexive verbs the same as above, use a reflexive pronoun as shown on page
  81, and make the changes for imperatives and present participles shown there in red.
Make compound tenses by adding a past participle on page 83 or 84.
Translation possibilities are on page 88. Conjugation tips are on page 90.

Pattern 73: Some conjugations customarily are not used, plus o ➠ ue.
Soler (sol-er) (to be accustomed to [followed by a verb]) is the pattern verb.
Present participle: sol-iendo   Past participle: sol-ido

Singular		Plural	
Indicativo	*Subjunctivo*	*Indicativo*	*Subjunctivo*
Presente	*Presente*	*Presente*	*Presente*
suel-o	suel-a	sol-emos	sol-amos
suel-es	suel-as	sol-éis	sol-áis
suel-e	suel-a	suel-en	suel-an
Imperfecto	*Imperfecto*	*Imperfecto*	*Imperfecto*
sol-ía	sol-iera	sol-íamos	sol-iéramos
	OR		OR
	sol-iese		sol-iésemos
sol-ías	sol-ieras	sol-íais	sol-ierais
	OR		OR
	sol-ieses		sol-ieseis
sol-ía	sol-iera	sol-ían	sol-ieran
	OR		OR
	sol-iese		sol-iesen
Pretérito		*Pretérito*	
sol-í		sol-imos	
sol-iste		sol-isteis	
sol-ió		sol-ieron	
Futuro	*Futuro*	*Futuro*	*Futuro*
(not used)	(not used)	(not used)	(not used)
(not used)	(not used)	(not used)	(not used)
(not used)	(not used)	(not used)	(not used)
Potencial		*Potencial*	
(not used)		(not used)	
(not used)		(not used)	
(not used)		(not used)	

Imperativo	
Singular	Plural
(not used); no (not used)	(not used); no (not used)
(not used); no (not used)	(not used); no (not used)
(not used); no (not used)	(not used); no (not used)

Conjugate reflexive verbs the same as above, use a reflexive pronoun as shown on page
   81, and make the changes for imperatives and present participles shown there in red.
Make compound tenses by adding a past participle on page 83 or 84.
Translation possibilities are on page 88. Conjugation tips are on page 90.

74
tener

Pattern 74: e ➡ ie or u, delete e, plus other changes.
Tener (ten-er) (to have) (an auxiliary verb) is the pattern verb.
Present participle: ten-iendo   Past participle: ten-ido

Singular		Plural	
Indicativo	*Subjunctivo*	*Indicativo*	*Subjunctivo*
Presente	*Presente*	*Presente*	*Presente*
teng-o	teng-a	ten-emos	teng-amos
tien-es	teng-as	ten-éis	teng-áis
tien-e	teng-a	tien-en	teng-an
Imperfecto	*Imperfecto*	*Imperfecto*	*Imperfecto*
ten-ía	tuv-iera	ten-íamos	tuv-iéramos
	OR		OR
	tuv-iese		tuv-iésemos
ten-ías	tuv-ieras	ten-íais	tuv-ierais
	OR		OR
	tuv-ieses		tuv-ieseis
ten-ía	tuv-iera	ten-ían	tuv-ieran
	OR		OR
	tuv-iese		tuv-iesen
Pretérito		*Pretérito*	
tuv-e		tuv-imos	
tuv-iste		tuv-isteis	
tuv-o		tuv-ieron	
Futuro	*Futuro*	*Futuro*	*Futuro*
tend-ré	tuv-iere	tend-remos	tuv-iéremos
tend-rás	tuv-ieres	tend-réis	tuv-iereis
tend-rá	tuv-iere	tend-rán	tuv-ieren
Potencial		*Potencial*	
tend-ría		tend-ríamos	
tend-rías		tend-ríais	
tend-ría		tend-rían	

Imperativo	
Singular	Plural
(not used); no (not used)	teng-amos; no teng-amos
ten; no teng-as	ten-ed; no teng-áis
teng-a; no teng-a	teng-an; no teng-an

Conjugate reflexive verbs the same as above, use a reflexive pronoun as shown on page 81, and make the changes for imperatives and present participles shown there in red.
Make compound tenses by adding a past participle on page 83 or 84.
Translation possibilities are on page 88. Conjugation tips are on page 90.

Pattern 75: add ig or j, plus other changes.
Traer (tra-er) (to bring, carry) is the pattern verb.
Present participle: tra-yendo   Past participle: tra-ído

Singular		Plural	
Indicativo	*Subjunctivo*	*Indicativo*	*Subjunctivo*
Presente	*Presente*	*Presente*	*Presente*
traig-o	traig-a	tra-emos	traig-amos
tra-es	traig-as	tra-éis	traig-áis
tra-e	traig-a	tra-en	traig-an
Imperfecto	*Imperfecto*	*Imperfecto*	*Imperfecto*
tra-ía	traj-era	tra-íamos	traj-éramos
	OR		OR
	traj-ese		traj-ésemos
tra-ías	traj-eras	tra-íais	traj-erais
	OR		OR
	traj-eses		traj-eseis
tra-ía	traj-era	tra-ían	traj-eran
	OR		OR
	traj-ese		traj-esen
Pretérito		*Pretérito*	
traj-e		traj-imos	
traj-iste		traj-isteis	
traj-o		traj-eron	
Futuro	*Futuro*	*Futuro*	*Futuro*
tra-eré	traj-ere	tra-eremos	traj-éremos
tra-erás	traj-eres	tra-eréis	traj-ereis
tra-erá	traj-ere	tra-erán	traj-eren
Potencial		*Potencial*	
tra-ería		tra-eríamos	
tra-erías		tra-eríais	
tra-ería		tra-erían	

Imperativo	
Singular	Plural
(not used); no (not used)	traig-amos; no traig-amos
tra-e; no traig-as	tra-ed; no traig-áis
traig-a; no traig-a	traig-an; no traig-an

Conjugate reflexive verbs the same as above, use a reflexive pronoun as shown on page 81, and make the changes for imperatives and present participles shown there in red.
Make compound tenses by adding a past participle on page 83 or 84.
Translation possibilities are on page 88. Conjugation tips are on page 90.

76

trocar

Pattern 76: o ➟ ue when stressed, c ➟ qu before e.
Trocar (troc-ar) (to exchange, barter) is the pattern verb.
Present participle: troc-ando   Past participle: troc-ado

Singular		Plural	
Indicativo	*Subjunctivo*	*Indicativo*	*Subjunctivo*
Presente	*Presente*	*Presente*	*Presente*
truec-o	truequ-e	troc-amos	troqu-emos
truec-as	truequ-es	troc-áis	troqu-éis
truec-a	truequ-e	truec-an	truequ-en
Imperfecto	*Imperfecto*	*Imperfecto*	*Imperfecto*
troc-aba	troc-ara	troc-ábamos	troc-áramos
	OR		OR
	troc-ase		troc-ásemos
troc-abas	troc-aras	troc-abais	troc-arais
	OR		OR
	troc-ases		troc-aseis
troc-aba	troc-ara	troc-aban	troc-aran
	OR		OR
	troc-ase		troc-asen
Pretérito		*Pretérito*	
troqu-é		troc-amos	
troc-aste		troc-asteis	
troc-ó		troc-aron	
Futuro	*Futuro*	*Futuro*	*Futuro*
troc-aré	troc-are	troc-aremos	troc-áremos
troc-arás	troc-ares	troc-aréis	troc-areis
troc-ará	troc-are	troc-arán	troc-aren
Potencial		*Potencial*	
troc-aría		troc-aríamos	
troc-arías		troc-aríais	
troc-aría		troc-arían	

Imperativo	
Singular	Plural
(not used); no (not used)	troqu-emos; no troqu-emos
truec-a; no truequ-es	troc-ad; no troqu-éis
truequ-e; no truequ-e	truequ-en; no truequ-en

Conjugate reflexive verbs the same as above, use a reflexive pronoun as shown on page 80, and make the changes for imperatives and present participles shown there in red.
Make compound tenses by adding a past participle on page 83 or 84.
Translation possibilities are on page 88. Conjugation tips are on page 89.

Pattern 77: e ➠ ie or i, delete i, add d or g, plus other changes.
Venir (ven-ir) (to come) is the pattern verb.
Present participle: vin-iendo   Past participle: ven-ido

Singular		Plural	
Indicativo	*Subjunctivo*	*Indicativo*	*Subjunctivo*
Presente	*Presente*	*Presente*	*Presente*
veng-o	veng-a	ven-imos	veng-amos
vien-es	veng-as	ven-ís	veng-áis
vien-e	veng-a	vien-en	veng-an
Imperfecto	*Imperfecto*	*Imperfecto*	*Imperfecto*
ven-ía	vin-iera	ven-íamos	vin-iéramos
	OR		OR
	vin-iese		vin-iésemos
ven-ías	vin-ieras	ven-íais	vin-ierais
	OR		OR
	vin-ieses		vin-ieseis
ven-ía	vin-iera	ven-ían	vin-ieran
	OR		OR
	vin-iese		vin-iesen
Pretérito		*Pretérito*	
vin-e		vin-imos	
vin-iste		vin-isteis	
vin-o		vin-ieron	
Futuro	*Futuro*	*Futuro*	*Futuro*
vend-ré	vin-iere	vend-remos	vin-iéremos
vend-rás	vin-ieres	vend-réis	vin-iereis
vend-rá	vin-iere	vend-rán	vin-ieren
Potencial		*Potencial*	
vend-ría		vend-ríamos	
vend-rías		vend-ríais	
vend-ría		vend-rían	

Imperativo	
Singular	Plural
(not used); no (not used)	veng-amos; no veng-amos
ven; no veng-as	ven-id; no veng-áis
veng-a; no veng-a	veng-an; no veng-an

Conjugate reflexive verbs the same as above, use a reflexive pronoun as shown on page 82, and make the changes for imperatives and present participles shown there in red.
Make compound tenses by adding a past participle on page 83 or 84.
Translation possibilities are on page 88. Conjugation tips are on page 91.

78
ver

Pattern 78: e is added, é ⟹ e, í ⟹ i, ó ⟹ o.
Ver (v-er) (to see, look at) is the pattern verb.
Present participle: v-iendo   Past participle: v-isto

Singular		Plural	
Indicativo	*Subjunctivo*	*Indicativo*	*Subjunctivo*
Presente	*Presente*	*Presente*	*Presente*
ve-o	ve-a	v-emos	ve-amos
v-es	ve-as	v-eis	ve-áis
v-e	ve-a	v-en	ve-an
Imperfecto	*Imperfecto*	*Imperfecto*	*Imperfecto*
ve-ía	v-iera	ve-íamos	v-iéramos
	OR		OR
	v-iese		v-iésemos
ve-ías	v-ieras	ve-íais	v-ierais
	OR		OR
	v-ieses		v-ieseis
ve-ía	v-iera	ve-ían	v-ieran
	OR		OR
	v-iese		v-iesen
Pretérito		*Pretérito*	
v-i		v-imos	
v-iste		v-isteis	
v-io		v-ieron	
Futuro	*Futuro*	*Futuro*	*Futuro*
v-eré	v-iere	v-eremos	v-iéremos
v-erás	v-ieres	v-eréis	v-iereis
v-erá	v-iere	v-erán	v-ieren
Potencial		*Potencial*	
v-ería		v-eríamos	
v-erías		v-eríais	
v-ería		v-erían	

Imperativo	
Singular	Plural
(not used); no (not used)	ve-amos; no ve-amos
v-e; no ve-as	v-ed; no ve-áis
ve-a; no ve-a	ve-an; no ve-an

Conjugate reflexive verbs the same as above, use a reflexive pronoun as shown on page 81, and make the changes for imperatives and present participles shown there in red.
Make compound tenses by adding a past participle on page 83 or 84.
Translation possibilities are on page 88. Conjugation tips are on page 90.

Pattern 79: yag, yaz, yazc, and yazg are roots.
Yacer (yac-er) (to rest, lie somewhere, e.g., cattle) is the pattern verb.
Present participle: yac-iendo   Past participle: yac-ido

	Singular		Plural	
Indicativo	*Subjunctivo*	*Indicativo*	*Subjunctivo*

Presente	*Presente*	*Presente*	*Presente*
yazc-o, yazg-o, yag-o	yazc-a, yazg-a, yag-a	yac-emos	yazc-amos, yazg-amos, yag-amos
yac-es	yazc-as, yazg-as, yag-as	yac-éis	yazc-áis, yazg-áis, yag-áis
yac-e	yazc-a, yazg-a, yag-a	yac-en	yazc-an, yazg-an, yag-an
Imperfecto	*Imperfecto*	*Imperfecto*	*Imperfecto*
yac-ía	yac-iera OR yac-iese	yac-íamos	yac-iéramos OR yac-iésemos
yac-ías	yac-ieras OR yac-ieses	yac-íais	yac-ierais OR yac-ieseis
yac-ía	yac-iera OR yac-iese	yac-ían	yac-ieran OR yac-iesen
Pretérito		*Pretérito*	
yac-í		yac-imos	
yac-iste		yac-isteis	
yac-ió		yac-ieron	
Futuro	*Futuro*	*Futuro*	*Futuro*
yac-eré	yac-iere	yac-eremos	yac-iéremos
yac-erás	yac-ieres	yac-eréis	yac-iereis
yac-erá	yac-iere	yac-erán	yac-ieren
Potencial		*Potencial*	
yac-ería		yac-eríamos	
yac-erías		yac-eríais	
yac-ería		yac-erían	

Imperativo	
Singular	Plural
(not used); no (not used)	yazc-amos, yazg-amos, yag-amos; no yazc-amos, yazg-amos, yag-amos
yaz, yac-e; no yazc-as	yac-ed; no yazc-áis
yazc-a, yazg-a, yag-a no yazc-a; no yazg-a; no yag-a	yazc-an, yazg-an, yag-an; no yazc-an, yazg-an, yag-an

Conjugate reflexive verbs the same as above, use a reflexive pronoun as shown on page 81, and make the changes for imperatives and present participles shown there in red.
Make compound tenses by adding a past participle on page 83 or 84.
Translation possibilities are on page 88. Conjugation tips are on page 90.

80
levantarse

Pattern 80: reflexive "ar" verbs.
Levantarse (levant-arse) (to get up) is the pattern verb.
Present participle: levant-ándose   Past participle: levant-ado

Singular		Plural	
Indicativo	*Subjunctivo*	*Indicativo*	*Subjunctivo*
Presente	*Presente*	*Presente*	*Presente*
me levant-o	me levant-e	nos levant-amos	nos levant-emos
te levant-as	te levant-es	os levant-áis	os levant-éis
se levant-a	se levant-e	se levant-an	se levant-en
Imperfecto	*Imperfecto*	*Imperfecto*	*Imperfecto*
me levant-aba	me levant-ara OR me levant-ase	nos levant-ábamos	nos levant-áramos OR nos levant-ásemos
te levant-abas	te levant-aras OR te levant-ases	os levant-abais	os levant-arais OR os levant-aseis
se levant-aba	se levant-ara OR se levant-ase	se levant-aban	se levant-aran OR se levant-asen
Pretérito		*Pretérito*	
me levant-é		nos levant-amos	
te levant-aste		os levant-asteis	
se levant-ó		se levant-aron	
Futuro	*Futuro*	*Futuro*	*Futuro*
me levant-aré	me levant-are	nos levant-aremos	nos levant-áremos
te levant-arás	te levant-ares	os levant-aréis	os levant-areis
se levant-ará	se levant-are	se levant-arán	se levant-aren
Potencial		*Potencial*	
me levant-aría		nos levant-aríamos	
te levant-arías		os levant-aríais	
se levant-aría		se levant-arían	

Imperativo	
Singular	Plural
(not used); no (not used)	levant-émonos ; no nos levant-emos
levánt-ate ; no te levant-es	levant-aos ; no os levant-éis
levánt-ese ; no se levant-e	levánt-ense ; no se levant-en

The letters in red on this page show how reflexive "ar" conjugations differ from non-reflexive "ar" conjugations.
Make compound tenses by adding a past participle on page 84.
Translation possibilities are on page 88. Conjugation tips are on page 89.

Pattern 81: reflexive "er" verbs.
Atreverse (atrev-erse) (to dare, venture) is the pattern verb.
Present participle: atrev-iéndo se   Past participle: atrev-ido

Singular		Plural	
Indicativo	*Subjunctivo*	*Indicativo*	*Subjunctivo*
Presente	*Presente*	*Presente*	*Presente*
me atrev-o	me atrev-a	nos atrev-emos	nos atrev-amos
te atrev-es	te atrev-as	os atrev-éis	os atrev-áis
se atrev-e	se atrev-a	se atrev-en	se atrev-an
Imperfecto	*Imperfecto*	*Imperfecto*	*Imperfecto*
me atrev-ía	me atrev-iera	nos atrev-íamos	nos atrev-iéramos
	OR		OR
	me atrev-iese		nos atrev-iésemos
te atrev-ías	te atrev-ieras	os atrev-íais	os atrev-ierais
	OR		OR
	te atrev-ieses		os atrev-ieseis
se atrev-ía	se atrev-iera	se atrev-ían	se atrev-ieran
	OR		OR
	se atrev-iese		se atrev-iesen
Pretérito		*Pretérito*	
me atrev-í		nos atrev-imos	
te atrev-iste		os atrev-isteis	
se atrev-ió		se atrev-ieron	
Futuro	*Futuro*	*Futuro*	*Futuro*
me atrev-eré	me atrev-iere	nos atrev-eremos	nos atrev-iéremos
te atrev-erás	te atrev-ieres	os atrev-eréis	os atrev-iereis
se atrev-erá	se atrev-iere	se atrev-erán	se atrev-ieren
Potencial		*Potencial*	
me atrev-ería		nos atrev-eríamos	
te atrev-erías		os atrev-eríais	
se atrev-ería		se atrev-erían	

Imperativo	
Singular	Plural
(not used); no (not used)	atrev- ámonos; no nos atrev-amos
atrév-e te; no te atrev-as	atrev- eos; no os atrev-áis
atrév-a se; no se atrev-a	atrév-an se; no se atrev-an

The letters in red on this page show how reflexive "er" conjugations differ from non-reflexive "er" conjugations.
Make compound tenses by adding a past participle on page 84.
Translation possibilities are on page 88. Conjugation tips are on page 90.

82
aburrirse

Pattern 82: reflexive "ir" verbs.
Aburrirse (aburr-irse) (to be bored) is the pattern verb.
Present participle: aburr-iéndose   Past participle: aburr-ido

Singular		Plural	
Indicativo	*Subjunctivo*	*Indicativo*	*Subjunctivo*
Presente	*Presente*	*Presente*	*Presente*
me aburr-o	me aburr-a	nos aburr-imos	nos aburr-amos
te aburr-es	te aburr-as	os aburr-ís	os aburr-áis
se aburr-e	se aburr-a	se aburr-en	se aburr-an
Imperfecto	*Imperfecto*	*Imperfecto*	*Imperfecto*
me aburr-ía	me aburr-iera	nos aburr-íamos	nos aburr-iéramos
	OR		OR
	me aburr-iese		nos aburr-iésemos
te aburr-ías	te aburr-ieras	os aburr-íais	os aburr-ierais
	OR		OR
	te aburr-ieses		os aburr-ieseis
se aburr-ía	se aburr-iera	se aburr-ían	se aburr-ieran
	OR		OR
	se aburr-iese		se aburr-iesen
Pretérito		*Pretérito*	
me aburr-í		nos aburr-imos	
te aburr-iste		os aburr-isteis	
se aburr-ió		se aburr-ieron	
Futuro	*Futuro*	*Futuro*	*Futuro*
me aburr-iré	me aburr-iere	nos aburr-iremos	nos aburr-iéremos
te aburr-irás	te aburr-ieres	os aburr-iréis	os aburr-iereis
se aburr-irá	se aburr-iere	se aburr-irán	se aburr-ieren
Potencial		*Potencial*	
me aburr-iría		nos aburr-iríamos	
te aburr-irías		os aburr-iríais	
se aburr-iría		se aburr-irían	

Imperativo	
Singular	Plural
(not used); no (not used)	aburr-ámonos; no nos aburr-amos
abúrr-ete; no te aburr-as	aburr-íos; no os aburr-áis
abúrr-ase; no se aburr-a	abúrr-anse; no se aburr-an

The letters in red on this page show how reflexive "ir" conjugations differ from non-reflexive "ir" conjugations.
Make compound tenses by adding a past participle on page 84.
Translation possibilities are on page 88. Conjugation tips are on page 91.

Add the past participle (past p.) of the verb you
want to conjugate
(e.g., he hablado).

83

compound non-reflexive verbs[1]

Singular			Plural	
Indicativo	*Subjunctivo*		*Indicativo*	*Subjunctivo*
Perfecto	*Perfecto*		*Perfecto*	*Perfecto*
he (past p.)	haya (past p.)		hemos (past p.)	hayamos (past p.)
has (past p.)	hayas (past p.)		habéis (past p.)	hayáis (past p.)
ha (past p.)	haya (past p.)		han (past p.)	hayan (past p.)
Pluscuamperfecto	*Pluscuamperfecto*		*Pluscuamperfecto*	*Pluscuamperfecto*
había (past p.)	hubiera (past p.) OR hubiese (past p.)		habíamos (past p.)	hubiéramos (past p.) OR hubiésemos (past p.)
habías (past p.)	hubieras (past p.) OR hubieses (past p.)		habíais (past p.)	hubierais (past p.) OR hubieseis (past p.)
había (past p.)	hubiera (past p.) OR hubiese (past p.)		habían (past p.)	hubieran (past p.) OR hubiesen (past p.)
Pretérito Anterior			*Pretérito Anterior*	
hube (past p.)			hubimos (past p.)	
hubiste (past p.)			hubisteis (past p.)	
hubo (past p.)			hubieron (past p.)	
Futuro Perfecto	*Futuro Perfecto*		*Futuro Perfecto*	*Futuro Perfecto*
habré (past p.)	hubiere (past p.)		habremos (past p.)	hubiéremos (past p.)
habrás (past p.)	hubieres (past p.)		habréis (past p.)	hubiereis (past p.)
habrá (past p.)	hubiere (past p.)		habrán (past p.)	hubieren (past p.)
Potencial Compuesto			*Potencial Compuesto*	
habría (past p.)			habríamos (past p.)	
habrías (past p.)			habríais (past p.)	
habría (past p.)			habrían (past p.)	

Imperativo	
Singular	Plural
(not used); no (not used)	(not used); no (not used)
(not used); no (not used)	(not used); no (not used)
(not used); no (not used)	(not used); no (not used)

[1]These conjugations are made using haber. Estar, ser, and tener can also be used to make compound verbs. All four verbs are, consequently, called auxiliary verbs. Translation possibilities are on page 88. Conjugation tips are on pages 89-91.

Compound present participle: habiendo (past p.)

84 Add the past participle (past p.) of the verb you want to conjugate.

compound reflexive verbs[1]

Singular		Plural	
Indicativo	*Subjunctivo*	*Indicativo*	*Subjunctivo*

Perfecto
me he (past p.)
te has (past p.)
se ha (past p.)

Perfecto
me haya (past p.)
te hayas (past p.)
se haya (past p.)

Perfecto
nos hemos (past p.)
os habéis (past p.)
se han (past p.)

Perfecto
nos hayamos (past p.)
os hayáis (past p.)
se hayan (past p.)

Pluscuamperfecto
me había (past p.)

Pluscuamperfecto
me hubiera (past p.)
OR
me hubiese (past p.)

Pluscuamperfecto
nos habíamos (past p.)

Pluscuamperfecto
nos hubiéramos (past p.)
OR
nos hubiésemos (past p.)

te habías (past p.)

te hubieras (past p.)
OR
te hubieses (past p.)

os habíais (past p.)

os hubierais (past p.)
OR
os hubieseis (past p.)

se había (past p.)

se hubiera (past p.)
OR
se hubiese (past p.)

se habían (past p.)

se hubieran (past p.)
OR
se hubiesen (past p.)

Pretérito Anterior
me hube (past p.)
te hubiste (past p.)
se hubo (past p.)

Pretérito Anterior
nos hubimos (past p.)
os hubisteis (past p.)
se hubieron (past p.)

Futuro Perfecto
me habré (past p.)
te habrás (past p.)
se habrá (past p.)

Futuro Perfecto
me hubiere (past p.)
te hubieres (past p.)
se hubiere (past p.)

Futuro Perfecto
nos habremos (past p.)
os habréis (past p.)
se habrán (past p.)

Futuro Perfecto
nos hubiéremos (past p.)
os hubiereis (past p.)
se hubieren (past p.)

Potencial Compuesto
me habría (past p.)
te habrías (past p.)
se habría (past p.)

Potencial Compuesto
nos habríamos (past p.)
os habríais (past p.)
se habrían (past p.)

Imperativo	
Singular	Plural

(not used); no (not used)
(not used); no (not used)
(not used); no (not used)

(not used); no (not used)
(not used); no (not used)
(not used); no (not used)

[1]These compound verbs are made using haber. Estar, ser, and tener can also be used to make compound verbs. All four verbs, consquently, are called auxiliary verbs. Translation possibilities are on page 88. Conjugation tips are on pages 89-91.

Compound present participle: habiéndose (past p.)

progressive tenses of non-reflexive verbs

Singular		Plural	
Indicativo	*Subjunctivo*	*Indicativo*	*Subjunctivo*

Presente	*Presente*	*Presente*	*Presente*
estoy (pres. p.)	esté (pres. p.)	estamos (pres. p.)	estemos (pres. p.)
estás (pres. p.)	estés (pres. p.)	estáis (pres. p.)	estéis (pres. p.)
está (pres. p.)	esté (pres. p.)	están (pres. p.)	estén (pres. p.)

Imperfecto	*Imperfecto*	*Imperfecto*	*Imperfecto*
estaba (pres. p.)	estuviera (pres. p.) OR estuviese (pres. p.)	estábamos (pres. p.)	estuviéramos (pres. p.) OR estuviésemos (pres. p.)
estabas (pres. p.)	estuvieras (pres. p.) OR estuvieses (pres. p.)	estabais (pres. p.)	estuvierais (pres. p.) OR estuvieseis (pres. p.)
estaba (pres. p.)	estuviera (pres. p.) OR estuviese (pres. p.)	estaban (pres. p.)	estuvieran (pres. p.) OR estuviesen (pres. p.)

Pretérito		*Pretérito*	
estuve (pres. p.)		estuvimos (pres. p.)	
estuviste (pres. p.)		estuvisteis (pres. p.)	
estuvo (pres. p.)		estuvieron (pres. p.)	

Futuro	*Futuro*	*Futuro*	*Futuro*
estaré (pres. p.)	estuviere (pres. p.)	estaremos (pres. p.)	estuviéremos (pres. p.)
estarás (pres. p.)	estuvieres (pres. p.)	estaréis (pres. p.)	estuviereis (pres. p.)
estará (pres. p.)	estuviere (pres. p.)	estarán (pres. p.)	estuvieren (pres. p.)

Potencial		*Potencial*	
estaría (pres. p.)		estaríamos (pres. p.)	
estarías (pres. p.)		estaríais (pres. p.)	
estaría (pres. p.)		estarían (pres. p.)	

Imperativo	
Singular	Plural
(not used); no (not used)	estemos (pres. p.); no estemos (pres. p.)
está (pres. p.); no estés (pres. p.)	estad (pres. p.); no estéis (pres. p.)
esté (pres. p.); no esté (pres. p.)	estén (pres. p.); no estén (pres. p.)

Translation possibilities are on page 88. Conjugation tips are on pages 89-91.

86 Add the present participle (pres. p.) of the verb you want to conjugate.

progressive tenses of reflexive verbs

	Singular		Plural	
	Indicativo	*Subjuntivo*	*Indicativo*	*Subjuntivo*

Presente / *Presente* (Singular) — *Presente* / *Presente* (Plural)

Indicativo (Sing.)	Subjuntivo (Sing.)	Indicativo (Plur.)	Subjuntivo (Plur.)
estoy (pres. p.)me	esté (pres. p.)me	estamos (pres. p.)nos	estemos (pres. p.)nos
estás (pres. p.)te	estés (pres. p.)te	estáis (pres. p.)os	estéis (present p.)os
está (pres. p.)se	esté (pres. p.)se	están (pres. p.)se	estén (pres. p.)se

Imperfecto / *Imperfecto*

estaba (pres.p)me	estuviera (pres.p)me OR estuviese (pres. p.)me	estábamos (pres.p)nos	estuviéramos (pres.p)nos OR estuviésemos (pres. p.)nos
estabas (pres.p.)te	estuvieras (pres.p.)te OR estuvieses (pres. p.)te	estabais (pres.p.)os	estuvierais (pres.p.)os OR estuvieseis (pres. p.)os
estaba (pres. p.)se	estuviera (pres. p.)se OR estuviese (pres. p.)se	estaban (pres. p.)se	estuvieran (pres. p.)se OR estuviesen (pres. p.)se

Pretérito

estuve (pres. p.)me		estuvimos (pres. p.)nos	
estuviste (pres. p.)te		estuvisteis (pres. p.)os	
estuvo (pres. p.)se		estuvieron (pres. p.)se	

Futuro / *Futuro*

estaré (pres. p.)me	estuviere (pres. p.)me	estaremos (pres. p.)nos	estuviéremos (pres. p.)nos
estarás (pres. p.)te	estuvieres (pres.p.)te	estaréis (pres.p.)os	estuviereis (pres.p.)os
estará (pres. p.)se	estuviere (pres. p.)se	estarán (pres. p.)se	estuvieren (pres. p.)se

Potencial

estaría (pres. p.)me		estaríamos (pres. p.)nos	
estarías (pres. p.)te		estaríais (pres. p.)os	
estaría (pres. p.)se		estarían (pres. p.)se	

Imperativo

Singular	Plural
(not used); no (not used)	estémonos (pres. p.); no nos estemos (pres. p.)
éstate (pres. p.); no te estés (pres. p.)	estaos (pres. p.); no os estéis (pres. p.)
éstese (pres. p.); no se esté (pres. p.)	éstense (pres. p.); no se estén (pres. p.)

Conjugation tips are on pages 89-91.

Add the past participle (past p.) of the verb you want to conjugate.
Infinitive: ser (past p.)
Compound infinitive: haber sido (past p.)

passive voice

Singular		Plural	
Indicativo	*Subjunctivo*	*Indicativo*	*Subjunctivo*
Presente	*Presente*	*Presente*	*Presente*
soy (past p.)	sea (past p.)	somos (past p.)s	seamos (past p.)s
eres (past p.)	seas (past p.)	sois (past p.)s	seáis (past p.)s
es (past p.)	sea (past p.)	son (past p.)s	sean (past p.)s
Imperfecto	*Imperfecto*	*Imperfecto*	*Imperfecto*
era (past p.)	fuera (past p.) OR fuese (past p.)	éramos (past p.)s	fuéramos (past p.)s OR fuésemos (past p.)s
eras (past p.)	fueras (past p.) OR fueses (past p.)	erais (past p.)s	fuerais (past p.)s OR fueseis (past p.)s
era (past p.)	fuera (past p.) OR fuese (past p.)	eran (past p.)s	fueran (past p.)s OR fuesen (past p.)s
Pretérito		*Pretérito*	
fui (past p.)		fuimos (past p.)s	
fuiste (past p.)		fuisteis (past p.)s	
fue (past p.)		fueron (past p.)s	
Futuro	*Futuro*	*Futuro*	*Futuro*
seré (past p.)	fuere (past p.)	seremos (past p.)s	fuéremos (past p.)s
serás (past p.)	fueres (past p.)	seréis (past p.)s	fuereis (past p.)s
será (past p.)	fuere (past p.)	serán (past p.)s	fueren (past p.)s
Potencial		*Potencial*	
sería (past p.)		seríamos (past p.)s	
serías (past p.)		seríais (past p.)s	
sería (past p.)		serían (past p.)s	

Imperativo	
Singular	Plural
(not used); no (not used)	seamos (past p.)s; no seamos (past p.)s
sé (past p.); no seas (past p.)	sed (past p.)s; no seáis (past p.)s
sea (past p.); no sea (past p.)	sean (past p.)s; no sean (past p.)s

Present participle: siendo (past p.)
Compound present participle: habiendo sido (past p.)
Past participle: sido (past p.)
Conjugation tips are on pages 89-91.

Translation possibilities using the verb hablar (to speak).

translation possibilities

	Singular		Plural	
	Indicativo	*Subjunctivo*	*Indicativo*	*Subjunctivo*
	Presente I speak[1] you speak[3] he speaks[5]	*Presente* I speak[1] you speak[3] he speaks[5]	*Presente* we speak[2] you speak[4] they speak[6]	*Presente* we speak[2] you speak[4] they speak[6]
	Imperfecto I was speaking	*Imperfecto* I was speaking OR I was speaking	*Imperfecto* we were speaking	*Imperfecto* we were speaking OR we were speaking
	you were speaking	you were speaking OR you were speaking	you were speaking	you were speaking OR you were speaking
	he[7] was speaking	he[7] was speaking OR he[7] was speaking	they were speaking	they were speaking OR they were speaking
	Pretérito I spoke you spoke he[8] spoke		*Pretérito* we spoke you spoke they spoke	
	Futuro I will speak you will speak he[8] will speak	*Futuro* I will speak you will speak he[8] will speak	*Futuro* we will speak you will speak they will speak	*Futuro* we will speak you will speak they will speak
	Potencial I would speak you would speak he[8] would speak		*Potencial* we would speak you would speak they would speak	

Imperativo	
Singular	Plural
(not used); no (not used) you must speak; you must not speak he[8] must speak; he[8] must not speak	we must speak; we must not speak you must speak; you must not speak they must speak; they must not speak

[1]Also I do speak, I am speaking. [2]Also we do speak, we are speaking. [3]Also (familiar, singular) you do speak, you are speaking. [4]Also (familiar, plural) you do speak, you are speaking. [5]Also (formal, singular) you speak, you do speak, you are speaking, he (she, it) speaks, he (she, it) does speak, he (she, it) is speaking. [6]Also (formal, plural) they do speak, they are speaking. [7]Also you were speaking, she was speaking, it was speaking, it. [8]Also you, she, it.

Tips on conjugating are shown by parentheses and footnotes.
Present participle: -ando
Past participle: -ado

tips on conjugating "ar" verbs

Singular		Plural	
Indicativo	*Subjunctivo*	*Indicativo*	*Subjunctivo*
Presente	*Presente*	*Presente*	*Presente*
-o	-e (yo)	-amos (presente)	-emos
-as	-es	-áis[1]	-éis[1]
-a[2] (Ud., él, ella, ello)	-e (Ud., él, ella, ello)	-an	-en
Imperfecto	*Imperfecto*	*Imperfecto*	*Imperfecto*
-aba (yo)	-ara[3] (yo)	-ábamos	-áramos[3]
	OR		OR
	-ase[4] (yo)		-ásemos[4]
-abas	-aras[3]	-abais[1]	-arais[1, 3]
	OR		OR
	-ases[4]		-aseis[1, 4]
-aba (Ud., él, ella, ello)	-ara[3] (Ud., él, ella, ello)	-aban	-aran[3]
	OR		OR
	-ase[4] (Ud., él, ella, ello)		-asen[4]
Pretérito		*Pretérito*	
-é		-amos (pretérito)	
-aste		-asteis[1]	
-ó		-aron	
Futuro	*Futuro*	*Futuro*	*Futuro*
-aré	-are[5] (yo)	-aremos	-áremos[5]
-arás	-ares[5]	-aréis[1]	-areis[1, 5]
-ará	-are[5] (Ud., él, ella, ello)	-arán	-aren[5]
Potencial		*Potencial*	
-aría (yo)		-aríamos	
-arías		-aríais[1]	
-aría (Ud., él, ella, ello)		-arían	

Imperativo	
Singular	Plural
(not used); no (not used)	-emos; no -emos
-a[2] (tú); no -es	-ad;[1] no -éis[1]
-e(Ud., él, ella, ello); no -e (Ud., él, ella, ello)	-en; no -en

The parentheses indicate that a conjugation is not unique, so you need to tell your listener or reader which alternative you mean. By matching identical conjugations, you can tell which are paired together. Usually the choice is between yo and one of the following: Ud., él, ella, ello. Regarding footnote 2 only, the choice is between tú and Ud., él, ella, or ello. In one instance, the choice is between the presente and pretérito tense.

The footnotes are on page 92.

tips on conjugating "er" verbs

Present participle: -iendo
Past participle: -ido

Singular		Plural	
Indicativo	*Subjunctivo*	*Indicativo*	*Subjunctivo*
Presente	*Presente*	*Presente*	*Presente*
-o	-a (yo)	-emos	-amos
-es	-as	-éis[1]	-áis[1]
-e[2] (Ud., él, ella, ello)	-a (Ud., él, ella, ello)	-en	-an
Imperfecto	*Imperfecto*	*Imperfecto*	*Imperfecto*
-ía (yo)	-iera[3] (yo) OR -iese[4] (yo)	-íamos	-iéramos[3] OR -iésemos[4]
-ías	-ieras[3] OR -ieses[4]	-íais[1]	-ierais[1, 3] OR -ieseis[1, 4]
-ía (Ud., él, ella, ello)	-iera[3] (Ud., él, ella, ello) OR -iese[4] (Ud., él, ella, ello)	-ían	-ieran[3] OR -iesen[4]
Pretérito		*Pretérito*	
-í		-imos	
-iste		-isteis[1]	
-ió		-ieron	
Futuro	*Futuro*	*Futuro*	*Futuro*
-eré	-iere[5] (yo)	-eremos	-iéremos[5]
-erás	-ieres[5]	-eréis[1]	-iereis[1, 5]
-erá	-iere[5] (Ud., él, ella, ello)	-erán	-ieren[5]
Potencial		*Potencial*	
-ería (yo)		-eríamos	
-erías		-eríais[1]	
-ería (Ud., él, ella, ello)		-erían	

Imperativo	
Singular	Plural
(not used); no (not used)	-amos; no -amos
-e[2] (tú); no -as	-ed;[1] no -áis[1]
-a (Ud., él, ella, ello); no -a (Ud., él, ella, ello)	-an; no -an

The parentheses indicate that a conjugation is not unique, so you need to tell your
listener or reader which alternative you mean. By matching identical conjugations,
you can tell which are paired together. Usually the choice is between yo and one of
the following: Ud., él, ella, ello. Regarding footnote 2 only, the choice is between tú
and Ud., él, ella, or ello.
The footnotes are on page 92.

Tips on conjugating are shown by parentheses and footnotes.
Present participle: -iendo
Past participle: -ido

tips on conjugating "ir" verbs

Singular		Plural	
Indicativo	*Subjunctivo*	*Indicativo*	*Subjunctivo*
Presente	*Presente*	*Presente*	*Presente*
-o	-a (yo)	-imos (presente)	-amos
-es	-as	-ís[1]	-áis[1]
-e[2] (Ud., él, ella, ello)	-a (Ud., él, ella, ello)	-en	-an
Imperfecto	*Imperfecto*	*Imperfecto*	*Imperfecto*
-ía (yo)	-iera[3] (yo) OR -iese[4] (yo)	-íamos	-iéramos[3] OR -iésemos[4]
-ías	-ieras[3] OR -ieses[4]	-íais[1]	-ierais[1, 3] OR -ieseis[1, 4]
-ía (Ud., él, ella, ello)	-iera[3] (Ud., él, ella, ello) OR -iese[4] (Ud., él, ella, ello)	-ían	-ieran[3] OR -iesen[4]
Pretérito		*Pretérito*	
-í		-imos (pretérito)	
-iste		-isteis[1]	
-ió		-ieron	
Futuro	*Futuro*	*Futuro*	*Futuro*
-iré	-iere[5] (yo)	-iremos	-iéremos[5]
-irás	-ieres[5]	-iréis[1]	-iereis[1, 5]
-irá	-iere[5] (Ud., él, ella, ello)	-irán	-ieren[5]
Potencial		*Potencial*	
-iría (yo)		-iríamos	
-irías		-iríais[1]	
-iría (Ud., él, ella, ello)		-irían	

Imperativo	
Singular	Plural
(not used); no (not used)	-amos; no -amos
-e[2] (tú); no -as	-id;[1] no -áis[1]
-a (Ud., él, ella, ello); no -a (Ud., él, ella, ello)	-an; no -an

The parentheses indicate that a conjugation is not unique, so you need to tell your listener or reader which alternative you mean. By matching identical conjugations, you can tell which are paired together. Usually the choice is between yo and one of the following: Ud., él, ella, ello. Regarding footnote 2 only, the choice is between tú and Ud., él, ella, or ello. In one instance, the choice is between the presente and pretérito tense.
The footnotes are on page 92.

[1]Use the ustedes (Uds.) conjugations rather than the vosotros (and vosotras) conjugations when communicating with people in the Americas.

[2]These two conjugations are identical for most non-reflexive verbs, but not for reflexive verbs. Some frequently used non-reflexive verbs, including haber, are exceptions.

The other imperative conjugations of non-reflexive verbs, and reflexive imperative conjugations preceded by "no", are identical to the related present subjunctive tense, except the affirmative vosotros (and vostoras).

The affirmative vosotros (and vosotras) of non-reflexive verbs replace the final "r" of the infinitive form of the verb with "d". The affirmative vosotros (and vosotras) of reflexive verbs replace the final "r" of the infinitive form of the verb with "os".

[3]This form usually is preferred in unpublished writing.

[4]This form usually is preferred in published writing.

[5]The present indicative and subjunctive conjugations are preferred nowadays over the future subjunctive. Similarly, the compound present indicative and subjunctive conjugations are preferred nowadays over the compound future subjunctive.

The tips on conjugating Spanish verbs on pages 89, 90 and 91 are identical, except that on page 90 (i.e., for "er" verbs), you do not have to tell your listener or reader whether you mean the presente or pretérito tense.

15,000 Spanish Verbs
in alphabetical order

15,000 Spanish Verbs

Find the verb in the list below and conjugate it like the pattern identified by number (and identical page number) printed next to the verb.

a

ababill-arse 80
abacor-ar 1
abadan-ar 1
abadern-ar 1
abagr-arse 80
abaj-ar 1
abaj-arse 80
abalag-ar 1
abalall-ar 1
abalandr-ar 1
abalanz-ar 21
abalanz-arse ... 21
abal-ar 1
abalaustr-ar 1
abaldes-ar 1
abaldon-ar 1
abaldon-arse ... 80
abale-ar 1
abali-ar 9
abalien-ar 1
abaliz-ar 21
abaliz-arse 21
aball-ar 1
aballest-ar 1
abalsam-ar 1
abalser-ar 1
abaluart-ar 1
aban-ar 1
abancal-ar 1
abancuch-ar 1
abandaliz-ar 21
abander-ar 1
abanderiz-ar 21
abanderiz-
 arse 21
abandole-ar 1
abandon-ar 1
abandon-
 arse 80
abane-ar 1
abang-ar 51
abanic-ar 67
abanic-arse 67
abanique-ar 1

abant-ar 1
abañ-ar 1
abaraj-ar 1
abarand-ar 1
abarañ-ar 1
abarat-ar 1
abarat-arse 80
abarb-ar 1
abarbech-ar 1
abarbet-ar 1
abarc-ar 67
abarcuz-ar 21
abarlo-ar 1
abarlo-arse 80
abarquill-ar 1
abarquill-
 arse 80
abarrac-ar 67
abarrac-arse 67
abarragan-ar 1
abarragan-
 arse 80
abarraj-ar 1
abarranc-ar 67
abarranc-
 arse 67
abarr-ar 1
abarren-ar 1
abarr-er 2
abarril-ar 1
abarr-ir 3
abarrot-ar 1
ab-arse 80, and
 used in the
 positions in ... 14
abas-ar 1
abasoir-ar 1
abass-ar 1
abast-ar 1
abastard-ar 1
abastec-er 48
abastec-erse ... 48
abastill-ar 1
abastion-ar 1
abatan-ar 1
abat-ar 1

abatat-ar 1
abatat-arse 80
abate-ar 1
abat-ir 3
abatoj-ar 1
abatoll-ar 1
abayunc-ar 67
abdic-ar 67
abduc-ir 28
abebr-ar 1
abeit-ar 1
abeiz-ar 1
abejone-ar 1
abejorre-ar 1
abejuc-ar 67
abel-ar 1
abeld-ar 53
abellac-ar 67
abellot-ar 1
abemol-ar 1
aberenjen-ar 1
aberr-ar 37
aberre-ar 1
abes-ar 1
abesti-arse 80
abestion-ar 1
abetun-ar 1
abevigu-ar 1
abeyt-ar 1
abez-ar 1
abich-arse 80
abield-ar 1
abigarr-ar 1
abij-ar 1
abill-ar 1
abillit-ar 1
abin-ar 1
abisagr-ar 1
abisel-ar 1
abism-ar 1
abistern-ar 1
abistu-ar 1
abit-ar 1
abiyel-ar 1
abizcoch-ar 1
abjur-ar 1

ablact-ar 1
abland-ar 1
ablandec-er 48
abland-ir 3
ablaque-ar 1
ableg-ar 1
ablend-ar 1
ablent-ar 1
ablevi-ar 1
abluc-ar 1
ablu-ir 42
abneg-ar 62
abob-ar 1
abocad-ar 1
abocade-ar 1
abocan-ar 1
aboc-ar 67
abocard-ar 1
abocel-ar 1
abocet-ar 1
aboch-ar 1
abochorn-ar 1
abocin-ar 1
abodoc-ar 67
abodoc-arse 67
abof-ar 67
abof-arse 67
abofell-ar 1
abofete-ar 1
abogade-ar 1
abog-ar 51
abol-ir 4
aboll-ar 1
abollon-ar 1
abols-ar 1
abomb-ar 1
abomin-ar 1
abonanz-ar 21,
 and for its use
 regarding
 weather,
 see 45
abon-ar 1
abon-arse 80
abond-ar 1
aboquill-ar 1

abord-ar 1
abordon-ar 1
aborraj-ar 1
aborraj-arse 80
aborrasc-ar 67
aborrasc-arse
67, and for its
use regarding
weather,
see 45
aborrec-er 48
aborreg-ar 51
aborreg-arse 51
aborric-arse 67
aborr-ir 3
aborron-ar 1
aborrug-ar 51
aborrug-arse 51
abort-ar 1
aboruj-ar 1
abos-ar 1
abostez-ar 21
abotag-ar 51
abotag-arse 51
abotarg-ar 51
abotij-arse 80
aboton-ar 1
aboton-arse 80
aboved-ar 1
aboy-ar 1
abozal-ar 1
aboz-ar 1
abrac-ar 67
abracij-arse 80
abrahon-ar 1
abras-ar 1
abravec-er 48
abraz-ar 21
abrech-ar 1
abrenunci-ar 1
abreton-ar 1
abrev-ar 1
abrevi-ar 1
abrez-ar 21
abribon-arse 80
abrig-ar 51
abrig-arse 80
abrillant-ar 1
abriol-ar 1
abrir 3, except
the past parti-

ciple is abierto
abro-ar 1
abro-arse 80
abrocal-ar 1
abroc-ar 1
abroch-ar 1
abrog-ar 51
abrog-arse 80
abrom-ar 1
abrom-arse 80
abronc-ar 67
abroquel-ar 1
abrotoñ-ar 1
abrull-ar 1
abrum-arse
80, and for its
use regarding
weather,
see 45
abrut-ar 1
abruz-arse 21
absced-arse 80
abscond-er 2
absent-arse 80
absolutiz-ar 21
absolv-er 47,
except the
past partici-
ple is
absuelto
abson-ar 25
absorb-er 2,
plus the past
participle
absorto
absort-ar 1
absten-er 74
absten-erse 74
absterg-er 23
abstra-er 75,
plus the past
participle
abstracto
abub-arse 80
abuch-ar 1
abuche-ar 1
abuen-ar 1
abuey-ar 1
abullon-ar 1
abult-ar 1
abund-ar 1

abuñol-ar 25
abuñuel-ar 1
abur-ar 1
aburel-ar 1
aburgues-
arse 80
aburil-ar 1
aburr-ar 1
aburr-arse 80
aburr-ir 3
aburr-irse 82
aburuj-ar 1
aburujun-ar 1
abus-ar 1
abuz-arse 21
acabal-ar 1
acaball-ar 1
acaballer-ar 1
acaballon-ar 1
acabañ-ar 1
acab-ar 1
acabd-ar 1
acabdell-ar 1
acabdill-ar 1
acabel-ar 1
acabestr-ar 1
acabestrill-ar 1
acabild-ar 1
acabt-ar 1
acach-arse 80
acachet-ar 1
acachete-ar 1
acachorr-ar 1
academiz-ar 21
acadenill-ar 1
acaec-er 48,
and for its
use regarding
weather,
see 45
aca-er 20
acafel-ar 1
acaguas-
arse 80
acairel-ar 9
acalabaz-
arse 80
acalabrot-ar 1
acalambr-
arse 80
acaland-ar 1

acald-ar 1
acalentur-ar 1
acalentur-
arse 80
acallant-ar 1
acall-ar 1
acalor-ar 1
acalore-arse 80
acalug-ar 51
acamaleon-
arse 80
acam-ar 1
acamastron-
arse 80
acamellon-ar 1
acampan-ar 1
acamp-ar 1
acanal-ar 1
acanall-ar 1
acanastill-ar 1
acancer-ar 1
acancer-arse ... 80
acanch-ar 1
acandil-ar 1
acanelon-ar 1
acangren-
arse 80
acanog-ar 51
acansin-arse 80
acansir-arse 80
acantale-ar 1,
and for its
use regarding
weather,
see 45
acantar-ar 1
acante-ar 1
acantil-ar 1
acanton-ar 1
acañavere-ar 1
acañone-ar 1
acapar-ar 1
acaparr-ar 1
acaparr-arse 80
acapill-ar 1
acapiz-arse 21
acapuch-ar 1
acapull-arse 80
acarabe-ar 1
acaramel-ar 1
acar-ar 1

acardenal-ar 1
acare-ar 1
acarici-ar 1
acariñ-ar 1
acarnaz-arse ... 80
acaron-ar 1
acarral-ar 1
acarr-arse 80
acarraz-ar 21
acarraz-arse ... 21
acarre-ar 1
acarret-ar 1
acarrete-ar 1
acarroñ-ar 1
acarton-ar 1
acaser-arse 80
acastill-ar 1
acat-ar 1
acatarr-ar 1
acatarr-arse 80
acaudal-ar 1
acaudill-ar 1
acautel-arse 80
acced-er 2
accidentaliz-
   ar 21
accident-ar 1
accion-ar 1
acebad-ar 1
acech-ar 1
acecin-ar 1
aced-ar 1
aceit-ar 1
acelaj-arse 80
aceler-ar 1
acendr-ar 1
acenef-ar 1
acens-ar 1
acensu-ar 9
acentu-ar 9
acep-ar 1
acepill-ar 1
acept-ar 1
aceptil-ar 1
acequi-ar 1
acer-ar 1
acer-arse 80
acerc-ar 67
acernad-ar 1
acerr-ar 53
acerroj-ar 1

acert-ar 53
acerv-ar 1
acetific-ar 67
acetrin-ar 1
acez-ar 21
achabacan-ar 1
achac-ar 1
achacill-arse 80
achaflan-ar 1
achahuistl-
   arse 80
achajuan-
   arse 80
achamp-arse ... 80
achanc-ar 1
achanch-ar 1
achang-ar 1
achant-ar 1
achant-arse 80
achaparr-
   arse 80
achapin-arse ... 80
achaplin-
   arse 80
achar-ar 1
acharol-ar 1
achat-ar 1
achech-ar 1
achic-ar 67
achicharr-ar 1
achicharron-ar .. 1
achicharron-
   arse 80
achichigu-ar 1
achicopal-
   arse 80
achigu-ar 51
achil-ar 1
achin-ar 1
achinel-ar 1
aching-ar 51
achipilc-arse 80
achiquit-ar 1
achir-ar 1
achird-ar 1
achirl-ar 1
achisp-ar 1
achivat-ar 1
achoc-ar 67
achoch-ar 1
achoch-arse 80

achol-ar 1
achollonc-ar 67
achollonc-
   arse 67
acholole-ar 1
achorgorn-ar 1
achot-ar 1
achubasc-ar 67
achubasc-arse
   67, and for its
   use regarding
   weather,
   see 45
achuch-ar 1
achucharr-ar 1
achucut-ar 1
achucut-arse ... 80
achucuy-ar 1
achuic-ar 1
achuic-arse 80
achuj-ar 1
achulap-ar 1
achulap-arse ... 80
achul-ar 1
achul-arse 80
achum-ar 1
achunch-ar 1
achunt-ar 1
achur-ar 1
achurr-ar 1
achurruc-ar 67
achurrusc-ar ... 67
achuruc-arse ... 80
achuz-ar 21
acibar-ar 1
acibarr-ar 1
aciber-ar 1
acical-ar 1
acicate-ar 1
acidific-ar 67
acidul-ar 1
aciem-ar 1
acigu-ar 7
aciguat-ar 1
aciguat-arse ... 80
acimbog-ar 1
acin-ar 1
acincel-ar 1
acing-ar 1
acintur-ar 1

aclam-ar 1
aclar-ar 1, and
   for its use
   regarding
   weather,
   see 45
aclarec-er 48
aclavel-arse 80
aclimat-ar 1
acloc-ar 76,
   and used in
   the positions
   in 45
acobard-ar 1
acobij-ar 1
acoc-arse 67
acoce-ar 1
acoch-arse 80
acochin-ar 1
acocl-ar 1
acocl-arse 80
acocor-ar 1
acocot-ar 1
acodal-ar 1
acod-ar 1
acoder-ar 1
acodici-ar 1
acodill-ar 1
acofr-ar 1
acog-er 23
acogoll-ar 1
acogombr-ar 1
acogot-ar 1
acohombr-ar 1
acoi-er 2
acojin-ar 1
acojon-ar 1
acol-ar 1
acolch-ar 1
acolchon-ar 1
acolg-ar 1
acolit-ar 1
acoll-ar 25
acollar-ar 1
acoller-ar 1
acollon-ar 1
acomb-ar 1
acomed-irse 52
acomet-er 1
acomod-ar 1
acompañ-ar 1

acompas-ar 1
acompinch-
  arse 80
acomplej-ar 1
acomunal-ar 1
acomun-arse ... 80
aconchab-
  arse 80
aconch-ar 1
aconcheg-ar 1
acondicion-ar ... 1
aconduch-ar 1
acongoj-ar 1
aconsej-ar 1
aconsonant-ar .. 1
acontec-er 39,
  and for its use
  regarding
  weather,
  see 45
acontent-ar 1
acop-ar 1
acopet-ar 1
acopi-ar 1
acopl-ar 1
acoquin-ar 1
acor-ar 1
acoraz-ar 21
acorazon-ar 1
acorch-ar 1
acord-ar 25
acordel-ar 1
acordon-ar 1
acorn-ar 25
acorne-ar 1
acorral-ar 1
acorr-er 2
acorruc-arse 67
acort-ar 1
acortej-arse 80
acorull-ar 1
acorv-ar 1
acorz-ar 21
acos-ar 1
acosij-ar 1
acost-ar 25
acostill-arse 80
acostumbr-ar 1
acot-ar 1
acotej-ar 1
acotol-ar 1

acoyund-ar 1
acoyunt-ar 1
acrecent-ar 53
acrec-er 48
acredit-ar 1
acrianz-ar 21
acrib-ar 1
acribill-ar 1
acrimin-ar 1
acrioll-arse 80
acrisol-ar 1
acristal-ar 1
acristian-ar 1
acromatiz-ar 21
acruñ-ar 1
actit-ar 1
activ-ar 1
actualiz-ar 21
actu-ar 9
acuadrell-ar 1
acuadrill-ar 1
acuajaron-ar 1
acuanti-ar 1
acuart-ar 1
acuartel-ar 1
acuarteron-ar ... 1
acuartill-ar 1
acuatiz-ar 21
acub-ar 1
acubil-ar 1
acucham-
  arse 80
acuch-ar 1
acuchar-ar 1
acuchill-ar 1
acuchille-ar 1
acuchuc-ar 1
acuchuch-ar 1
acuci-ar 1
acuclill-arse 80
acud-ir 3
acuerd-ar 1
acuern-ar 1
acuerp-ar 1
acugul-ar 1
acuidad-arse ... 80
acuilm-arse 80
acuit-ar 1
acul-ar 1
aculebr-ar 1
aculebre-

arse 80
aculebrin-ar 1
aculill-ar 1
acullic-ar 1
acull-ir 3
acultur-arse 80
acumb-arse 80
acumbr-ar 1
acumuch-ar 1
acumul-ar 1
acun-ar 1
acuñ-ar 1
acur-ar 1
acurcuch-
  arse 80
acurcull-arse ... 80
acurd-arse 80
acurr-arse 80
acurruc-arse ... 67
acurruj-arse 80
acurrull-ar 1
acuruj-arse 80
acus-ar 1
adagu-ar 7
adam-ar 1
adam-arse 80
adamasc-ar 67
adapon-er 57
adapt-ar 1
adarde-ar 1
adarg-ar 51
adarv-ar 1
adat-ar 1
adecen-ar 1
adecent-ar 1
adecu-ar 9
adehes-ar 1
adelant-ar 1
adelgaz-ar 21
adem-ar 1
adement-ar 1
adempribi-ar 1
adens-ar 1
adentell-ar 1
adentr-ar 1
aderez-ar 21
adestr-ar 53
adeud-ar 1
adherec-er 2
adher-ir 71
adhib-ir 3

arse 80
aculebrin-ar 1

adhort-ar 1
adiamant-ar 1
adi-ar 9
adicion-ar 1
adiestr-ar 1
adiet-ar 1
adiner-ar 1
adintel-ar 1
ad-ir 3, and
  used in the
  positions in 11
adivin-ar 1
adjetiv-ar 1
adjudic-ar 67
adjunt-ar 1
adjur-ar 1
adminicul-ar 1
administr-ar 1
admir-ar 1
admit-ir 3
adob-ar 1
adocen-ar 1
adoctrin-ar 1
adoj-ar 1
adolec-er 48
adolor-ar 1
adomicili-ar 1
adon-arse 80
adonec-er 48
adoniz-arse 21
adopt-ar 1
adoquin-ar 1
ador-ar 1
adormec-er 48
adorment-ar 1
adormil-ar 1
adormil-arse 80
adorm-ir 31
adormit-ar 1
adormit-arse 80
adorn-ar 1
ados-ar 1
adquir-ir 5
adr-ar 1
adriz-ar 21
adrog-ar 51
adscrib-ir 3,
  except the
  past partici-
  ple is adscrito
adsorb-er 2

adstring-ir 3,
  with the
  changes in 23
aduan-ar 1
aduc-ir 59,
  plus the past
  participle
  aducho
adueñ-ar 1
adueñ-arse 80
aduj-ar 1
adul-ar 1
adulc-ir 3,
  with the
  changes in 46
adule-ar 1
adulter-ar 1
adulz-ar 21
adulzor-ar 1
adumbr-ar 1
adun-ar 1
adund-arse 80
adven-ir 77
adver-ar 1
adverbializ-
  ar 21
adverbi-ar 1
advert-ir 71
advoc-ar 67
aech-ar 1
aerific-ar 1
aerodinamiz-
  ar 21
aerosuspend-
  er 2
aerotransport-
  ar 1
afabul-ar 1
afam-ar 1
afan-ar 1
afarg-ar 1
afarol-arse 80
afarras-ar 1
afascal-ar 1
afatag-ar 51
afat-ar 1
afe-ar 1
afeblec-erse 48
afeccion-
  arse 80
afect-ar 1

afeit-ar 1
afelp-ar 1
afemin-ar 1
aferr-ar 1,
  and alter-
  natively, ... 53
aferroj-ar 1
aferruch-arse ... 80
afervent-ar 1
afervor-ar 1
afervoriz-ar 21
afeston-ar 1
afeud-arse 80
afianz-ar 21
afi-ar 1
afibl-ar 1
afic-ar 1
aficion-ar 1
afiduci-ar 1
afiebr-arse 80
afiel-ar 1
afij-ar 1, plus
  the past parti-
  ciple afijo
afil-ar 1
afili-ar 1
afiligran-ar 1
afill-ar 1
afilor-ar 1
afin-ar 1
afinc-ar 67
afirm-ar 1
afirol-ar 1
afistul-ar 1
aflat-arse 80
aflaut-ar 1
aflig-ir 3, with
  the changes
  in 23, plus
  the past par-
  ticiple aflicto
aflogistic-ar 1
afloj-ar 1
aflor-ar 1
aflu-ir 42
afluxion-arse ... 80
afoete-ar 1
afof-ar 1
afogar-ar 1
afoll-ar 25
afollon-ar 1

afond-ar 1
afor-ar 25
aforr-ar 1
afortun-ar 1
afos-arse 80
afosc-arse 67
afrail-ar 1
afrances-ar 1
afratel-arse 80
afrech-arse 80
afrenill-ar 1
afrent-ar 1
afreñ-ir 3
afret-ar 1
africaniz-ar 21
afrijol-ar 1
afront-ar 1
afrontil-ar 1
afuet-ar 1
afuete-ar 1
afuf-ar 1
afurac-ar 67
afusil-ar 1
afusion-ar 1
afutr-arse 80
agabach-ar 1
agachap-
  arse 80
agach-ar 1
agaf-ar 1
agaler-ar 1
agalib-ar 1
agall-arse 80
agamit-ar 1
agamuz-ar 21
agangren-
  arse 80
agañot-ar 1
agarab-ar 1
agarbanz-ar 21
agarb-arse 80
agarbill-ar 1
agarbizon-ar 1
agardam-
  arse 80
agard-ar 1
agarduñ-ar 1
agarraf-ar 1
agarr-ar 1
agarroch-ar 1
agarrot-ar 1

agarrote-ar 1
agasaj-ar 1
agatiz-ar 21
agauch-arse 80
agavill-ar 1
agazap-ar 1
agenci-ar 1
agerman-
  arse 80
agest-arse 80
agigant-ar 1
agigot-ar 1
agil-ar 1
agilit-ar 1
agiliz-ar 21
agin-ar 1
agiot-ar 1
agitan-ar 1
agit-ar 1
aglob-ar 1
aglomer-ar 1
aglutin-ar 1
agobi-ar 1
agol-er 1
agol-er 47
agollet-ar 1
agolp-ar 1
agoniz-ar 21
agor-ar 6
agorgoj-arse 80
agorron-ar 1
agorzom-ar 1
agost-ar 1
agot-ar 1
agrace-ar 1
agraci-ar 1
agrad-ar 1
agradec-er 48
agram-ar 1
agramil-ar 1
agrand-ar 1
agranel-ar 1
agranit-ar 1
agranuj-arse 80
agrav-ar 1
agravi-ar 1
agraz-ar 21
agre-ar 1
agred-ir 3, and
  used in the
  positions in 4

agreg-ar 51
agremi-ar 1
agri-ar 1
agriet-ar 1
agrill-arse 80
agring-arse 51
agris-ar 1
agriset-ar 1
agrum-ar 1
agrup-ar 1
aguach-ar 1
aguacharn-ar 1
aguachinang-
arse 80
aguachin-ar 1
aguait-ar 1
aguajir-arse 80
agual-ar 1
aguam-arse 80
aguamel-ar 1
aguand-ar 1
aguant-ar 1
agu-ar 7
aguard-ar 1
aguasali-ar 1
aguas-arse 80
aguat-arse 80
aguaz-ar 21
agudiz-ar 21
agüeit-ar 1
aguerr-ir 4
aguij-ar 1
aguijone-ar 1
aguil-arse 80
aguisc-ar 67
aguizg-ar 51
agujer-ar 1
agujere-ar 1
agujete-ar 1
agusan-ar 1
aguz-ar 21
ahaj-ar 1
ahax-ar 1
ahech-ar 1
ahele-ar 1
aherroj-ar 1
aherrumbr-ar 1
ahervor-arse 80
ahidalg-ar 51
ahij-ar 9
ahijone-ar 1

ahil-ar 9
ahiler-ar 9
ahinc-ar 8
ahit-ar 9, plus
the past par-
ticiple ahíto
ahobachon-
arse 80
ahoc-arse 67
ahocic-ar 67
ahocin-arse 80
ahog-ar 51
ahoj-ar 1
ahombr-arse 80
ahond-ar 1
ahorcaj-arse 80
ahorc-ar 67
ahorm-ar 1
ahornag-arse ... 51
ahorn-ar 1
ahorquet-
arse 80
ahorquill-ar 1
ahorr-ar 1
ahot-ar 1
ahoy-ar 1
ahuch-ar 9
ahuche-ar 9
ahuec-ar 67
ahuer-ar 1
ahues-arse 80
ahuev-ar 1
ahum-ar 1
ahume-ar 1
ahup-ar 1
ahus-ar 1
ahus-arse 80
ahuyent-ar 1
air-ar 9
aire-ar 1
aisl-ar 9
ajabard-ar 1
ajamon-arse 80
ajaquec-arse ... 67
aj-ar 1
ajardin-ar 1
aje-ar 1
ajedrez-ar 21
ajel-ar 1
ajeni-ar 1
ajerg-ar 1

ajeri-ar 1
ajeriz-ar 1
ajesuit-ar 1
ajetre-ar 1
ajicar-ar 1
ajigot-ar 1
ajil-ar 1
ajilguer-arse 80
ajin-ar 1
ajiron-ar 1
ajob-ar 1
ajonje-ar 1
ajor-ar 25
ajord-ar 1
ajornal-ar 1
ajot-ar 1
ajuanet-ar 1
ajuar-ar 1
ajubon-ar 1
ajudi-arse 80
ajuglar-ar 1
ajuici-ar 1
ajum-ar 1
ajum-arse 80
ajumpi-arse 80
ajunc-ar 1
ajunquill-ar 1
ajust-ar 1
ajustici-ar 1
alab-ar 1
alabastr-ar 1
alabe-ar 1
alacen-ar 1
alaching-ar 1
alachingu-ar 1
alaci-ar 1
alaci-arse 80
alacrane-ar 1
aladr-ar 1
alag-ar 51
alagart-ar 1
alagart-arse 80
alagun-ar 1
alambic-ar 67
alambr-ar 1
alambre-ar 1
alamp-ar 1
alance-ar 1
alandre-arse 80
alanz-ar 21
alaqui-ar 1

alaqu-ir 3
alarde-ar 1
alarg-ar 51
alarid-ar 1
alarm-ar 1
al-arse 80
alastr-ar 1
albain-ar 1
albañal-ar 1
albañe-ar 1
albañile-ar 1
alb-ar 1
albardane-ar 1
albard-ar 1
albarde-ar 1
albardill-ar 1
albarraz-ar 21
albayald-ar 1
albe-ar 1
albeld-ar 53
alberg-ar 51
albitr-ar 1
albogue-ar 1
albore-ar 1,
and for its use
regarding
weather,
see 45
alborot-ar 1
alboroz-ar 21
albrici-ar 1
albumin-ar 1
alcachof-ar 1
alcahaz-ar 21
alcahuet-ar 1
alcahuete-ar 1
alcaide-ar 1
alcalesc-er 2
alcaliz-ar 21
alcane-ar 1
alcanfor-ar 1
alcantarill-ar 1
alcanz-ar 21
alcatif-ar 1
alcayat-ar 1
alcohol-ar 1
alcoholiz-ar 21
alcontriz-ar 21
alcoravis-ar 1
alcorz-ar 21

amalign-arse ...80
amallad-ar 1
amall-arse 80
amalvez-arse ...21
amamant-ar 1
amanceb-ar 1
amanceb-
    arse 80
amancill-ar 1
amane-ar 1
amanec-er 48,
    and for its use
    regarding
    weather,
    see 45
amaner-ar 1
amangual-
    arse 80
amaniat-ar 1
amanill-ar 1
amanoj-ar 1
amans-ar 1
amant-ar 1
amantill-ar 1
amanzan-ar 1
amañ-ar 1
amapol-arse 80
am-ar 1
amar-ar 1
amarchant-
    arse 80
amarec-er 48
amarg-ar 51
amargue-ar 1
amarguje-ar 1
amarill-ar 1
amarille-ar 1
amarillec-er 48
amarin-ar 1
amariz-ar 21
amarom-ar 1
amarr-ar 1
amarreque-ar ... 1
amartel-ar 1
amartigu-ar 7
amartill-ar 1
amas-ar 1
amat-ar 1
amayorazg-
    ar 51
amazacot-ar 1

ambici-ar 1
ambicion-ar 1
ambicione-ar 1
ambient-ar 1
ambl-ar 1
ambul-ar 1
ambut-ar 1
amech-ar 1
amedrant-ar 1
amedrent-ar 1
amel-ar 53
amelcoch-ar 1
amelg-ar 51
amell-ar 1
amenaz-ar 21
amengu-ar 7
ameniz-ar 21
amenor-ar 1
amenorg-ar 51
ament-ar 53
amer-ar 1
americaniz-
    ar 21
amerit-ar 1
ametal-ar 1
ametrall-ar 1
amezquin-
    arse 80
amezquind-
    arse 80
amig-ar 51
amilan-ar 1
amillar-ar 1
amillon-ar 1
aministr-ar 1
aminor-ar 1
amist-ar 1
amitig-ar 51
amnisti-ar 9
amobl-ar 25
amoch-ar 1
amodorr-ar 1
amodorrec-
    er 48
amohec-er 48
amohin-ar 9
amohos-ar 1
amohos-arse ...80
amojam-ar 1
amojel-ar 1
amojon-ar 1

amol-ar 25
amold-ar 1
amolel-ar 1
amoll-ar 1
amollec-er 48
amollent-ar 1
amollin-ar 1,
    and used in
    the positions
    in 45
amon-arse 80
amoned-ar 1
amonest-ar 1
amont-ar 1
amontazg-ar 51
amonton-ar 1
amoñ-ar 1
amorag-ar 51
amorat-ar 1
amorc-ar 67
amordaz-ar 21
amorec-er 48
amorg-ar 51
amorgon-ar 1
amorill-ar 1
amorr-ar 1
amorrin-ar 1
amorriñ-arse 80
amorron-ar 1
amorrong-
    arse 51
amortaj-ar 1
amortec-er 48
amortigu-ar 7
amortiz-ar 21
amorug-arse 51
amosc-ar 67
amostaz-ar 21
amotin-ar 1
amov-er 47
amoz-arse 21
ampar-ar 1
ampi-ar 1
ampiel-ar 1
ampli-ar 9
amplific-ar 67
ampoll-ar 1
ampr-ar 1
ampuch-ar 1
amput-ar 1
amuch-ar 1

amuebl-ar 1
amuel-ar 1
amuf-ar 1
amugron-ar 1
amuj-ar 1
amul-ar 1
amullic-ar 67
amunicion-ar 1
amunuc-arse ...80
amuñij-ar 1
amurall-ar 1
amur-ar 1
amurc-ar 67
amurill-ar 1
amurr-arse 80
amurri-arse 80
amurriñ-arse ...80
amusg-ar 51
amusti-ar 1
anac-er 48
anade-ar 1
anadi-ar 1
anagramatiz-
    ar 21
analiz-ar 21
anaranje-ar 1
anarquiz-ar 21
anascot-ar 1
anastomiz-
    arse 21
anastomos-
    arse 80
anatematiz-
    ar 21
anatomiz-ar 21
anc-arse 67
anch-ar 1
ancho-ar 1
ancl-ar 1
ancle-ar 1
ancor-ar 1
andaluz-arse 21
andami-ar 1
and-ar 10
andarague-ar 1
andaregue-ar 1
andarieg-ar 1
andig-ar 1
andivel-ar 1
andone-ar 1
andorre-ar 1

ane-ar 1
anebl-ar 53
anecdotiz-ar 21
aneci-arse 80
aned-ir 3
aneg-ar 51
anej-ar 1
anestesi-ar 1
anex-ar 1
anexion-ar 1
angarill-ar 1
angarille-ar 1
angel-ar 1
angeliz-ar 21
angeliz-arse 21
angost-ar 1
angusti-ar 1
anhel-ar 1
anid-ar 1
anidi-ar 1
aniebl-ar 1
anihil-ar 1
anill-ar 1
animaliz-ar 21
anim-ar 1
aniñ-arse 80
aniquil-ar 1
anis-ar 1
anivel-ar 1
aniviel-ar 1
annot-ar 1
anochec-er 48,
  and for its use
  regarding
  weather,
  see 45
anodin-ar 1
anonad-ar 1
anort-ar 1
anot-ar 1
anque-ar 1
anquilos-ar 1
ansann-ar 1
ansi-ar 9
antagall-ar 1
antain-ar 1
anteanunci-ar ... 1
anteced-er 1
antecog-er 23
antedat-ar 1
antedec-ir 58

antefer-ir 71
antel-ar 1
antellev-ar 1
antenunci-ar 1
antepag-ar 51
antepas-ar 1
antepon-er 57
antepuen-er 57
anteven-ir 77
antev-er 78
anticip-ar 1
anticu-ar 1
antidot-ar 1
antigu-ar 7
antimoni-ar 1
antipatiz-ar 21
antipoc-ar 67
antoj-ar 1
antoj-arse 80,
  and used in
  the positions
  in 45
antorch-ar 1
antruej-ar 1
anub-arse 80
anubl-ar 1,
  and for its
  use regarding
  weather,
  see 45
anuc-ar 67
anud-ar 1
anudr-irse 82
anul-ar 1
anunci-ar 1
anzol-ar 25
añad-ir 3
añasc-ar 67
añej-ar 1
añil-ar 1
añor-ar 1
añozg-ar 51
añubl-ar 1,
  and for its use
  regarding
  weather,
  see 45
añud-ar 1
añusc-ar 1
añusg-ar 51
aoj-ar 1

aojusg-ar 1
aov-ar 1
aovill-ar 1
apabil-ar 1
apabull-ar 1
apacent-ar 53
apach-ar 1
apachurr-ar 1
apacigu-ar 7
apadrin-ar 1
apadron-arse ... 80
apag-ar 51
apagull-ar 1
apain-arse 80
apais-ar 1
apalabr-ar 1
apalanc-ar 67
apale-ar 1
apalenc-arse ... 80
apalp-ar 1
apan-ar 1
apand-ar 1
apandill-ar 1
apandong-
  arse 51
apandorg-
  arse 80
apang-arse 51
apaniagu-arse .. 7
apann-ar 1
apantan-ar 1
apañal-arse 80
apañ-ar 1
apañusc-ar 67
apapiz-ar 21
apar-ar 1
aparat-ar 1
aparat-arse
  80, and for its
  use regarding
  weather,
  see 45
aparc-ar 4
apare-ar 1
aparec-er 48
aparei-ar 1
aparej-ar 1
aparent-ar 1
aparrag-arse 51
aparr-ar 1
aparroquian-

ar 1
aparroqui-ar 1
apart-ar 1
apartid-ar 1
aparv-ar 1
apasion-ar 1
apast-ar 1
apastrag-
  arse 51
apastuc-ar 1
apatiz-ar 21
apatron-arse ... 80
apatusc-ar 67
apayas-ar 1
apead-ar 1
apeal-ar 1
ape-ar 1
apech-ar 1
apechug-ar 51
aped-arse 80
apedaz-ar 21
apedre-ar 1,
  and used in
  the positions
  in 45
apeg-ar 51
apegual-ar 1
apeinaz-ar 1
apelambr-ar 1
apel-ar 1
apeld-ar 1
apelgar-arse ... 80
apeligr-ar 1
apell-ar 1
apellid-ar 1
apellin-arse 80
apelmaz-ar 21
apeloton-ar 1
apen-ar 1
apenc-ar 67
apension-ar 1
apension-
  arse 80
apeñusc-ar 67
apeon-ar 1
apequen-
  arse 80
aper-ar 1
apercan-arse ...80
apercanc-
  arse 67

apercat-ar 1
apercaz-ar 21
aperch-ar 1
apercib-ir 3
apercoll-ar 25
aperdig-ar 51
aperez-arse 21
apergamin-
  arse 80
apergoll-ar 1
apern-ar 53
aperre-ar 1
aperrill-ar 1
apersog-ar 51
aperson-arse ... 80
apertrech-ar 1
apesadumbr-
  ar 1
apesar-ar 1
apescoll-ar 25
apesg-ar 51
apestañ-ar 1
apest-ar 1
apestill-ar 1
apetec-er 48
apezon-ar 1
apezuñ-ar 1
apiad-ar 1
apian-ar 1
apicar-arse 80
apicon-ar 1
apil-ar 1
apilg-arse 51
apilgu-arse 80
apilon-ar 1
apilong-arse 51
apimpl-arse 80
apimpoll-ar 1
apimpoll-
  arse 80
apiñ-ar 1
apiñusc-ar 67
apioj-arse 80
apiol-ar 1
apip-arse 80
apiporr-arse 80
apirab-ar 1
apiramid-ar 1
apire-ar 1
apirgüin-arse ... 80
apison-ar 1

apit-ar 1
apitigu-arse 7
apiton-ar 1
aplac-ar 67
aplac-er 11
aplan-ar 1
aplanch-ar 1
aplant-ar 1
aplantill-ar 1
aplasm-ar 1
aplast-ar 1
aplatan-ar 1
aplaud-ir 3
aplay-ar 1
aplaz-ar 21
aplebey-ar 1
aplic-ar 67
aplom-ar 1
apoc-ar 67
apoc-arse 67
apoch-arse 80
apochong-
  arse 51
apocilg-arse 80
apocop-ar 1
apod-ar 1
apoder-ar 1
apoge-ar 1
apolill-ar 1
apolism-ar 1
apologetiz-ar ... 21
apologiz-ar 21
apoltron-ar 1
apoltron-arse ... 80
apolvill-arse 80
apomaz-ar 21
apomp-ar 1
aponch-ar 1
apontoc-ar 67
aponz-ar 21
apop-ar 1
apopoch-
  arse 80
apoquec-er 48
apoquin-ar 1
aporc-ar 67
aporism-arse ... 80
aporrace-ar 1
aporr-ar 1
aporr-arse 80
aporrat-ar 1

aporre-ar 1
aporrill-arse 80
aport-ar 1
aportill-ar 1
aporuñ-ar 1
apos-ar 1
aposent-ar 1
aposesion-ar 1
apost-ar 25
apostat-ar 1
apostem-ar 1
apostill-ar 1
apostill-arse 80
apostoliz-ar 21
apostrof-ar 1
apotenci-ar 1
apotinc-ar 1
apotinc-arse 67
apotr-arse 80
apotrer-ar 1
apoy-ar 1
apoz-arse 21
apreci-ar 1
aprehend-er 2
apremi-ar 1
aprend-er 2
aprens-ar 1
aprension-
  arse 80
apres-ar 1
aprest-ar 1
aprestigi-ar 1
apresur-ar 1
apret-ar 53
apretin-ar 1
apretuj-ar 1
apreven-ir 77
aprim-ar 1
aprisc-ar 67
aprision-ar 1
apro-ar 1
aprob-ar 25
apront-ar 1
apropi-ar 1
apropincu-ar 1
apropincu-
  arse 80
aprovech-ar 1
aprovision-ar 1
aproxim-ar 1
aprudenci-

arse 80
aprudent-
  arse 80
apt-ar 1
apuchinch-ar 1
apuchinch-
  arse 80
apulgar-ar 1
apulgar-arse 80
apulism-arse ... 80
apun-arse 80
apunch-ar 1
apuntal-ar 1
apunt-ar 1
apuntill-ar 1
apuñad-ar 1
apuñal-ar 1
apuñale-ar 1
apuñ-ar 1
apuñe-ar 1
apuñeg-ar 1
apuñete-ar 1
apuñusc-ar 67
apur-ar 1
apurr-ir 3
apurruñ-ar 1
apusus-arse 80
aquebraj-ar 1
aquebraz-
  arse 21
aquejer-ar 1
aquejumbr-
  arse 80
aquer-arse 80
aquerenci-ar 1
aqueres-arse 1
aquerid-arse 80
aquiesc-er 2,
  and used in
  the positions
  in 45
aquiet-ar 1
aquilat-ar 1
equill-ar 1
aquintral-
  arse 80
aquist-ar 1
arabiz-ar 21
arancel-ar 1
arancel-arse 80
arañ-ar 1

ar-ar 1
arbitr-ar 1
arbol-ar 1
arbole-ar 1
arbolec-er 48
arborec-er 48
arboriz-ar 21
arcabuce-ar 1
arcaiz-ar 35
arc-ar 67
archiv-ar 1
arcill-ar 1
ardale-ar 1
ard-er 2
arel-ar 1
aren-ar 1
arenc-ar 67
areng-ar 51
arf-ar 1
argamas-ar 1
argay-ar 1
argent-ar 1
argentiniz-ar 21
argoll-ar 1
argue-ar 1
arguell-arse 80
argü-ir 12
argument-ar 1
aric-ar 67
arid-arse 80
aridec-er 48
ariet-ar 1
arinc-arse 80
arisc-arse 67
arisque-ar 1
aristocratiz-
  ar 21
arl-ar 1
arm-ar 1
armiñ-ar 1
armoniz-ar 21
arom-ar 1
aromatiz-ar 21
arp-ar 1
arpegi-ar 1
arpi-ar 1
arpill-ar 1
arpiñ-ar 1
arpon-ar 1
arpone-ar 1
arque-ar 1

arquet-ar 1
arrabiat-ar 1
arracim-arse 80
arraig-ar 51
arraiz-ar 35
arral-ar 1
arrambl-ar 1
arrampl-ar 1
arran-arse 80
arranc-ar 67
arranch-ar 1
arranci-arse 80
arrap-ar 1
arras-ar 1
arrastr-ar 1
array-ar 1
arre-ar 1
arrebalg-ar 51
arrebañ-ar 1
arrebat-ar 1
arrebiat-ar 1
arrebol-ar 1
arreboll-arse 80
arreboz-ar 21
arrebuj-ar 1
arrebuñ-ar 1
arrecad-ar 1
arrecent-ar 53
arrechonch-
  arse 80
arrechunch-ar ... 1
arreci-ar 1
arrecif-ar 1
arrec-ir 4
arrec-irse 82,
  and used in the
  positions in 4
arredi-ar 1
arredil-ar 1
arredom-ar 1
arredonde-ar 1
arredr-ar 1
arregaz-ar 21
arregl-ar 1
arregost-ar 1
arreguer-ar 1
arrejac-ar 4
arrej-ar 1
arrejer-ar 1
arreling-arse 80
arrellan-arse 80

arremang-ar 51
arremanguiñ-
  ar 1
arremans-ar 1
arremat-ar 1
arremend-ar 1
arremet-er 2
arreming-
  arse 51
arremolin-ar 1
arrempuj-ar 1
arrend-ar 53
arrepanchig-
  arse 51
arrepas-ar 1
arrepent-ir 71
arrepent-irse 71
arrepist-ar 1
arrepoll-ar 1
arrequeson-
  arse 80
arrequint-ar 1
arrest-ar 1
arretac-arse 80
arrezag-ar 51
arri-ar 9
arriat-ar 1
arriaz-ar 21
arrib-ar 1
arrici-arse 80
arrid-ar 1
arriend-ar 1
arriesg-ar 51
arrig-irse 82,
  with the
  changes in 23
arrim-ar 1
arrincon-ar 1
arriostr-ar 1
arris-ar 1
arrisc-ar 67
arriz-ar 21
arrob-ar 1
arrobin-ar 1
arrobiñ-ar 1
arroch-ar 1
arrochel-arse ... 80
arrocin-ar 1
arrodaj-arse 80
arrode-ar 1
arrodel-ar 1

arrodill-ar 1
arrodrig-ar 51
arrodrigon-ar 1
arrog-ar 51
arroj-ar 1
arroll-ar 1
arroll-arse 80
arromadiz-ar ... 21
arromanz-ar 21
arrom-ar 1
arromp-er 2
arron-ar 1
arronz-ar 21
arrop-ar 1
arrostr-ar 1
arroy-ar 1
arroy-arse 80
arru-ar 1
arruch-ar 1
arruf-ar 1
arrufian-arse 80
arrug-ar 51
arruin-ar 1
arrull-ar 1
arrum-ar 1
arrum-arse
  80, and for its
  use regarding
  weather,
  see 45
arrumazon-
  arse 80
arrumb-ar 1
arrunch-arse ... 80
arrunfl-ar 1
arrut-ar 1
arrutin-ar 1
arterializ-ar 21
arteson-ar 1
articul-ar 1
artig-ar 51
artill-ar 1
artiz-ar 21
artuñ-ar 1
aruñ-ar 1
asac-ar 67
asaete-ar 1
asainete-ar 1
asalari-ar 1
asalmer-ar 1
asalt-ar 1

asalte-ar	1
asan-ar	1
as-ar	1
asasel-ar	1
ascend-er 2, with the changes in	53
ase-ar	1
asech-ar	1
ased-ar	1
asedi-ar	1
aseglar-arse	80
asegu-ir	52
asegund-ar	1
asegur-ar	1
asel-arse	80
asemej-ar	1
asemill-ar	1
asendere-ar	1
asent-ar	53
asent-ir	71
aseptiz-ar	21
aseren-ar	1
aseri-arse	80
aserr-ar	53
aserre-ar	1
aserruch-ar	1
asert-ar	1
ases-ar	1
asesin-ar	1
asesor-ar	1
asest-ar 1, and alter- natively,	53
asever-ar	1
asfalt-ar	1
asfixi-ar	1
asg-ar	1
asibil-ar	1
asign-ar	1
asiguat-arse	80
asil-ar	1
asimil-ar	1
asin-ar	1
as-ir	13
asist-ir	3
asne-ar	1
asobarc-ar	4
asobi-ar	1
asobin-arse	80
asocair-arse	80

asoc-ar	67
asoci-ar	1
asolan-ar	1
asolap-ar	1
asol-ar	25
asoldad-ar	1
asold-ar	25
asole-ar	1
asollam-ar	1
asollan-ar	1
asom-ar	1
asombr-ar	1
asonant-ar	1
ason-ar	25
asord-ar	1
asorn-ar	1
asoroch-arse	80
asoseg-ar	62
asotan-ar	1
asp-ar	1
aspavent-ar	53
aspavient- arse	80
aspe-ar	1
aspe-arse	80
aspere-ar	1
asperge-ar	1
asperg-er	23
aspergi-ar	1
asperj-ar	1
asperon-ar	1
aspill-ar	1
aspille-ar	1
aspir-ar	1
asque-ar	1
ast-ar	1
aste-ar	1
astill-ar	1
astreñ-ir	64
astring-ir 3, with the changes in 23, plus the past partici- ple astricto	
astriñ-ir	17
astrolabi-ar	1
astrolog-ar	51
asubi-ar	1
asum-ir	3
asunt-ar	1

asur-ar	1
asurc-ar	67
asust-ar	1
asutil-ar	1
atabale-ar	1
atabardill- arse	80
atabill-ar	1
atabl-ar	1
atac-ar	67
atafag-ar	51
atagall-ar	1
atair-ar	1
ataj-ar	1
atalaj-ar	1
atalant-ar	1
atalay-ar	1
atalud-ar	1
ataluz-ar	21
atañ-er	14
atapial-ar	1
atapuz-ar	21
ataquiz-ar	21
at-ar	1
atarace-ar	1
atarant-ar	1
ataraz-ar	21
atardec-er 48, and for its use regarding weather, see	45
atare-ar	1
atarquin-ar	1
atarrag-ar	51
atarraj-ar	1
atarray-ar	1
atarrill-arse	80
atarug-ar	51
atasaj-ar	1
atasc-ar	67
atavi-ar	67
ate-ar	1
atedi-ar	1
atejon-arse	80
atemoriz-ar	21
atemper-ar	1
atenace-ar	1
atenaz-ar	21
atend-er 2, with the changes	

in 53, plus the past participle atento	
atenebr-arse 80, and for its use regarding weather, see	45
aten-er	74
atental-ar	1
atent-ar	53
atenu-ar	9
ateperet-arse	80
aterec-er	48
ater-ir	4
aternec-er	48
aterraj-ar	1
aterr-ar	53
aterre-ar	1
aterrec-er	48
aterrer-ar	1
aterrill-arse	80
aterriz-ar	21
aterron-ar	1
aterroriz-ar	21
ates-ar	53
atesor-ar	1
atest-ar 1, and alter- natively,	53
atestigu-ar	7
atet-ar	1
atetill-ar	1
atez-ar	21
atib-ar	1
atiborr-ar	1
atiburr-ar	1
atiempr-ar	1
aties-ar	1
atild-ar	1
atilint-ar	1
atin-ar	1
atinc-ar	67
atincon-ar	1
ating-ir 3, with the changes in	23
atip-arse	80
atipl-ar	1
atipuj-arse	80
atiquiz-ar	21

atirant-ar 1
atirici-arse 80
atisb-ar 1
ativ-ar 1
atiz-ar 21
atizon-ar 1
ato-ar 1
atoc-ar 1
atoch-ar 1
atocin-ar 1
atoj-ar 1
atojin-ar 1
atoll-ar 1
atollec-er 48
atolondr-ar 1
atomec-er 48
atom-ir 4
atomiz-ar 21
aton-ar 1
atond-ar 1
atont-ar 1
atontec-er 48
atontolin-ar 1
ator-ar 1, and
  alter-
  natively, ... 25
atorcaz-ar
  25 plus the
  changes in 21
atorg-ar 51
atorment-ar 1
atornill-ar 1
atoroz-arse 21
atorozon-
  arse 80
atorr-ar 1
atortaj-ar 1
atortill-ar 1
atortoj-ar 1
atortol-ar 1
atortor-ar 1
atortuj-ar 1
atorzon-arse 80
atosig-ar 51
atoxic-ar 67
atrabaj-ar 1
atrabanc-ar 67
atrac-ar 67
atra-er 75
atrafag-ar 51
atragant-ar 1

atragant-arse ... 80
atraicion-ar 1
atraill-ar 9
atralac-arse 80
atramoj-ar 1
atramp-ar 1
atranc-ar 67
atrap-ar 1
atras-ar 1
atraves-ar 53
atraznal-ar 1
atregu-ar 7
atresnal-ar 1
atreud-ar 1
atrev-er 2
atrev-erse 81
atribu-ir 42
atribul-ar 1
atrill-ar 1
atrinc-ar 1
atrincher-ar 1
atroch-ar 1
atrofi-ar 1
atroj-ar 1
atron-ar 25,
  and for its
  use regarding
  weather,
  see 45
atronc-ar 1
atroner-ar 1
atrop-ar 1
atropell-ar 1
atropill-ar 1
atroz-ar 21
atruhan-arse 80
atucuñ-ar 1
atuf-ar 1
atuj-ar 1
atumultu-ar 9
atuntun-arse 80
atur-ar 1
aturbant-ar 1
aturbon-arse 80
aturd-ir 3
aturne-ar 1
aturull-ar 1
aturrull-ar 1
atus-ar 1
augur-ar 1
aull-ar 9

aument-ar 1
aun-ar 9
auñ-ar 1
aup-ar 9
aureol-ar 1
aurific-ar 67
auscult-ar 1
ausent-ar 1
auspici-ar 1
autentic-ar 67
autentific-ar 67
autocopi-ar 1
autografi-ar 9
automatiz-ar 21
autopsi-ar 1
autoriz-ar 21
autosuges-
  tion-arse 80
auxili-ar 1
avad-ar 1
avag-arse 80
avah-ar 1
aval-ar 1
avalent-ar 53
avaliz-ar 21
avall-ar 1
avalor-ar 1
avalu-ar 9
avanec-erse 48
avanz-ar 21
avasall-ar 1
avecin-ar 1
avecind-ar 1
avejanc-arse 67
avejent-ar 1
avejig-ar 51
avellan-ar 1
aven-ar 1
avenen-ar 1
aven-ir 77
aventaj-ar 1
avent-ar 53
aventur-ar 1
aver-ar 1
averdug-ar 51
avergonz-ar 15
averi-ar 9
averi-arse 9
averigu-ar 9
averrug-arse 51
avez-ar 21

avi-ar 9
aviej-ar 1
avigor-ar 1
avilant-arse 80
avillan-ar 1
avinagr-ar 1
avinz-arse 21
avis-ar 1
avisp-ar 1
avisped-ar 1
avispore-ar 1
avist-ar 1
avitol-ar 1
avituall-ar 1
aviv-ar 1
avizor-ar 1
avoc-ar 67
avos-ar 1
axegu-ar 1
axiomatiz-ar 19
aye-ar 1
ayerm-ar 1
ayud-ar 1
ayun-ar 1
ayunisar-ar 1
ayust-ar 1
azacan-arse 80
azacane-ar 1
azadon-ar 1
azafran-ar 1
azain-ar 1
azanj-ar 1
azarand-ar 1
azar-ar 1
azar-arse 80
azare-arse 80
azem-ar 1
azo-ar 1
azocal-ar 1
azoc-ar 67
azofr-ar 1
azog-ar 51
azol-ar 25
azolv-ar 1
azor-ar 1
azoroc-arse 67
azorr-ar 1
azorr-arse 80
azot-ar 1
azozobr-ar 1
azucar-ar 1

azufr-ar 1
azul-ar 1
azule-ar 1
azulej-ar 1
azumag-arse ...51
azum-ar 1
azurron-arse 80
azurumb-
  arse 80
azuz-ar 21

b

bab-ar 1
babe-ar 1
babilone-ar 1
babose-ar 1
babuj-ar 1
babuse-ar 1
bachate-ar 1
bache-ar 1
bachille-ar 1
bachiller-ar 1
bachillere-ar 1
badaje-ar 1
badall-ar 1
badern-ar 1
badulaque-ar 1
bafane-ar 1
baf-ar 1
bafe-ar 1
bag-ar 51
bail-ar 1
bailote-ar 1
baj-ar 1
baje-ar 1
balace-ar 1
baladr-ar 1
baladre-ar 1
baladron-ar 1
baladrone-ar 1
balance-ar 1
balandrone-ar ... 1
balaque-ar 1
bal-ar 1
balast-ar 1
balastr-ar 1
balaustr-ar 1
balay-ar 1
balbuce-ar 1

balbuc-ir 16
balcaniz-ar 21
balcone-ar 1
bald-ar 1
balde-ar 1
baldon-ar 1
baldone-ar 1
baldos-ar 1
bale-ar 1
bali-ar 1
balit-ar 1
balite-ar 1
baliz-ar 21
ball-ar 1
ballest-ar 1
balleste-ar 1
balot-ar 1
balsam-ar 1
balsamiz-ar 21
balse-ar 1
bambale-ar 1
bambane-ar 1
bambarote-ar 1
bambe-ar 1
bambole-ar 1
bambone-ar 1
bamborde-ar 1
bambuque-ar 1
bandare-ar 1
band-arse 80
bande-ar 1
bandej-ar 1
banderille-ar 1
banderiz-ar 21
band-ir 3
bandolere-ar 1
banque-ar 1
banquete-ar 1
bañ-ar 1
baptiz-ar 21
baque-ar 1
baqueliz-ar 21
baquete-ar 1
baqui-ar 9
barahust-ar 1
baraj-ar 1
barajust-ar 1
barand-ar 1
barat-ar 1
barate-ar 1
baraust-ar 1

barb-ar 1
barbare-ar 1
barbariz-ar 21
barbasque-ar 1
barbe-ar 1
barbech-ar 1
barbolete-ar 1
barboll-ar 1
barbot-ar 1
barbote-ar 1
barbull-ar 1
barbull-ir 17
barcin-ar 1
bard-ar 1
bareque-ar 1
baritone-ar 1
barlo-ar 1
barlvente-ar 1
barniz-ar 21
barque-ar 1
barrac-arse 80
barraj-ar 1
barranque-ar 1
barraque-ar 1
barr-ar 1
barre-ar 1
barren-ar 1
barrene-ar 1
barr-er 2
barrete-ar 1
barrisc-ar 67
barrisque-ar 1
barrit-ar 1
barrunt-ar 1
bartole-ar 1
bartul-ar 1
bartule-ar 1
barull-ar 1
barzon-ar 1
barzone-ar 1
bas-ar 1
basc-ar 1
bascul-ar 1
basific-ar 1
basque-ar 1
bastante-ar 1
bast-ar 1
bastard-ar 1
bastarde-ar 1
baste-ar 1
bastec-er 48

bastere-ar 1
bastill-ar 1
bastille-ar 1
bastiment-ar 1
bastion-ar 1
bast-ir 3
bastone-ar 1
basure-ar 1
batajole-ar 1
batall-ar 1
batan-ar 1
batane-ar 1
bate-ar 1
batibole-ar 1
baticole-arse ...80
batiport-ar 1
bat-ir 3
batoch-ar 1
batoj-ar 1
batoll-ar 1
batuc-ar 67
batuque-ar 1
bautiz-ar 21
bayoy-ar 1
bayunque-ar 1
bazuc-ar 67
bazuque-ar 1
beatific-ar 67
bebd-ar 1
beb-er 2
beberruch-ar 1
beborrete-ar 1
beborrote-ar 1
bec-ar 67
becerre-ar 1
becuadr-ar 1
bed-ar 1
bef-ar 1
bejuque-ar 1
beld-ar 53
bellaque-ar 1
bellote-ar 1
beltrane-ar 1
bembete-ar 1
bemol-ar 1
bemoliz-ar 21
bendec-ir 58,
  plus the
  regular past
  participle
  bendecido

and the
irregular past
participle
bendito
bendic-ir 58
benec-er 48
benefici-ar 1
berling-ar 51
bermeje-ar 1
bermejec-er 48
berr-ar 1
berre-ar 1
berrende-
arse 80
berrinch-ar 1
berroch-ar 1
bes-ar 1
besote-ar 1
bestializ-arse ... 21
besuc-ar 67
besuque-ar 1
betume-ar 1
betuminiz-ar 1
betun-ar 1
betune-ar 1
biab-ar 1
bias-ar 1
bich-ar 1
biche-ar 1
bichofe-ar 1
bicromat-ar 1
bield-ar 1
bienaventur-ar .. 1
bienquer-er 60,
plus the past
participle
bienquisto
bienquist-ar 1
bienviv-ir 3
bifurc-arse 67
bigarde-ar 1
bigardone-ar 1
bild-ar 1
bilm-ar 1
biloc-arse 67
bilonque-ar 1
biltrote-ar 1
bin-ar 1
biodegrad-ar 1
biografi-ar 9
birl-ar 1

birol-ar 1
birringue-ar 1
bis-ar 1
bisbis-ar 1
bisbise-ar 1
bisec-ar 67
bisegment-ar 1
bisel-ar 1
bistra-er 75
bistray-er 75
bit-ar 1
bituminiz-ar 21
bizantine-ar 1
bizarre-ar 1
bizc-ar 67
bizcoch-ar 1
bizcorne-ar 1
bizm-ar 1
bizque-ar 1
blande-ar 1
blandec-er 48
bland-ir 4
blanque-ar 1
blanquec-er 48
blasfem-ar 1
blasm-ar 1
blason-ar 1
blinc-ar 67
blind-ar 1
bloc-ar 67
bloque-ar 1
bluf-ar 1
blufe-ar 1
bobe-ar 1
bobin-ar 1
bocade-ar 1
bocarte-ar 1
boce-ar 1
bocel-ar 1
bocez-ar 21
boch-ar 1
bochinche-ar 1
bocin-ar 1
bocone-ar 1
bodegone-ar 1
bof-arse 80
bofete-ar 1
boford-ar 1
bog-ar 51
bogue-ar 1
bohord-ar 1

boicote-ar 1
boj-ar 1
boje-ar 1
bojote-ar 1
bolace-ar 1
bolcheviz-ar 21
bole-ar 1
bolere-ar 1
bolet-ar 1
bolete-ar 1
boliche-ar 1
boline-ar 1
boll-ar 1
bollici-ar 1
boll-ir 3
bolse-ar 1
bolsique-ar 1
bomb-ar 1
bombarde-ar 1
bombe-ar 1
bonderiz-ar 21
bonific-ar 67
boque-ar 1
boquete-ar 1
boraci-ar 1
borboll-ar 1
borbolle-ar 1
borbollone-ar 1
borborit-ar 1
borbot-ar 1
borbote-ar 1
bord-ar 1
borde-ar 1
bordej-ar 1
bordone-ar 1
borl-arse 80
borle-arse 80
borne-ar 1
bornegue-ar 1
borrache-ar 1
borraje-ar 1
borr-ar 1
borregue-ar 1
borrone-ar 1
bos-ar 1
boscaje-ar 1
bosquej-ar 1
boste-ar 1
bostez-ar 21
bostic-ar 67
bostone-ar 1

botacuch-ar 1
botalone-ar 1
botaniz-ar 21
bot-ar 1
botarate-ar 1
bote-ar 1
boton-ar 1
boved-ar 1
boxe-ar 1
boy-ar 1
boycote-ar 1
bozale-ar 1
brace-ar 1
bram-ar 1
brand-ar 1
brandec-er 2
bras-ar 1
brasc-ar 67
bravate-ar 1
brave-ar 1
bravi-ar 1
bravoce-ar 1
bravucone-ar 1
braz-ar 1
brazn-ar 1
bre-ar 1
brech-ar 1
breg-ar 51
bregete-ar 1
breguete-ar 1
breque-ar 1
bresc-ar 67
brete-ar 1
brez-ar 21
brib-ar 1
bribi-ar 1
bribone-ar 1
brid-ar 1
brill-ar 1
brinc-ar 67
brincole-ar 1
brind-ar 1
bris-ar 1
brisc-ar 67
briz-ar 21
brizn-ar 1
broc-ar 1
broce-arse 80
broch-ar 1
broll-ar 1
brom-ar 1

brome-ar 1
bronce-ar 1
bronque-ar 1
broquel-arse 80
brosl-ar 1
brot-ar 1
broz-ar 21
bruje-ar 1
bruj-ir 3
brujule-ar 1
brum-ar 1
bruñ-ir 17
brutaliz-ar 21
brutaliz-arse 21
brute-ar 1
bruz-ar 21
buce-ar 1
buch-ar 1
buf-ar 1
bufone-ar 1
bufone-arse 80
bufoniz-ar 21
bug-ir 3, with
  the changes
  in 23
buh-ar 1
bu-ir 42
buitre-ar 1
bujarrone-ar 1
bul-ar 1
buld-ar 1
bullar-ar 1
bullec-er 48
bull-ir 17
bunde-ar 1
bure-ar 1
buril-ar 1
burl-ar 1
burocratiz-ar 21
burraje-ar 1
burre-ar 1
busc-ar 67
buscone-ar 1
buz-ar 21

C

cabal-ar 1
cabalg-ar 51

cabaliz-ar 21
caballe-ar 1
caballere-ar 1
cabdill-ar 1
cabe-ar 1
cabece-ar 1
cabell-ar 1
cab-er 18
cabestr-ar 1
cabestre-ar 1
cabilde-ar 1
cable-ar 1
cablegrafi-ar 74
cabrafig-ar 1
cabrahig-ar 19
cabre-ar 1
cabrest-ar 1
cabreste-ar 1
cabrev-ar 1
cabrille-ar 1
cabriol-ar 1
cabriole-ar 1
cabrion-ar 1
cabruñ-ar 1
cabule-ar 1
cabz-ar 21
cacabe-ar 1
cacarañ-ar 1
cacaraque-ar 1
cacare-ar 1
cace-ar 1
cachache-ar 1
cachañ-ar 1
cachañe-ar 1
cachape-ar 1
cachaque-ar 1
cach-ar 1
cacharpe-
  arse 80
cacharre-ar 1
cache-ar 1
cachete-ar 1
cachiflore-ar 1
cachifol-ar 1
cachifoll-ar 1
cachilape-ar 1
cachilapi-ar 1
cachipod-ar 1
cachiporre-
  arse 80
cachirule-ar 1

cachonde-ar 1
cachonde-
  arse 80
cachorre-ar 1
cachu-ar 1
cachuche-ar 1
cachuele-ar 1
cachunc-ar 1
cachure-ar 1
cacique-ar 1
cacul-ar 1
cacule-ar 1
cadenci-ar 1
cadene-ar 1
cadmi-ar 1
caduc-ar 67
caduque-ar 1
ca-er 20
caf-ar 1
cafete-ar 1
cag-ar 51
caigü-ir 42
caimane-ar 1
cain-ar 1
cairel-ar 1
caje-ar 1
cajete-ar 1
cajone-ar 1
calabace-ar 1
calabri-ar 1
calabrot-ar 1
calace-ar 1
calafate-ar 1
calafet-ar 1
calafete-ar 1
calamon-
  arse 80
calamorr-ar 1
calandr-ar 1
cal-ar 1
calate-ar 1
calaver-ar 1
calavere-ar 1
calc-ar 67
calcet-ar 1
calcete-ar 1
calcific-ar 67
calcin-ar 1
calcitr-ar 1
calcografi-ar 74
calcorre-ar 1

cachonde-ar 1
calcul-ar 1
calde-ar 1
calec-er 48
calec-erse 48
calend-ar 1
calent-ar 53
calenture-ar 1
cal-er 2
calete-ar 1
calibr-ar 1
calich-ar 1
calific-ar 67
caligrafi-ar 74
calill-ar 1
calimb-ar 1
callant-ar 1
callape-ar 1
call-ar 1
calle-ar 1
callec-er 48
calleje-ar 1
callent-ar 1
callos-ar 1
calm-ar 1
calme-ar 1
calofri-arse 74
calomni-ar 1
caloni-ar 1
caloñ-ar 1
calor-ar 1
calosfri-arse 80
calote-ar 1
calumb-arse 80
calumni-ar 1
calv-ar 1
calvec-er 48
calz-ar 21
camandul-ar 1
camandule-ar ... 1
camarone-ar 1
camastre-ar 1
cambalach-ar ... 1
cambalache-
  ar 1
camb-ar 1
cambi-ar 1
cambiz-ar 21
camel-ar 1
cami-ar 1
camin-ar 1
camoch-ar 1

camod-ar 1	cañ-ar 1	carboniz-ar 21	carroce-ar 1
camorre-ar 1	cañaver-ar 1	carbur-ar 1	carroch-ar 1
camote-ar 1	cañavere-ar 1	carcaje-ar 1	carroñ-ar 1
campane-ar 1	cañe-ar 1	carcav-ar 1	carroz-ar 21
campanille-ar ... 1	cañone-ar 1	carcave-ar 1	carruc-ar 67
camp-ar 1	caoliniz-ar 21	carcavin-ar 1	cartabone-ar 1
campe-ar 1	capace-ar 1	carcel-ar 1	carte-ar 1
campej-ar 1	capacete-ar 1	carcer-ar 1	cartele-ar 1
camufl-ar 1	capacit-ar 1	carch-ar 1	cartografi-ar 74
canalete-ar 1	cap-ar 1	carcomec-er 2	casament-ar ... 53
canaliz-ar 21	capcion-ar 1	carcom-er 2	cas-ar 1
canaque-ar 1	cape-ar 1	card-ar 1	cascabele-ar 1
can-ar 1	caperuce-ar 1	cardenaliz-ar 1	cascamaj-ar 1
cancane-ar 1	capialz-ar 21	carduz-ar 21	casc-ar 67
cancel-ar 1	capicul-ar 1	care-ar 1	cascare-ar 1
cancer-ar 1	capirote-ar 1	carec-er 48	cascarone-ar 1
canch-ar 1	capitaliz-ar 21	caren-ar 1	cascarrin-ar 1
canche-ar 1	capitane-ar 1	carg-ar 51	cascote-ar 1
cand-ar 1	capitone-ar 1	cargose-ar 1	cascunde-ar 1
candelill-ar 1	capitul-ar 1	cari-ar 1	caseific-ar 67
candilete-ar 1	capitule-ar 1	caribe-ar 1	caspalete-ar 1
cand-irse 82	capol-ar 1	caricatur-ar 1	casque-ar 1
candombe-ar 1	capon-ar 1	caricaturiz-ar ... 21	casquine-ar 1
candongue-ar ... 1	capone-arse 80	carillone-ar 1	castañe-ar 1
cane-ar 1	caporale-ar 1	carimb-ar 1	castañete-ar 1
canec-er 48	capot-ar 1	cariñ-ar 1	castellaniz-ar ... 21
canec-erse 48	capote-ar 1	carle-ar 1	castific-ar 1
canfor-ar 1	caprific-ar 1	carmen-ar 1	castig-ar 51
cangall-ar 1	capsul-ar 1	carmin-ar 1	castiz-ar 21
cang-ar 51	capt-ar 1	carnavale-ar 1	castr-ar 1
cangreje-ar 1	capten-er 74	carne-ar 1	casualiz-ar 21
cangren-arse ... 80	captiv-ar 1	carnere-ar 1	casuistic-ar 67
canguel-ar 1	captur-ar 1	carnific-arse 67	casungue-ar 1
canj-ar 1	capuce-ar 1	caroch-ar 1	catalaniz-ar 21
canje-ar 1	capuj-ar 1	caronch-arse ... 80	cataliz-ar 21
canmi-ar 1	capuz-ar 21	carpente-ar 1	catalog-ar 51
canoniz-ar 21	carabe-ar 1	carpete-ar 1	catane-ar 1
cans-ar 1	carabin-ar 1	carpinte-ar 1	catapult-ar 1
cantale-ar 1	carabine-ar 1	carpintere-ar 1	cat-ar 1
cantalete-ar 1	carabrite-ar 1	carp-ir 3	catarre-ar 1
cant-ar 1	caracole-ar 1	carrance-ar 1	catastr-ar 1
cante-ar 1	caracteriz-ar 21	carrañ-arse 80	catat-ar 1
cantic-ar 1	carambol-ar 1	carraplane-ar ... 1	cate-ar 1
cantine-ar 1	carambole-ar 1	carraspe-ar 1	catedr-ar 1
canton-ar 1	caramele-ar 1	carrasque-ar 1	catequiz-ar 21
cantone-ar 1	carameliz-ar 21	carre-ar 1	cateteriz-ar 21
cantone-arse ... 80	caramill-ar 1	carrej-ar 1	catip-ar 1
canturre-ar 1	carapite-ar 1	carrere-ar 1	catite-ar 1
canturri-ar 1	carbon-ar 1	carrete-ar 1	cativ-ar 1
cantus-ar 1	carbonat-ar 1	carric-ar 1	catoliz-ar 21
canut-ar 1	carbone-ar 1	carrill-ar 1	catoniz-ar 21

catrine-ar 1
cauc-arse 80
cauch-ar 1
cauchut-ar 1
caucion-ar 1
caus-ar 1
cause-ar 1
caustic-ar 67
caustific-ar 1
cautel-ar 1
cauteriz-ar 21
cautiv-ar 1
cav-ar 1
cavil-ar 1
cavilose-ar 1
cayape-ar 1
cayasch-ar 1
cayasch-ir 3
caz-ar 21
cazcale-ar 1
cazolete-ar 1
cazumbr-ar 1
cazungue-ar 1
cazuñ-ar 1
cebad-ar 1
ceb-ar 1
cece-ar 1
cecin-ar 1
cedace-ar 1
ced-er 1
cedul-ar 1
cefe-ar 1
cegaje-ar 1
ceg-ar 62
cej-ar 1
cel-ar 1
celebr-ar 1
celemine-ar 1
celer-ar 1
cellisque-ar 1,
   and for its use
   regarding
   weather,
   see 45
cement-ar 1
cen-ar 1
cencerre-ar 1
cendr-ar 1
ceneg-ar 51
cens-ar 1
censu-ar 1

censur-ar 1
centell-ar 1,
   and for its use
   regarding
   weather,
   see 45
centelle-ar 1,
   and for its use
   regarding
   weather,
   see 45
centesim-ar 1
centon-ar 1
centoniz-ar 1
centraliz-ar 21
centr-ar 1
centrifug-ar 51
centuplic-ar 67
ceñ-ar 1
ceñ-ir 64
cepill-ar 1
cepren-ar 1
cerc-ar 67
cerce-ar 1,
   and used
   in the
   positions in ... 45
cercen-ar 1
cerch-ar 1
cerche-ar 1
cerche-arse 80
cercior-ar 1
cerde-ar 1
cerebr-ar 1
cerific-ar 1
cerne-ar 1
cern-er 2,
   with the
   changes in 5
cern-ir 3, with
   the changes
   in 53, and
   used in the
   positions in 14
cerote-ar 1
cerraje-ar 1
cerr-ar 53
cerreboj-ar 1
cerrill-ar 1
certific-ar 67
cesante-ar 1

ces-ar 1
cespit-ar 1
ceston-ar 1
chabacane-ar ... 1
chacane-ar 1
chacare-ar 1
chacarre-ar 1
chacarrusc-
   ar 67
chacch-ar 1
chace-ar 1
chachalaque-
   ar 1
chach-ar 1
chachare-ar 1
chacolote-ar 1
chacon-ar 1
chacote-ar 1
chacuale-ar 1
chacurrusc-ar ... 1
chafall-ar 1
chaf-ar 1
chafarde-ar 1
chafarre-ar 1
chafarrin-ar 1
chaflan-ar 1
chagu-ar 7
chair-ar 1
chajuan-arse ...80
chalane-ar 1
chal-ar 1
chaleque-ar 1
chall-ar 1
cham-ar 1
chamarile-ar 1
chamarre-ar 1
chambone-ar 1
chamel-ar 1
chamiz-ar 21
chamorr-ar 1
champ-ar 1
champe-ar 1
champurr-ar 1
champurre-ar ... 1
chamull-ar 1
chamurr-ar 1
chamusc-ar 67
chamuy-ar 1
chancaque-ar ... 1
chanc-ar 67
chance-ar 1

chancel-ar 1
chanch-ar 1
chanchull-ar 1
chancill-ar 1
chanclete-ar 1
chancu-ar 1
chancuque-ar ... 1
chanel-ar 1
chanfl-ar 1
chanfle-ar 1
chang-ar 51
changolote-ar ... 1
changue-ar 1
chanque-ar 1
chantaje-ar 1
chant-ar 1
chañ-ar 1
chapalate-ar 1
chapale-ar 1
chapalete-ar 1
chap-ar 1
chaparre-ar 1,
   and for its use
   regarding
   weather,
   see 45
chapatale-ar 1
chapate-ar 1
chape-ar 1
chapec-ar 67
chapesc-ar 67
chapete-ar 1
chapeton-ar 1
chapetone-ar 1
chapisc-ar 67
chaple-ar 1
chapod-ar 1
chapole-ar 1
chapote-ar 1
chapuce-ar 1
chapull-ar 1
chapurr-ar 1
chapurre-ar 1
chapuz-ar 21
chaque-ar 1
chaquete-ar 1
charamusc-
   ar 67
charangu-er 1
charchuele-ar ... 1
charl-ar 1

charlatane-ar 1
charle-ar 1
charlote-ar 1
charol-ar 1
charque-ar 1
charqui-ar 1
charrane-ar 1
charrangue-ar ... 1
charr-ar 1
charrasc-
   arse 80
charrasque-ar ... 1
charre-ar 1
charrusc-ar 67
chasc-ar 67
chascone-ar 1
chasp-ar 1
chasparre-ar 1
chaspe-ar 1
chasque-ar 1
chate-ar 1
chav-ar 1
chave-ar 1
chavete-ar 1
chay-ar 1
chaz-ar 21
chec-ar 67
cheche-ar 1
chechone-ar 1
chele-ar 1
chemec-ar 1
chenque-ar 1
cheque-ar 1
cherch-ar 1
cherri-ar 1
chib-ar 1
chicane-ar 1
chic-ar 67
chich-ar 1
chicharr-ar 1
chicharre-ar 1
chiche-ar 1
chichigu-ar 1
chichin-ar 1
chichisbe-ar 1
chichone-ar 1
chicle-ar 1
chicole-ar 1
chicore-ar 1
chicote-ar 1
chict-ar 1

chifl-ar 1
chijete-ar 1
chileniz-ar 21
chilicote-ar 1
chilingue-ar 1
chill-ar 1
chilote-ar 1
chilp-ar 1
chilpi-ar 1
chim-ar 1
chimb-ar 1
chimene-ar 1
chimiscole-ar 1
chimorr-ar 1
chinampe-ar 1
chin-ar 1
chinaste-ar 1
chinch-ar 1
chinchine-ar 1
chinchone-ar 1
chinchorre-ar 1
chinchose-ar 1
chincuale-ar 1
chine-ar 1
chingane-ar 1
ching-ar 51
chingar-ar 1
chingl-ar 1
chingue-ar 1
chiniti-ar 1
chiñinc-ar 1
chipi-ar 1
chipilc-arse 80
chipiline-ar 1
chipoje-ar 1
chipote-ar 1
chique-ar 1
chiquere-ar 1
chiquete-ar 1
chiquite-ar 1
chiraje-ar 1
chirape-ar 1
  and used in
  the positions
  in 45
chirele-ar 1
chirhu-ar 1
chirigote-ar 1
chirij-ar 1
chirijim-ar 1
chiripe-ar 1

chirl-ar 1
chirlat-ar 1
chirle-ar 1
chirote-ar 1
chirre-ar 1
chirri-ar 9
chirrione-ar 1
chirrisque-ar 1
chisc-ar 67
chische-ar 1
chisguete-ar 1
chism-ar 1
chisme-ar 1
chismorre-ar 1
chismose-ar 1
chismote-ar 1
chisp-ar 1
chispe-ar 1,
  and for its use
  regarding
  weather,
  see 45
chispoje-ar 1
chisporrete-ar ... 1
chisporrote-ar ... 1
chist-ar 1
chiste-ar 1
chit-ar 1
chite-arse 80
chiv-ar 1
chiv-arse 80
chivate-ar 1
chive-ar 1
choc-ar 67
chocarre-ar 1
choch-ar 1
choche-ar 1
chochole-ar 1
chocl-ar 1
chocle-ar 1
chocole-ar 1
chocore-ar 1
chocote-ar 1
chole-ar 1
choll-ar 1
chollonc-arse ... 80
chollong-
  arse 67
chongue-ar 1
chongue-
  arse 51

chont-ar 1
chope-ar 1
choque-ar 1
chor-ar 1
chore-ar 1
chorr-ar 1
chorre-ar 1
chorrete-ar 1
chosp-ar 1
chote-ar 1
choz-ar 21
chozp-ar 1
chubasque-ar ... 1
chucane-ar 1
chuce-ar 1
chuch-ar 1
chuche-ar 1
chuchique-ar 1
chuch-ir 3
chuchumeque-
  ar 1
chuchuque-ar ... 1
chueque-ar 1
chuf-ar 1
chufe-ar 1
chufl-ar 1
chuflete-ar 1
chugu-ar 1
chulanch-ar 1
chule-ar 1
chuli-ar 1
chulpaje-ar 1
chulquine-ar 1
chumandi-ar 1
chum-ar 1
chumb-ar 1
chumbe-ar 1
chumpipe-ar 1
chunc-ar 1
chung-ar 1
chung-arse 51
chungue-ar 1
chungue-
  arse 80
chunt-ar 1
chuñ-ar 1
chup-ar 1
chuperrete-ar ... 1
chupete-ar 1
chuque-arse 80
churc-ar 1

churear - cohetear

chure-ar	1	grafi-ar	1
churin-ar	1	cinematografi-	
churn-ar	1	ar	74
churr-ar	1	cinerradiografi-	
churrasc-ar	67	ar	1
churrasque-ar	1	cingl-ar	1
churre-ar	1	cint-ar	1
churrete-ar	1	cintare-ar	1
churrique-arse	1	cinte-ar	1
churrit-ar	1	cintil-ar	1
churrum-ar	1	circ-ar	1
churrupe-ar	1	circu-ir	42
churrupete-ar	1	circul-ar	1
churrusc-ar	67	circunceñ-ir	64
chuscarr-ar	1	circuncid-ar 1,	
chusch-ar	1	plus the past	
chuse-ar	1	participle	
chuse-arse	80	circunciso	
chusme-ar	1	circuncig-ir 3,	
chusque-		with the	
arse	80	changes in	46
chut-ar	1	circunc-ir	3
chute-ar	1	circund-ar	1
chuz-ar	21	circunfer-ir	71
ciabog-ar	51	circunloque-ar	1
cianque-ar	1	circunnaveg-	
ci-ar	74	ar	1
cibernetiz-ar	1	circunscrib-ir	
cical-ar	1	3, except the	
cicate-ar	1	past partici-	
cicatere-ar	1	ples are	
cicatriz-ar	21	circunscripto	
cicl-ar	1	and	
ciclis-ar	1	circunscrito	
ciendobl-ar	1	circunstanci-	
cifr-ar	1	ar	1
ciguat-arse	80	circunval-ar	1
cilindr-ar	1	circunven-ir	77
cim-ar	1	circunvol-ar	25
cimarre-ar	1	circunyac-er	79
cimarrone-ar	1	circur-ar	1
cimbl-ar	1	cisc-ar	51
cimbr-ar	1	cisi on-ar	1
cimbre-ar	1	cism-ar	1
ciment-ar	53	cit-ar	1
cincel-ar	1	citariz-ar	21
cinch-ar	1	civiliz-ar	21
cinefic-ar	1	cizall-ar	1
cinegrafi-ar	1	cizañ-ar	1
cinemagrafi-ar	1	cizañe-ar	1
cinemarradio-		clam-ar	1

clamore-ar	1	cobdici-ar	1
claque-ar	1	cobe-ar	1
clar-ar	1	cobech-ar	1
clare-ar 1, and		cobij-ar	1
for its use		cobiz-ar	21
regarding		cobr-ar	1
weather,		cobre-ar	1
see	45	cobr-ir	67
clarec-er 48,		cocainiz-ar	1
and for its use		coc-ar	67
regarding		cocar-ar	1
weather,		coce-ar	1
see	45	coc-er 22 has	
clarific-ar	67	a past partici-	
clarine-ar	1	ple cocho	
clasific-ar	67	coch-ar	1
clatole-ar	1	coch-arse	80
claudic-ar	67	coche-ar	1
clauquill-ar	1	cochine-ar	1
claustr-ar	1	cochiz-arse	80
claustre-ar	1	cocin-ar	1
clausul-ar	1	cocine-ar	1
clausur-ar	1	cocobole-ar	1
clav-ar	1	cocore-ar	1
clavete-ar	1	code-ar	1
climatiz-ar	21	codecill-ar	1
clis-ar	1	codemand-ar	1
clis-arse	80	codetent-ar	1
clisteriz-ar	21	codici-ar	1
cloc-ar	76	codicil-ar	1
cloque-ar	1	codific-ar	67
cloroform-ar	1	codille-ar	1
cloroformiz-		coerc-er	46
ar	21	coexist-ir	3
clorur-ar	1	coextend-erse	
coaccion-ar	1	81, with the	
coacerv-ar	1	changes in	53
coact-ar	1	cofre-ar	1
coacus-ar	1	cofund-ar	1
coadquir-ir	5	cog-er	23
coadun-ar	1	cogit-ar	1
coadyuv-ar	1	cognoc-er	2
coagul-ar	1	cognomin-ar	1
coalicion-ar	1	cogoll-ar	1
coalig-ar	51	cogolm-ar	1
coapt-ar	1	cohabit-ar	1
coarrend-ar	53	cohech-ar	1
coart-ar	1	cohered-ar	1
coasoci-arse	80	coher-irse	82
cob-ar	1	cohesion-ar	1
cobarde-ar	1	cohete-ar	1

114

cohib-ir 3,
  with the
  changes in 9
cohob-ar 1
cohombr-ar 1
cohond-er 2
cohonest-ar 1
cohort-ar 1
coid-ar 1
coime-ar 1
coincid-ir 3
coindic-ar 1
coinquin-ar 1
coit-ar 1
coje-ar 1
colabor-ar 1
colacion-ar 1
colaps-ar 1
col-ar 1,
  and alter-
  natively, ... 25
colaud-ar 1
colch-ar 25
cole-ar 1
coleccion-ar 1
colect-ar 1
colectiviz-ar 21
coleg-ar 1
colegi-arse 80
coleg-ir 3,
  with the
  changes in 46
coleriz-ar 21
colete-ar 1
colgande-ar 1
colgandeje-ar ... 1
colg-ar 24
colicu-ar 74
colicuec-er 48
colid-ir 3
colig-ar 51
colig-arse 80
colim-ar 1
colind-ar 1
colision-ar 1
colite-ar 1
coll-er 2
coll-ir 3
colm-ar 1
colmat-ar 1
colmene-ar 1

colobe-ar 1
coloc-ar 67
coloniz-ar 21
color-ar 1
colore-ar 1
color-ir 4
colp-ar 1
colud-ir 3
columbe-ar 1
columbr-ar 1
columniz-ar 21
columpi-ar 1
comadre-ar 1
comale-ar 1
comalec-
  erse 48
comandante-
  ar 1
comand-ar 1
comandit-ar 1
comarc-ar 67
combalach-
  arse 80
comb-ar 1
combat-ir 3
combin-ar 1
combr-ar 1
come-ar 1
comedi-ar 1
comed-ir 52
comed-irse 52
comend-ar 1
coment-ar 1
comentari-ar 74
comenz-ar 34
com-er 2
comercializ-
  ar 21
comerci-ar 1
comet-er 2
comiche-ar 1
comine-ar 1
comique-ar 1
comis-ar 1
comisc-ar 67
comision-ar 1
comisque-ar 1
comor-ar 1
compact-ar 1
compadr-ar 1

compadre-ar 1
compagin-ar 1
compang-ar 51
compar-ar 1
comparec-er 48
compart-ir 1
compas-ar 1
compase-ar 1
compatibiliz-
  ar 21
compel-er 2,
  plus the past
  participle
  compulso
compendi-ar 1
compendiz-
  ar 21
compenetr-ar 1
compenetr-
  arse 80
compens-ar 1
compermut-ar ... 1
compet-er 2
compet-ir 52
compiad-
  arse 80
compiez-ar 21
compil-ar 1
compil-ir 3
complac-er 54
complan-ar 1
complañ-ir 3
complement-
  ar 1
complet-ar 1
complexion-ar ... 1
complic-ar 67
compl-ir 3
complot-ar 1
compod-ar 1
compon-er 57
componte-ar 1
comport-ar 1
comport-arse ... 80
compr-ar 1
comprend-er 2,
  plus the past
  participle
  comprenso
comprim-ir 3,
  plus the past

participle
  compreso
compr-ir 3
comprob-ar 25
compromet-er ... 2
compuls-ar 1
compung-ir 3,
  with the
  changes in 23
compurg-ar 51
computadoriz-
  ar 21
comput-ar 1
computariz-
  ar 21
comulg-ar 51
comung-ar 1
comunic-ar 67
comunistiz-
  ar 21
concaden-ar 1
concaten-ar 1
concaus-ar 1
concav-ar 1
conceb-ir 52
conced-er 1
concej-ar 1
concelebr-ar 1
concen-ar 1
concentr-ar 1
concepte-ar 1
conceptu-ar 74
concern-ir 3,
  with the
  changes in 53
concert-ar 53
conchab-ar 1
conchabe-ar 1
conch-ar 1
conchav-ar 1
conchuch-
  arse 80
concienci-ar 1
concientiz-ar ... 21
concili-ar 1
concion-ar 1
concit-ar 1
conclu-ir 42,
  plus the past
  participle
  concluso

concom-erse ... 81
concomit-ar 1
concord-ar 25
concrecion-ar ... 1
concret-ar 1
conculc-ar 67
concurr-ir 3
concurs-ar 1
condam-ar 1
conde-ar 1
condecend-er
  2, with the
  changes in 53
condec-ir 28
condecor-ar 1
condej-ar 1
conden-ar 1
condens-ar 1,
  plus the past
  participle
  condenso
condes-ar 1
condescend-er
  2, with the
  changes in 53
condex-ar 1
condicion-ar 1
condiment-ar 1
cond-ir 3
condistingu-ir ... 3
condolec-
  erse 52
condol-er 47
condol-erse 47
condon-ar 1
condongue-
  arse 80
conduc-ir 59
condur-ar 1
conect-ar 1
coneje-ar 1
conexion-ar 1
confabul-ar 1
confeccion-ar ... 1
confeder-ar 1
conferec-ar 48
conferenci-ar 1
confer-ir 71
confes-ar 53,
  plus the past
  participle

confeso
confi-ar 74
conficion-ar 1
confidenci-ar 1
configur-ar 1
confin-ar 1
confing-ir 3,
  with the
  changes in 23
confirm-ar 1
confisc-ar 67
confit-ar 1
conflagr-ar 1
conflu-ir 42
conform-ar 1
confort-ar 1
confragu-ar 1
confratern-ar 1
confraterniz-
  ar 21
confric-ar 67
confront-ar 1
confu-ir 42
confund-ir 3,
  plus the past
  participle
  confuso
confut-ar 1
congel-ar 1
congeni-ar 1
congestion-ar 1
conglob-ar 1
conglomer-ar 1
conglori-ar 1
conglutin-ar 1
congoj-ar 1
congole-ar 1
congraci-ar 1
congratul-ar 1
congreg-ar 51
conhort-ar 1
conific-ar 1
conjetur-ar 1
conjug-ar 51
conjunt-ar 1
conjurament-
  ar 1
conjur-ar 1
conllev-ar 1
conllor-ar 1
conlo-ar 1

conmemor-ar 1
conmensur-ar ... 1
conmin-ar 1
conmiser-ar 1
conmiser-
  arse 80
conmocion-ar ... 1
conmov-er 47
conmut-ar 1
connaturaliz-
  ar 21
connaturaliz-
  arse 80
conniv-ar 3
connombr-ar 1
connot-ar 1
connumer-ar 1
conoc-er 48
conosc-er 48
conquer-ir 71
conquist-ar 1
conre-ar 1
conrein-ar 1
consacr-ar 1
consagr-ar 1
consecr-ar 1
consegr-ar 1
consegu-ir 52
consej-ar 1
consent-ir 71
conserv-ar 1
consider-ar 1
consign-ar 1
consist-ir 3
consogr-ar 25
consol-ar 25
consolid-ar 1
consonantific-
  ar 1
consonantiz-
  ar 21
conson-ar 25
conspir-ar 1
conspu-ir 42
const-ar 1
constat-ar 1
constel-ar 1
constern-ar 1
constip-ar 1
constitucion-
  aliz-ar 21

constitu-ir 42,
  plus the past
  participle
  constituto
constreñ-ir 64
constring-ir 17
constru-ir 42
constupr-ar 1
consuegr-ar 1
consult-ar 1
consum-ar 1
consum-ir 3,
  plus the past
  participle
  consunto
consustantiv-
  arse 80
contabiliz-ar 21
contact-ar 1
contagi-ar 1
contamin-ar 1
cont-ar 25
contec-er 48
contemper-ar 1
contempl-ar 1
contemporiz-
  ar 21
contend-er 2,
  with the
  changes in 5
conten-er 74
content-ar 1,
  plus the past
  participle
  contento
contest-ar 1
contextu-ar 74
contingent-ar 1
continu-ar 74
cont-ir 3
contone-arse ... 80
contongue-
  arse 80
contorc-erse 22
contorn-ar 1
contorne-ar 1
contorsion-
  arse 80
contraabr-ir 3,
  except the
  past participle

is contraabierto
contraafianz-
ar 21
contraatac-ar ... 67
contrabalance-
ar 1
contrabande-
ar 1
contrabat-ir 3
contrabrace-ar .. 1
contracalc-ar ... 67
contracambi-
ar 1
contrachap-ar ... 1
contrachape-
ar 1
contracord-
ar 25
contract-ar 1
contracuartel-
ar 1
contradec-ir 58
contraendos-
ar 1
contra-er 75,
plus the past
participle
contracto
contraescarp-
ar 1
contraesmalt-
ar 1
contraestimul-
ar 1
contrafac-er 2
contrafall-ar 1
contrafirm-ar 1
contraforj-ar 1
contragir-ar 1
contragru-ar 1
contraguiñ-ar ... 1
contrahac-er 41
contraherr-ar 1
contrahorod-
ar 1
contraindic-
ar 67
contra-ir 43
contral-ar 1
contralibr-ar 1
contrall-ar 1

contrallev-ar 1
contralore-ar 1
contramall-ar 1
contramand-ar .. 1
contramanifest-
ar 53
contramaniobr-
ar 1
contramarc-
ar 67
contramarch-
ar 1
contramat-ar 1
contramin-ar 1
contramurall-
ar 1
contramur-ar 1
contraorden-
ar 1
contrapas-ar 1
contrape-ar 1
contrapech-ar ... 1
contrapele-ar 1
contrapes-ar 1
contrapon-er 57
contraprob-
ar 25
contrapropon-
er 57
contraproyect-
ar 1
contrapugn-ar ... 1
contrapunt-ar 1
contrapunt-
arse 80
contrapunte-
ar 1
contrapunz-
ar 21
contrari-ar 74
contrarray-ar 1
contrarrequer-
ir 71
contrarrest-ar 1
contrar-
revolucion-ar .. 1
contrasell-ar 1
contraseñ-ar 1
contrasign-ar 1
contrast-ar 1
contrat-ar 1

contraval-ar 1
contraven-ir 78
contremec-er
48, plus the
changes in 46
contribu-ir 26
contribul-ar 1
contrist-ar 1
control-ar 1
controvert-ir 71
contund-ir 3,
plus the past
participle
contuso
conturb-ar 1
contusion-ar 1
convalec-er 48
convalid-ar 1
convel-erse 81
convenc-er 5,
plus the past
participle
convicto
conven-ir 77
converg-er 23
converg-ir 3,
with the
changes in 23
convers-ar 1
convert-ir 71,
plus the past
participle
converso
convid-ar 1
conviv-ir 3
convoc-ar 67
convol-ar 25
convolv-erse 47
convoy-ar 1
convuls-ar 1
convulsion-ar 1
conyug-ar 51
coñe-arse 80
cooper-ar 1
coopt-ar 1
coordin-ar 1
cop-ar 1
cope-ar 1
copel-ar 1
copi-ar 1
copil-ar 1

copin-ar 1
cople-ar 1
copolimeriz-
arse 80
coprecipit-ar 1
coproduc-ir 13
copuch-ar 1
copul-ar 1
copul-arse 80
coque-ar 1
coquete-ar 1
coquific-ar 67
coquiz-ar 21
cor-ar 1
corbate-ar 1
corc-arse 80
corch-ar 1
corcov-ar 1
corcove-ar 1
corcus-ir 3
corde-ar 1
cordel-ar 1
core-ar 1
coreografi-ar 9
cori-ar 1
corl-ar 1
corle-ar 1
corne-ar 1
cornete-ar 1
cornific-ar 1
coron-ar 1
coroniz-ar 1
corporific-ar 67
corporiz-arse ... 21
corre-ar 1
corregent-ar 1
correg-ir 32,
plus the past
participle
correcto
correin-ar 1
correlacion-ar ... 1
correnci-ar 1
correnti-ar 1
corr-er 2
correspond-er .. 2
corretaje-ar 1
correte-ar 1
corrinche-ar 1
corrobor-ar 1
corroc-ar 1

corro-er 65
corromp-er 2,
  plus the past
  participle
  corrupto
corrug-ar 1
cors-ar 1
corse-ar 1
cortapis-ar 1
cort-ar 1
cortej-ar 1
cortin-ar 1
cortisque-ar 1
cortocircuit-ar ... 1
corusc-ar 67,
  and for its use
  regarding
  weather,
  see 45
corv-ar 1
corvete-ar 1
coscache-ar 1
cosc-arse 67
coscorrone-ar ... 1
cosech-ar 1
cos-er 2
cosete-ar 1
cospe-arse 80
cosque-ar 1
cosquill-ar 1
cosquille-ar 1
costal-ar 1
costale-arse 80
costane-ar 1
cost-ar 25
coste-ar 1
costiñ-ar 1
costreñ-ir 64
costribar 1
costring-ir 3,
  with the
  changes in 23
costriñ-ir 17
costru-ir 7
costumbr-ar 1
costumn-ar 1
costur-ar 1
costure-ar 1
costurone-ar 1
cot-ar 1
cote-ar 1

cotej-ar 1
cotille-ar 1
cotique-ar 1
cotiz-ar 21
cotone-ar 1
cotorre-ar 1
coun-irse 3
coxque-ar 1
coyote-ar 1
coyund-arse 80
coyunde-ar 1
craque-ar 1
crascit-ar 1
cre-ar 1
crebant-ar 1
crecent-ar 1
crec-er 48
cre-er 26
crench-ar 1
creosot-ar 1
crep-ar 1
crepit-ar 1
cres-arse 80
cresp-ar 1
crest-ar 1
cretific-ar 1
crey-er 2
cri-ar 9
crib-ar 1
crid-ar 1
criminaliz-ar 21
crimin-ar 1
crin-ar 1
crineise-ar 1
crineje-ar 1
crism-ar 1
crisol-ar 1
crisp-ar 1
crisp-ir 3
cristaliz-ar 21
cristian-ar 1
cristianiz-ar 21
critic-ar 67
critique-ar 1
critiquiz-ar 21
croaj-ar 1
cro-ar 1
crocit-ar 1
crom-ar 1
cromat-ar 1
cromolitografi-

ar 9
croniz-ar 1
cronometr-ar 1
croscit-ar 1
crotor-ar 1
crucete-ar 1
cruci-ar 1
crucific-ar 67
crucute-ar 1
cruent-ar 1
cruj-ir 3
cruz-ar 21
cuabe-ar 1
cuac-ar 67
cuadr-ar 1
cuadre-ar 1
cuadricul-ar 1
cuadrill-ar 1
cuadrille-ar 1
cuadruplic-ar ... 67
cuadruplic-ar ... 67
cuaj-ar 1
cualific-ar 67
cuanti-ar 9
cuantific-ar 67
cuaresm-ar 1
cuarre-ar 1
cuartague-ar 1
cuart-ar 1
cuarte-ar 1
cuartel-ar 1
cuartr-ar 1
cuatezon-ar 1
cuatre-ar 1
cuatrere-ar 1
cuatrodobl-ar ... 1
cuatrope-ar 1
cubanch-ar 1
cubanche-ar 1
cubaniz-ar 21
cubic-ar 67
cubij-ar 1
cubil-ar 1
cubilete-ar 1
cubr-ir 3,
  except the
  past participle
  is cubierto
cuc-ar 67
cucarache-ar 1
cucarre-ar 1

cuch-ar 1
cuchare-ar 1
cucharete-ar 1
cuche-ar 1
cuchiche-ar 1
cuchichi-ar 9
cuchill-ar 1
cuchuche-ar 1
cuchuflet-ar 1
cuchuflete-ar 1
cuchunche-ar ... 1
cucuruti-ar 1
cudici-ar 1
cued-ar 1
cuente-ar 1
cueque-ar 1
cuere-ar 1
cuerpe-ar 1
cuestion-ar 1
cuete-ar 1
cuete-arse 80
cueve-ar 1
cufi-ar 1
cuhete-ar 1
cuid-ar 1
cuit-ar 1
cuit-arse 80
cuite-ar 1
cuje-ar 1
culanque-ar 1
culate-ar 1
cule-ar 1
culebre-ar 1
culeque-ar 1
culinc-ar 1
culipande-ar 1
cullinc-ar 1
culmin-ar 1
culot-ar 1
culpabiliz-ar 21
culp-ar 1
cultiparl-ar 1
cultiv-ar 1
cultur-ar 1
cumbamch-ar ... 1
cumbanche-ar .. 1
cumi-ar 1
cumpliment-ar .. 1
cumpl-ir 3
cumul-ar 1
cun-ar 1

cuncune-ar 1
cund-ir 3
cune-ar 1
cunt-ir 3
cuñ-ar 1
cuprific-ar 1
cuque-ar 1
cur-ar 1
curcute-ar 1
curele-ar 1
curi-ar 1
curiose-ar 1
curr-ar 1
currel-ar 1
currucute-ar 1
currusc-ar 67
curs-ar 1
curt-ir 3
curucute-ar 1
curv-ar 1
curve-ar 1
cuscurre-ar 1
cuscute-ar 1
cus-ir 3
cusp-ar 1
cuspete-ar 1
custodi-ar 1
custr-irse 82
cutare-ar 1
cutarre-ar 1
cut-ir 3
cuzque-ar 1

d

dactilografi-ar ... 9
dadiv-ar 1
daguerrotip-ar .. 1
dall-ar 1
damasquin-ar ... 1
damn-ar 1
damn-arse 80
damnific-ar 67
danific-ar 67
dann-ar 1
danz-ar 21
danzone-ar 1
dañ-ar 1
dañific-ar 1
dañine-ar 1

dapn-ar 1
d-ar 27
dasain-ar 1
dat-ar 1
daval-ar 1
deambul-ar 1
deband-ar 1
debat-ir 3
debel-ar 1
deb-er 2
debilit-ar 1
debit-ar 1
deboc-ar 67
bebroc-ar 67
debruz-ar 21
debut-ar 1
deca-er 20
decalcific-ar 67
decalv-ar 1
decamp-ar 1
decant-ar 1
decap-ar 1
decapit-ar 1
decapsul-ar 1
decarbonat-ar 1
decarbur-ar 1
deceb-ir 3
deced-er 2
deceler-ar 1
decend-er 2,
  with the
  changes in 53
decent-ar 53
decep-ar 1
decepcion-ar 1
decerc-ar 1
decern-ir 3,
  with the
  changes in 53
decerrumb-ar 1
decervig-ar 1
decib-irse 82
decid-ir 3
decimaliz-ar 1
decim-ar 1
dec-ir 28
declam-ar 1
declar-ar 1
declin-ar 1
decolg-ar 25
decoll-ar 1

decolor-ar 1
decomis-ar 1
decompon-er ... 57
decontamin-ar .. 1
decor-ar 1
decorr-erse 81
decrec-er 48
decrepit-ar 1
decret-ar 1
decupl-ar 1
decuplic-ar 67
dedale-ar 1
dedic-ar 67
dedign-ar 1
dedol-ar 1
deduc-ir 59
deech-ar 1
defalc-ar 67
defam-ar 1
defec-ar 67
defeccion-ar 1
defend-er 2,
  with the
  changes in ... 53
defenec-er 48
defens-ar 1
defer-ir 71
defes-ar 1
defi-ar 1
defin-ir 3
deflag-ar 51
deflagr-ar 1
deflegm-ar 1
deflogistic-ar ... 67
defondon-ar 1
deforest-ar 1
deform-ar 1
defosfor-ar 1
defraud-ar 1
defu-ir 42
degast-ar 1
degener-ar 1
degest-ir 3
deglut-ir 3
degoll-ar 25
degrad-ar 1
deguast-ar 1
degust-ar 1
dehend-er 2,
  with the
  changes in 53

dehes-ar 1
dehort-ar 1
deific-ar 67
dej-ar 1
dejarret-ar 1
dejempl-ar 1
dejug-ar 1
delat-ar 1
delax-ar 1
delayad-ar 1
delect-ar 1
deleg-ar 51
deleit-ar 1
delej-ar 1
deletre-ar 1
delezn-arse 80
delgaz-ar 1
deliber-ar 1
delibr-ar 1
delici-arse 80
delimit-ar 1
deline-ar 1
deling-arse 80
delinqu-ir 29
delint-ar 1
delinter-ar 1
deliñ-ar 1
delir-ar 1
delong-ar 1
delud-ir 3
demacr-ar 1
demacr-arse 80
demand-ar 1
demarc-ar 67
demarr-arse 80
demasi-arse 9
demedi-ar 1
dement-ar 1
demerit-ar 1
demig-ar 1
demit-ir 3
democratiz-
  ar 21
demol-er 47
demonstr-ar 25
demor-ar 1
demostr-ar 25
demud-ar 1
demulc-ir 3,
  with the
  changes in 46

demultiplic-ar ... 1
deneg-ar 62
denegrec-er 48
denegr-ir 3,
and used in
the positions
in 45
dengue-ar......... 1
denigr-ar 1
denod-arse 80
denomin-ar 1
denost-ar 25
denot-ar 1
dens-ar 1
densific-ar 67
dent-ar 53
dentec-er 48
dentell-ar 1
dentelle-ar 1
dentrotra-er 75
denud-ar 1
denunci-ar 1
deñ-ar 1
depar-ar 1
depart-ir 3
depauper-ar 1
depend-er 2
depil-ar 1
deplor-ar 1
depon-er 57
deport-ar 1
depos-ar 1
deposit-ar 1
deprav-ar 1
deprec-ar 67
depreci-ar 1
depred-ar 1
deprend-er 2
deprim-ar 1
deprim-ir 3
depur-ar 1
deput-ar 1
derelinqu-ir 29
derez-ar 1
deriv-ar 1
derog-ar 51
derrab-ar 1
derraig-ar 1
derraiz-ar 21
derram-ar 1
derranc-ar 67

derranch-ar 1
derrap-ar 1
derrelinqu-ir 29,
plus the past
participle
derrelicto
derreneg-ar 61
derreng-ar 53
derret-ir 52
derrib-ar 1
derrisc-ar 1
derroc-ar 67
derroch-ar 1
derromp-er 2
derronch-ar 1
derrostr-arse 80
derrot-ar 1
derrubi-ar 1
derru-ir 42
derrumb-ar 1
derrumbi-ar 1
desabarranc-
ar 67
desabarrot-ar 1
desabastec-
er 48
desabat-ir 3
desabej-ar 1
desabit-ar 1
desaboc-ar 1
desaboll-ar 1
desabollon-ar 1
desabon-ar 1
desabor-ar 1
desabord-
arse 80
desaboton-ar 1
desaboved-ar 1
desaboz-ar 21
deasbraz-
arse 80
desabrig-ar 51
desabrillant-ar .. 1
desabr-ir 11
desabroch-ar 1
desacalor-
arse 80
desacanton-ar .. 1
desacat-ar 1
desacatarr-
arse 80

desaced-ar 1
desaceit-ar 1
desacentu-ar 1
desacer-ar 1
desacerb-ar 1
desacert-ar 53
desachigu-ar 1
desachir-
arse 80
desachisp-ar 1
desacidific-
ar 67
desacidul-ar 1
desaclimat-ar ... 1
desacobard-ar .. 1
desacoll-ar 25
desacollar-ar 1
desacomod-ar .. 1
desacompañ-
ar 1
desacondicion-
ar 1
desaconsej-ar ... 1
desacopl-ar 1
desacord-ar 25
desacordon-ar .. 1
desacorral-ar 1
desacorrol-ar 1
desacostumbr-
ar 1
desacot-ar 1
desacotej-ar 1
desacraliz-ar 1
desacredit-ar 1
desactiv-ar 1
desacuartel-ar .. 1
desacumul-ar 1
desacuñ-ar 1
desaderaz-ar ... 21
desaderez-ar ... 21
desadeud-ar 1
desadoquin-ar .. 1
desador-ar 1
desadormec-
er 48
desadorn-ar 1
desaduj-ar 1
desadvert-ir 71
desafam-ar 1
desafe-ar 1
desafect-ar 1

desafeit-ar 1
desaferr-ar 53
desafianz-ar 21
desafi-ar 9
desaficion-ar 1
desafij-ar 1
desafil-ar 1
desafin-ar 1
desafiuci-ar 1
desafiuz-ar 21
desafor-ar 25
desaforr-ar 1
desafrances-
ar 1
desafrent-ar 1
desafuci-ar 1
desagarr-ar 1
desagit-ar 1
desagot-ar 1
desagraci-ar 1
desagrad-ar 1
desagradec-
er 48
desagrav-ar 1
desagravi-ar 1
desagreg-ar 51
desagri-ar 1
desagu-ar 58
desaguaz-ar ... 21
desaherroj-ar ... 1
desahij-ar 9
desahit-arse 9
desahog-ar 51
desahuci-ar 1
desahum-ar 9
desain-ar 9
desair-ar 9
desaire-ar 1
desaisl-arse 9
desajac-arse ... 80
desajarr-ar 1
desajust-ar 1
desalab-ar 1
desalabe-ar 1
desalag-ar 51
desal-ar 1
desalb-ar 1
desalbard-ar 1
desalbardill-ar .. 1
desalcoholiz-
ar 21

desalegr-
  arse 80
desalent-ar 53
desalfiler-ar 1
desalfombr-ar ... 1
desalforj-ar 1
desalhaj-ar 1
desali-ar 9
desalin-ar 1
desaline-ar 1
desaliñ-ar 1
desalis-ar 1
desaliv-ar 1
desalmacen-
  ar 1
desalm-ar 1
desalmen-ar 1
desalmidon-ar .. 1
desaloj-ar 1
desalperch-ar ... 1
desalquil-ar 1
desalquitran-
  ar 1
desalter-ar 1
desalucin-ar 1
desamaner-
  arse 80
desam-ar 1
desamarr-ar 1
desamartel-ar ... 1
desamazacot-
  ar 1
desambient-ar .. 1
desamelg-ar 51
desamig-ar 51
desamist-
  arse 80
desamobl-ar 25
desamodorr-ar .. 1
desamojel-ar 1
desamold-ar 1
desamonton-
  ar 1
desamor-ar 1
desamorr-ar 1
desamortaj-ar ... 1
desamortec-
  er 48
desamortiz-
  ar 21
desamotin-ar 1

desamotin-
  arse 80
desampar-ar 1
desamuebl-ar ... 1
desamur-ar 1
desanagu-
  arse 80
desanalfabetiz-
  ar 1
desancl-ar 1
desancor-ar 1
desand-ar 19
desanej-arse 80
desanex-ar 1
desangr-ar 1
desanid-ar 1
desanim-ar 1
desantañ-
  arse 80
desanubl-ar 1
desanud-ar 1
desanzol-ar 25
desañ-arse 80
desañud-ar 1
desaoj-ar 1
desapadrin-ar ... 1
desapañ-ar 1
desapare-ar 1
desaparec-er ... 48
desaparej-ar 1
desaparroqui-
  ar 1
desapart-ar 1
desapasion-ar ... 1
desapeg-ar 51
desapegual-ar .. 1
desapercib-
  irse 82
desapest-ar 1
desapiad-
  arse 80
desapihuel-ar ... 1
desapiol-ar 1
desaplac-er 54
desaplic-ar 67
desaplom-ar 1
desapoc-ar 1
desapoder-ar 1
desapolill-ar 1
desaponz-ar 21
desaporc-ar 76

desaposent-ar .. 1
desaposesion-
  ar 1
desapostem-
  ar 1
desapoy-ar 1
desapreci-ar 1
desaprend-er 2
desaprens-ar 1
desapret-ar 53
desapretin-ar 1
desapr-ir 3
desaprisc-ar 1
desaprision-ar .. 1
desaprob-ar 25
desapropi-ar 1
desaprovech-
  ar 1
desapuntal-ar ... 1
desapunt-ar 1
desaquell-
  arse 80
desaquilat-ar 1
desarbol-ar 1
desarchiv-ar 1
desaren-ar 1
desargent-ar 1
desarm-ar 1
desarmoniz-
  ar 21
desarrabiat-ar ... 1
desarraig-ar 51
desarraj-ar 1
desarranc-
  arse 67
desarreboz-
  ar 21
desarrebuj-ar 1
desarregl-ar 1
desarrend-ar 53
desarrevolv-er
  25, except
  the past
  participle is
  desarrevuelto
desarrim-ar 1
desarrincon-ar .. 1
desarroll-ar 1
desarrop-ar 1
desarrug-ar 51
desarrum-ar 1

desarticul-ar 1
desartill-ar 1
desarzon-ar 1
desas-ar 1
desase-ar 1
desasegur-ar 1
desasent-ar 53
desasfalt-ar 1
desasimil-ar 1
desas-ir 13
desasist-ir 3
desasn-ar 1
desasoci-ar 1
desasoseg-ar ... 62
desast-ar 1
desastill-ar 1
desatac-ar 67
desatanc-ar 67
desatap-ar 1
desat-ar 1
desatasc-ar 67
desatavi-ar 9
desatemoriz-
  ar 21
desatempl-
  arse 80
desatend-er
  2, with the
  changes in
  53, plus the
  past participle
  desatento
desatent-ar 53
desater-irse 82
desaterr-ar 53
desatesor-ar 1
desatest-ar 1
desatib-ar 1
desatin-ar 1
desatoll-ar 1
desatolondr-ar .. 1
desatont-
  arse 80
desator-ar 1
desatornill-ar 1
desatrac-ar 67
desatra-er 75
desatraill-ar 9
desatramp-ar 1
desatranc-ar ... 67
desatraves-

desatufarse - descatolizar

ar 53	desbeb-er 2	descabuy-	descapill-ar 1
desatuf-arse 80	desbecerr-ar 1	arse 80	descapirot-ar 1
desaturd-ir 3	desbenzol-ar 1	descach-ar 1	descapitaliz-
desatus-ar 1	desbez-ar 21	descacharr-ar 1	ar 21
desautoriz-ar ... 21	desbinz-ar 21	descachaz-ar ... 21	descapot-ar
desavah-ar 1	desbisagr-	descacil-ar 1	1, and for
desavasall-ar 1	arse 80	descader-ar 1	its use
desavecind-	desbloc-ar 67	descadill-ar 1	regarding
arse 80	desbloque-ar 1	descaec-er 48	weather,
desaven-ir 77	desboc-ar 67	desca-er 20	see 45
desavez-ar 21	desbomb-ar 1	descafein-ar 9	descapot-arse
desavi-ar 9	desbonet-	descafil-ar 1	80, and for
desavis-ar 1	arse 80	descagaz-ar 1	its use
desayud-ar 1	desboquill-ar 1	descajill-arse ... 80	regarding
desayun-ar 1	desbord-ar 1	descalabaz-	weather,
desayunt-ar 1	desborniz-ar ... 21	arse 21	see 45
desayust-ar 1	desboron-ar 1	descalabr-ar 1	descapuch-ar ... 1
desazog-ar 51	desborr-ar 1	descalamin-ar .. 1	descapuchon-
desazon-ar 1	desborreg-ar 51	descalandraj-	ar 1
desazucar-ar 1	desbosc-ar 1	ar 1	descapull-ar 1
desazufr-ar 1	desboton-ar 1	descal-ar 1	descar-arse 80
desbab-ar 1	desbrag-ar 51	descalcañ-ar 1	descarbonat-
desbaf-arse 80	desbrav-ar 1	descalc-ar 67	ar 1
desbag-ar 51	desbrave-ar 1	descalcific-ar ... 67	descarboniz-
desbalag-ar 51	desbravec-er ... 48	descalent-	ar 1
desbalij-ar 1	desbraz-arse ... 21	arse 53	descarbur-ar 1
desballest-ar 1	desbreñ-ar 1	descalf-ar 1	descarcañal-
desbamb-	desbrev-arse ... 80	descalich-	ar 1
arse 80	desbrid-ar 1	arse 80	discard-ar 1
desbanc-ar 67	desbrizn-ar 1	descalific-ar 67	descarg-ar 51
desband-	desbroch-ar 1	descalim-ar 1	descariñ-
arse 80	desbrot-ar 1	descalz-ar 21	arse 80
desbanz-ar 21	desbroz-ar 21	descam-ar 1	descarmen-ar ... 1
desbarahust-	desbru-ar 9	descambi-ar 1	descarn-ar 1
ar 9	desbruci-	descambur-ar ... 1	descaroz-ar 21
desbarajust-ar .. 1	arse 80	descamin-ar 1	descarretill-ar ... 1
desbarat-ar 1	desbruj-ar 1	descamis-ar 1	descarri-ar 9
desbaraust-ar ... 1	desbuch-ar 1	descamp-ar 1	descarril-ar 1
desbarb-ar 1	desbull-ar 1	descan-ar 1	descarrill-ar 1
desbarbill-ar 1	descabal-ar 1	descancel-ar 1	descart-ar 1
desbard-ar 1	descabalg-ar ... 51	descans-ar 1	descarter-ar 1
desbarniz-ar 21	descabell-ar 1	descant-ar 1	descartuch-ar ... 1
desbarranc-	descabeñ-	descante-ar 1	descas-ar 1
ar 67	arse 80	descanter-ar 1	descasc-ar 67
desbarr-ar 1	descabestr-ar ... 1	descantill-ar 1	descascar-ar 1
desbarret-ar 1	descabez-ar 21	descanton-ar 1	descascarill-ar .. 1
desbarrig-ar 51	descrabrit-ar 1	descañ-ar 1	descascarri-ar ... 1
desbarrumb-	descabull-	descañon-ar 1	descasp-ar 1
arse 80	arse 80	descap-ar 1	descast-ar 1
desbast-ar 1	descabull-	descaperuz-	descastr-ar 1
desbautiz-ar 21	irse 17	ar 21	descatoliz-ar ... 21

descaudill-ar 1
descav-ar 1
descazarri-ar 1
desceb-ar 1
descend-er
2, with the
changes in 53
descend-ir 3
descentraliz-
ar 21
descentr-ar 1
desceñ-ir 64
descep-ar 1
descer-ar 1
descerc-ar 67
descerebr-ar 1
descerebriz-ar .. 1
descerez-ar 21
descerraj-ar 1
descerr-ar 53
descerrum-
arse 80
descervig-ar 51
deschal-ar 1
deschap-ar 1
descharch-ar 1
deschav-ar 1
deschavet-
arse 80
deschepic-ar 1
deschin-ar 1
deschupon-ar ... 1
descifr-ar 1
descimbr-ar 1
desciment-ar ... 53
descinch-ar 1
descing-ir 3,
with the
changes in 23
descintr-ar 1
desciviliz-ar 21
desclasific-ar ... 67
desclav-ar 1
desclavij-ar 1
descloc-ar 1
desclorur-ar 1
descluec-ar 1
descoagul-ar 1
descobaj-ar 1
descobij-ar 1
descoc-ar 67

descoc-arse 80
descoc-er 22
descocot-ar 1
descod-ar 1
descog-er 23
descogestin-
ar 1
descogoll-ar 1
descogot-ar 1
descohesion-
ar 1
descol-ar 1
descolch-ar 1
descolg-ar 24
descoll-ar 25
descolm-ar 1
descolmill-ar 1
descoloc-ar 67
descoloniz-ar ... 21
descolor-ar 1
descolor-ir 3,
and used in
the positions
in 45
descombr-ar 1
descomed-
irse 52
descom-er 2
descomong-ar .. 1
descompadr-
ar 1
descompagin-
ar 1
descompañ-ar .. 1
descompas-ar .. 1
descompas-
arse 80
descompens-
ar 1
descomplac-
er 54
descomplet-
ar 1
descompon-
er 57
descomprim-ir .. 3
descomulg-
ar 51
desconceptu-
ar 9
desconcert-

ar 53
desconchab-
ar 1
desconch-ar 1
desconchinfl-
ar 1
desconcord-
ar 25
desconect-ar 1
desconfi-ar 9
desconflaut-ar .. 1
desconform-ar .. 1
descongel-ar 1
descongestion-
ar 1
descongoj-ar 1
desconhort-ar ... 1
desconoc-er 48
desconsej-ar 1
desconsent-
ir 71
desconsider-
ar 1
desconsol-ar 25
descontagi-ar ... 1
descontamin-
ar 1
descont-ar 25
descontent-ar
1, plus the
past participle
descontento
descontinu-ar ... 9
descontrapes-
ar 1
descontrol-ar ... 1
desconven-ir 77
desconvent-
ir 71
desconvers-ar ... 1
desconvid-ar ... 1
descop-ar 1
descorazon-ar .. 1
descorch-ar 1
descord-ar 25
descorder-ar 1
descorit-ar 1
descorn-ar 25
descoron-ar 1
descorre-ar 1
descorr-er 2

descorrot-
arse 80
descortez-ar 21
descortin-ar 1
descos-er 2
descost-arse
80, with the
changes in 47
descostill-ar 1
descostr-ar 1
descot-ar 1
descotorr-ar 1
descoyunt-ar 1
descrec-er 48
descre-er 26
descrem-ar 1
descrest-ar 1
descri-ar 1
descri-arse 80
describ-ir 3,
except the
past partici-
ples are
descrito and
descripto
descrin-ar 1
descrism-ar 1
descristian-ar ... 1
descristianiz-
ar 21
descrucific-
ar 67
descruz-ar 21
descuacha-
rrang-arse 80
descuadern-ar .. 1
descuadr-ar 1
descuadril-
arse 80
descuadrill-
arse 80
descuaj-ar 1
descuajaring-
ar 51
descuajering-
ar 51
descuartel-ar 1
descuartiz-ar ... 21
descubr-ir 3,
except the
past participle

is descubierto
descuer-ar 1
descuere-ar 1
descuern-ar 1
descuid-ar 1
descul-ar 1
desculat-ar 1
descumpl-ir 3
desd-ar 1
desdec-ir 58
desdent-ar 53
desdeñ-ar 1
desdevan-ar 1
desdibuj-ar 1
desdich-arse 80
desdient-ar 1
desdiner-ar 1
desdobl-ar 1
desdon-ar 1
desdoncell-ar 1
desdor-ar 1
dese-ar 1
deseb-ar 1
desec-ar 67
desech-ar 1
desedific-ar 67
deseduc-ar 67
desegu-ir 52
desej-arse 80
deselectriz-
ar 21
desell-ar 1
deseman-ar 1
desembal-ar 1
desembaldos-
ar 1
desemballest-
ar 1
desembalsam-
ar 1
desembals-ar ... 1
desembanast-
ar 1
desembaraz-
ar 21
desembarc-
ar 67
desembarg-
ar 51
desembarranc-
ar 67

desembarr-ar 1
desembaul-ar ... 9
desembebec-
erse 48
desembeles-
arse 80
desembellec-
er 48
desemblant-
arse 80
desemboc-ar ... 67
desemboj-ar 1
desembols-ar ... 1
desemborrach-
ar 1
desemborr-ar 1
desembosc-
arse 67
desembot-ar 1
desemboz-ar ... 21
desembrag-
ar 51
desembr-ar 53
desembravec-
er 48
desembraz-
ar 21
desembre-ar 1
desembriag-
ar 51
desembrid-ar 1
desembroc-
ar 67
desembroll-ar 1
desembroz-
ar 21
desembruj-ar 1
desembrutec-
er 48
desembuch-ar .. 1
desembud-ar 1
desembull-ar 1
desemej-ar 1
desempac-ar ... 67
desempach-ar .. 1
desempaj-ar 1
desempalag-
ar 51
desempalm-ar .. 1
desempantan-
ar 1

desempañ-ar 1
desempapel-
ar 1
desempaquet-
ar 1
desemparej-ar .. 1
desemparv-ar ... 1
desempast-ar ... 1
desempastel-
ar 1
desempat-ar 1
desempavon-
ar 1
desempedr-
ar 53
desempeg-ar ... 51
desempeñ-ar ... 1
desempeor-
arse 80
desempercud-
ir 3
desemperez-
ar 21
desempern-ar ... 1
desempertig-
ar 51
desemplom-ar .. 1
desemplum-ar .. 1
desempobrec-
er 2
desempoll-ar 1
desempolv-ar ... 1
desempolvor-
ar 1
desempotr-ar 1
desempoz-ar ... 21
desempozoñ-
ar 1
desempulg-
ar 51
desempuñ-ar 1
desenalbard-
ar 1
desenamor-ar ... 1
desenastr-ar 1
desencabalg-
ar 51
desencab-ar 1
desencabestr-
ar 1
desencaden-

ar 1
desencaj-ar 1
desencajon-ar ... 1
desencalabrin-
ar 1
desencal-ar 1
desencalc-ar ... 67
desencall-ar 1
desencamin-
ar 1
desencanall-ar .. 1
desencandil-
ar 1
desencant-ar 1
desencantar-
ar 1
desencap-ar 1
desencapill-ar ... 1
desencapot-ar .. 1
desencapot-
arse 80, and
for its use
regarding
weather,
see 45
desencaprich-
ar 1
desencarcel-
ar 1
desencarec-
er 48
desencarg-ar ... 51
desencarn-ar 1
desencarton-
ar 1
desencas-ar 1
desencasquill-
ar 1
desencastill-ar .. 1
desencenag-
ar 51
desencentr-ar ... 1
desencerr-ar ... 53
desenchuec-
ar 67
desenchuf-ar 1
desencinch-ar ... 1
desencint-ar 1
desenclav-ar 1
desenclavij-ar ... 1
desencloc-ar 25

desencl-uec-ar ... 1
desencobr-ar 1
desencofr-ar 1
desencog-er ... 23
desencol-ar 1
desencoleriz-
ar 21
desencon-ar 1
desencontr-
arse 80, with
the changes
in 45
desencord-ar ... 25
desencordel-
ar 1
desencorv-ar 1
desencov-ar 25
desencresp-ar .. 1
desencrudec-
er 48
desencuadern-
ar 1
desencuart-ar ... 1
desencub-ar 1
desencumbr-
ar 1
desendemoni-
ar 1
desendiabl-ar ... 1
desendios-ar 1
desenfad-ar 1
desenfald-ar 1
desenfang-ar ...51
desenfard-ar 1
desenfardel-ar .. 1
desenfil-ar 1
desenfoc-ar 67
desenfrail-ar 1
desenfren-ar 1
desenfresc-ar ... 1
desenfund-ar 1
desenfurec-
er 48
desenfurruñ-
ar 1
desengalg-ar ...51
desenganch-
ar 1
desengañ-ar 1
desengañif-ar ... 1
desengañil-ar ... 1

desengargol-
ar 1
desengarraf-ar .. 1
desengarz-ar ...21
desengast-ar 1
desengaz-ar 21
desengom-ar 1
desengozn-ar 1
desengran-ar 1
desengras-ar 1
desengrillet-ar .. 1
desengros-ar ...25
desengrud-ar 1
desenguant-
ar 80
desenguant-
arse 80
desenguarac-
ar 67
desenhad-ar 1
desenhasti-ar 1
desenhebr-ar 1
desenhechiz-
ar 21
desenhetr-ar 1
desenhorn-ar 1
desenjabeg-
ar 51
desenjaez-ar ...21
desenjalm-ar 1
desenjaul-ar 1
desenlabon-ar .. 1
desenladrill-ar .. 1
desenlaz-ar 21
desenli-ar 1
desenlod-ar 1
desenlos-ar 1
desenlustr-ar 1
desenlut-ar 1
desenmalez-
ar 51
desenmall-ar 1
desenmarañ-
ar 1
desenmascar-
ar 1
desenmohec-
er 48
desenmordaz-
ar 21
desenmudec-

er 48
desennegrec-
er 48
desenoj-ar 1
desenquiet-ar ... 1
desenraiz-ar 51
desenred-ar 1
desenriz-ar 21
desenroll-ar 1
desenron-ar 1
desenrosc-ar ...67
desenrudec-
er 48
desensaban-
ar 1
desensambl-
ar 1
desensañ-ar 1
desensart-ar 1
desensat-ar 1
desenseb-ar 1
desenseñ-ar 1
desenset-ar 1
desensibiliz-
ar 21
desensill-ar 1
desensitiz-ar 51
desensober-
bec-er 48
desentabl-ar 1
desentaling-
ar 51
desentarim-ar ... 1
desentech-ar 1
desentej-ar 1
desentel-ar 1
desentend-erse
81, with the
changes in 53
desenterr-ar 53
desentold-ar 1
desentollec-
er 48
desenton-ar 1
desentong-ar ...51
desentornill-ar .. 1
desentorpec-
er 48
desentram-ar 1
desentramp-ar .. 1
desentrañ-ar 1

desentren-ar 1
desentristec-
er 48
desentroniz-
ar 21
desentropez-
ar 53
desentumec-
er 48
desentum-ir 3
desenvain-ar 1
desenvar-
arse 80
desenvelej-ar ... 1
desenvend-ar ... 1
desenverg-ar ...51
desenviol-ar 1
desenviud-ar 1
desenvolv-er
47, except the
past participle
is desenvuelto
desenyes-ar 1
desenyug-ar 51
desenyung-
ar 51
desenyunt-ar 1
desenzarz-ar 21
desenzolv-ar 21
deseñ-ar 1
desequilibr-ar ... 1
deseriz-ar 51
desert-ar 1
desertific-ar 1
deserv-ir 52
desescombr-
ar 1
desescurec-
er 48
deseslabon-ar ... 1
desespald-ar 1
desespañoliz-
ar 21
desesperanz-
ar 21
desesper-ar 1
desespos-ar 1
desespum-ar 1
desestabiliz-
ar 21
desestanc-ar ...67

desestañ-ar 1
desester-ar 1
desesteriliz-
ar 51
desestim-ar 1
desestudi-ar 1
deseterniz-ar ...51
desexcomulg-
ar 51
desexualiz-ar ...51
desfac-er 41
desfaj-ar 1
desfalc-ar 67
desfallec-er 48
desfam-ar 1
desfanatiz-ar ...51
desfard-ar 1
desfas-ar 1
desfavorec-
er 48
desfay-ar 1
desfe-ar 1
desfech-ar 1
desferr-ar 1
desfibr-ar 1
desfibrin-ar 1
desfigur-ar 1
desfij-ar 1
desfilach-ar 1
desfil-ar 1
desfiluch-ar 1
desfilvan-ar 1
desfiuz-ar 51
desflaquec-er ... 2
desflec-ar 67
desflegm-ar 1
desflem-ar 1
desfloc-ar 76
desflor-ar 1
desflorec-er 48
desfog-ar 51
desfogon-ar 1
desfol-ar 1
desfoli-ar 1
desfollon-ar 1
desfond-ar 1
desforest-ar 1
desform-ar 1
desforr-ar 1
desforrocin-ar ... 1
desfortalec-

er 48
desfortific-ar 1
desforz-arse 39
desfosfor-ar 1
desfragu-ar 58
desfren-ar 1
desfrez-ar 21
desfrunc-ir 3,
with the
changes in 46
desfrut-ar 1
desfu-ir 42
desfund-ar 1
desgaj-ar 1
desgald-ir 3
desgalg-ar 51
desgalill-arse ...80
desgalon-ar 1
desgan-ar 1
desganch-ar 1
desganglion-
ar 1
desganguill-ar ... 1
desgañif-
arse 80
desgañ-irse 17
desgañit-
arse 80
desgañot-ar 1
desgañot-
arse 80
desgargant-ar ... 1
desgargante-
ar 1
desgargol-ar 1
desgarit-ar 1
desgarr-ar 1
desgarret-ar 1
desgarron-ar 1
desgast-ar 1
desgat-ar 1
desgaus-ar 1
desgaznat-
arse 80
desgermin-ar 1
desglas-ar 1
desglobuliz-
ar 21
desglos-ar 1
desgobern-ar ...53
desgolill-ar 1

desgollet-ar 1
desgom-ar 1
desgonz-ar 21
desgorr-arse ...80
desgot-ar 1
desgozn-ar 1
desgraci-ar 1
desgrad-ar 1
desgradu-ar 1
desgram-ar 1
desgran-ar 1
desgranz-ar 21
desgras-ar 1
desgrav-ar 1
desgreñ-ar 1
desguabil-ar 1
desguabin-ar 1
desgualdraj-ar .. 1
desguanz-ar 21
desguañang-
ar 51
desguañ-ar 1
desguañing-ar ... 1
desguarnec-
er 48
desguarn-ir 3,
and used in
the positions
in 4
desguas-ar 1
desguat-ar 1
desguaz-ar 21
desguind-ar 1
desguinz-ar 21
desgurrumb-
ar 1
desgusan-ar 1
deshabit-ar 1
deshabitu-ar 9
deshac-er 41
deshebill-ar 1
deshebr-ar 1
deshechiz-ar 21
deshel-ar 53,
and used in
the positions
in 45
deshematiz-
ar 51
desherb-ar 53
deshered-ar 1

desherman-ar ... 1
desherr-ar 53
desherrumbr-
ar 1
deshetr-ar 1
deshidrat-ar 1
deshidrogen-
ar 1
deshij-ar 1
deshijuel-ar 1
deshilach-ar 1
deshil-ar 1
deshilvan-ar 1
deshinc-ar 67
deshinch-ar 1
deshipnotiz-
ar 21
deshipotec-
ar 67
deshog-ar 1
deshoj-ar 1
deshollej-ar 1
deshollin-ar 1
deshombrec-
erse 48
deshonest-ar 1
deshonor-ar 1
deshonr-ar 1
deshorn-ar 1
deshues-ar 1
deshumaniz-
ar 21
deshum-arse ...80
deshumedec-
er 48
deshumill-ar 1
design-ar 1
desigual-ar 1
desilusion-ar 1
desimagin-ar 1
desiman-ar 1
desimant-ar 1
desimpon-er 57
desimpresion-
ar 1
desinclin-ar 1
desincorpor-ar .. 1
desincrust-ar 1
desindici-ar 1
desinfart-ar 1
desinfatu-ar 1

desinfeccion-
  ar 1
desinfect-ar 1
desinficion-ar ... 1
desinfis-ar 1
desinflam-ar 1
desinfl-ar 1
desinquiet-ar 1
desinsacul-ar ... 1
desinsect-ar 1
desintegr-ar 1
desinteres-
  arse 80
desintestin-ar ... 1
desintoxic-ar 67
desintub-ar 1
desinvern-ar 53
desinvert-ir 71
desiñ-ar 1
desist-ir 3
desiti-ar 1
desjarci-ar 1
desjaret-arse ... 80
desjarret-ar 1
desjet-arse 80
desjoloch-ar 1
desjuanet-ar 1
desjuard-ar 1
desjug-ar 51
desjunt-ar 1
desjuñ-ir 3
desjur-ar 1
deslabon-ar 1
deslabr-ar 1
desladrill-ar 1
deslaid-ar 1
deslam-ar 1
deslan-ar 1
deslandr-ar 1
deslard-arse 80
deslastr-ar 1
deslat-ar 1
deslateraliz-
  ar 21
deslav-ar 1
deslavaz-ar 21
deslaz-ar 21
deslech-ar 1
deslechug-ar ... 51
deslechuguill-
  ar 1

desle-ír 63
deslendr-ar 53
deslengu-ar 7
deslengüet-ar ... 1
desli-ar 9
deslig-ar 51
deslinaj-ar 1
deslin-ar 1
deslind-ar 1
desling-ar 51
desliñ-ar 1
desliz-ar 21
deslo-ar 1
deslom-ar 1
desluc-ir 3,
  with the
  changes in 48
deslumbr-ar 1
deslustr-ar 1
deslut-ar 1
desmadej-ar 1
desmadr-ar 1
desmadrin-
  arse 80
desmagnetiz-
  ar 21
desmajol-ar 25
desmalez-ar 21
desmalingr-ar ... 1
desmall-ar 1
desmalr-ar 1
desmam-ar 1
desmamey-ar ... 1
desmamon-ar ... 1
desmampar-ar .. 1
desman-ar 1
desman-arse ... 80
desmanch-ar 1
desmand-ar 1
desmandig-
  ar 51
desmanduf-ar ... 1
desmane-ar 1
desmang-ar 51
desmangorre-
  ar 1
desmanguill-
  ar 1
desmanigu-
  ar 58
desmant-ar 1

desmantec-
  ar 67
desmantel-ar 1
desmantill-ar ... 1
desmañan-
  arse 80
desmañ-ar 1
desmañ-arse ... 80
desmaquill-ar ... 1
desmarañ-ar 1
desmaravill-ar .. 1
desmarc-ar 67
desmarch-
  arse 80
desmarid-ar 1
desmaroj-ar 1
desmarr-irse 4
desmat-ar 1
desmaterializ-
  ar 21
desmaton-ar 1
desmay-ar 1
desmech-ar 1
desmechon-ar .. 1
desmed-irse ... 52
desmedr-ar 1
desmedul-ar 1
desmejor-ar 1
desmelancoliz-
  ar 21
desmel-ar 53
desmelen-ar 1
desmembr-ar ... 53
desmemori-
  arse 80
desmengu-ar ... 58
desment-ir 71
desmenude-ar .. 1
desmenuz-ar ... 21
desmeoll-ar 1
desmerec-er ... 48
desmerit-ar 1
desmesur-ar 1
desmezcl-ar 1
desmic-ar 67
desmigaj-ar 1
desmig-ar 51
desmilitariz-
  ar 21
desmineraliz-
  ar 21

desminu-ir 42
desmitific-ar 67
desmoc-ar 1
desmoch-ar 1
desmog-ar 51
desmold-ar 1
desmol-er 47
desmonetiz-
  ar 21
desmont-ar 1
desmontrenc-
  ar 1
desmoñ-ar 1
desmoraliz-
  ar 21
desmorec-
  erse 48
desmorfini-ar ... 21
desmoron-ar 1
desmost-
  arse 80
desmostel-ar 1
desmostol-ar 1
desmot-ar 1
desmoviliz-ar ... 21
desmugr-ar 1
desmull-ir 17
desmultiplic-
  ar 67
desmur-ar 1
desmurri-ar 1
desmutiz-ar 21
desnacionaliz-
  ar 21
desnalg-ar 51
desnarcotiz-
  ar 21
desnarig-ar 51
desnat-ar 1
desnaturaliz-
  ar 21
desnatur-ar 1
desnazific-ar ... 67
desneg-ar 53
desnerv-ar 1
desnev-ar 53,
  and for its use
  regarding
  weather,
  see 45
desnicotiniz-

desplay-ar 1
desplaz-ar 21
despleg-ar 62
despleguete-
    ar 1
desplom-ar 1
desplum-ar 1
despobl-ar 25
despoetiz-ar 21
despoj-ar 1
despolariz-ar ... 21
despolitiz-ar ... 21
despolv-ar 1
despolvore-ar ... 1
despolvoriz-
    ar 21
despon-er 57
desponj-ar 1
despopulariz-
    ar 21
desporr-ar 1
desporrondig-
    arse 51
desportill-ar 1
despos-ar 1
despose-er 70
despost-ar 1
despostill-ar 1
despotiz-ar 21
despotric-ar 67
despreci-ar 1
despredic-ar 1
desprend-er 2
desprens-ar 1
despreocup-
    arse 80
despres-ar 1
desprestigi-ar ... 1
despretin-ar 1
despreven-ir 77
despriv-ar 1
despropi-ar 1
desproporcion-
    ar 1
desprove-er 65,
    plus the past
    participle
    desprovisto
despulg-ar 51
despul-ir 1
despull-ar 1

despulmon-
    arse 80
despulp-ar 1
despuls-ar 1
despum-ar 1
despunt-ar 1,
    and for its use
    regarding
    weather,
    see 45
desquebraj-ar ... 1
desquebr-ar 53
desquej-ar 1
desquem-ar 1
desquer-er 60
desquici-ar 1
desquiet-ar 1
desquijar-ar 1
desquijarr-ar 1
desquijer-ar 1
desquilat-ar 1
desquilibr-ar 1
desquit-ar 1
desrabadill-ar ... 1
desrab-ar 1
desrabe-ar 1
desraber-ar 1
desrabill-ar 1
desrabot-ar 1
desraig-ar 1
desraiz-ar 35
desram-ar 1
desramill-ar 1
desranch-
    arse 80
desranill-ar 1
desrasp-ar 1
desrastroj-ar 1
desratiz-ar 21
desray-ar 1
desrazon-ar 21
desregl-ar 1
desreling-ar 51
desriel-ar 1
desriñon-ar 1
desrisc-ar 67
desriz-ar 21
desrobl-ar 1
desrodrig-ar 51
desronch-ar 1
desroñ-ar 1

desrostr-ar 1
desrumb-ar 1
destab-ar 1
destabl-ar 1
destac-ar 67
destachon-ar ... 1
destacon-ar 1
destaj-ar 1
destajaz-ar 21
destall-ar 1
destalon-ar 1
destan-ar 1
destante-
    arse 80
destap-ar 1
destapi-ar 1
destapon-ar 1
destar-ar 1
destarr-ar 1
destartal-ar 1
destaz-ar 21
destebrech-ar ... 1
destech-ar 1
destej-ar 1
destej-er 2
destel-arse 80
desteleng-ar ... 51
destell-ar 1
destempl-ar 1
destend-er 2,
    with the
    changes in 53
destent-ar 53
desteñ-ir 64
desteriliz-ar 21
destermin-ar 1
desterner-ar 1
desternill-
    arse 80
desterr-ar 53
desterron-ar 1
destet-ar 1
destetill-ar 1
destetun-
    arse 80
destil-ar 1
destill-ar 1
destin-ar 1
destinter-
    arse 80
destiñ-ar 1

destiraniz-ar 21
destirp-ar 1
destitu-ir 42
destoc-ar 67
destocon-ar 1
destong-ar 1
destorb-ar 1
destorc-er 22
destorg-ar 77
destorm-ar 1
destorn-ar 1
destornill-ar 1
destornill-
    arse 80
destornud-ar 1
destorp-ar 1
destorrent-ar 1
destorrent-
    arse 80
destos-erse 81
destost-arse
    80, with the
    changes in 25
destoxic-ar 1
destoz-ar 21
destozol-ar 25
destrab-ar 1
destraill-ar 1
destram-ar 1
destranc-ar 67
destrast-ar 1
destrat-ar 1
destrej-ar 1
destrenz-ar 21
destrep-ar 1
destribut-ar 1
destrinc-ar 67
destrip-ar 1
destripul-ar 1
destriunf-ar 1
destriz-ar 21
destroc-ar 76
destromp-ar 1
destron-ar 1
destronc-ar 67
desronch-ar 1
destrop-ar 1
destroz-ar 21
destru-ir 42
destullec-er 48
destung-ar 51

desturb-ar 1
destus-ar 1
destustuz-ar 21
destutan-ar 1
desuard-ar 1
desubstanci-
ar 1
desuc-ar 67
desud-ar 1
desuel-ar 1
desuer-ar 1
desug-ar 51
desulfur-ar 1
desunc-ir 3,
with the
changes in 46
desunific-ar 1
desun-ir 3
desuñ-ar 1
desuñ-ir 17
desurc-ar 67
desurd-ir 3
desurt-ir 3
desus-ar 1
desustanci-ar 1
desvah-ar 1
desvain-ar 1
desva-ir 3
desval-er 2,
with the
changes in 68
desvalij-ar 1
desvalor-ar 1
desvaloriz-ar 21
desvalu-ar 9
desvanec-er 48
desvaporiz-
ar 21
desvar-ar 1
desvaret-ar 1
desvari-ar 9
desvariz-ar 21
desvas-ar 1
desvast-ar 1
desvastig-ar 51
desved-ar 1
desvel-ar 1
desveliz-ar 21
desven-ar 1
desvencij-ar 1
desvend-ar 1

desvent-ar 53
desverdec-er ... 48
desvergonz-
arse 15
desvest-ir 52
desvez-ar 21
desvi-ar 9
desviej-ar 1
desvigoriz-ar 21
desvincul-ar 1
desviol-ar 1
desvir-ar 1
desvirg-ar 51
desviriliz-ar 21
desvirtu-ar 9
desviscer-ar 1
desvitaliz-ar 21
desvitaminiz-
ar 21
desvitrific-ar 67
desviv-irse 82
desvolcan-
arse 80
desvolv-er
47, except
the past
participle
is desvuelto
desyem-ar 1
desyerb-ar 1
desyug-ar 51
desyunc-ir 3,
with the
changes in 46
deszafr-ar 1
deszoc-ar 67
deszulac-ar 67
deszum-ar 1
detall-ar 1
detante-arse 80
detard-ar 1
detect-ar 1
deten-er 74
detent-ar 1
deterg-er 23
deterior-ar 1
determin-ar 1
detest-ar 1
deton-ar 1
detorn-ar 1
detract-ar 1

detra-er 75
deturp-ar 1
deval-ar 1
devalu-ar 9
devan-ar 1
devane-ar 1
devast-ar 1
deved-ar 1
devel-ar 1
develiz-ar 21
deveng-ar 51
deven-ir 68
devis-ar 1
devolv-er 47,
except the
past participle
is devuelto
devor-ar 1
devot-ar 1
devov-er 2
dextriniz-ar 21
deyect-ar 1
dezm-ar 53
dezoc-ar 67
diabl-ar 1
diable-ar 1
diacon-ar 1
diaconiz-ar 21
diadem-ar 1
diafaniz-ar 21
diafragm-ar 1
diagnostic-ar ... 67
diagram-ar 1
dialis-ar 1
dializ-ar 21
dialog-ar 51
dialogiz-ar 21
diamant-ar 1
diamante-ar 1
diapent-ar 1
diatrib-ar 1
diazo-ar 1
diazot-ar 1
dibuj-ar 1
dic-ar 67
diciplin-ar 1
dictamin-ar 1
dict-ar 1
diet-ar 1
diezm-ar 1
difam-ar 1

difari-ar 1
diferec-er 48
diferenci-ar 1
difer-ir 71
dificult-ar 1
difinec-er 48
difin-ir 3
difiuci-ar 1
diflu-ir 42
difract-ar 1
difum-ar 1
difumin-ar 1
difund-ir 3,
plus the past
participle
difuso
difunte-ar 1
digerec-er 48
diger-ir 71
digest-ir 3
digitaliz-ar 21
digit-ar 1
digladi-ar 1
dign-arse 80
dignific-ar 67
digres-ar 1
digresion-ar 1
dijunte-ar 1
dilacer-ar 1
dilapid-ar 1
dilat-ar 1
diligenci-ar 1
dilori-ar 1
dilucid-ar 1
dilu-ir 42
diluvi-ar 1,
and for its
use regarding
weather,
see 45
diman-ar 1
dimidi-ar 1
dimig-ar 1
diminuec-er 48
diminu-ir 42
dim-ir 3
dimit-ir 3
dinamit-ar 1
dintel-ar 1
dinumer-ar 1
diñ-ar 1

diose-ar 1
diplom-ar 1
diptong-ar 51
diput-ar 1
diquel-ar 1
dirig-ir 3, with
  the changes
  in 23
dirim-ir 3
dirradi-ar 1
dirru-ir 42
discant-ar 1
disc-ar 1
discept-ar 1
discern-er 2,
  with the
  changes in 53
discern-ir 3,
  with the
  changes in 53
disciplin-ar 1
discont-ar 25
discontinu-ar 9
disconven-ir 77
discord-ar 25
discrep-ar 1
discrete-ar 1
discrimin-ar 1
disculp-ar 1
discurr-ir 3
discurs-ar 1
discurse-ar 1
discut-ir 3
disec-ar 67
disemin-ar 1
disent-ir 71
diseñ-ar 1
disert-ar 1
disfam-ar 1
disform-ar 1
disforz-arse 39
disfraz-ar 21
disfrez-arse 80
disfrut-ar 1
disfum-ar 1
disfumin-ar 1
disgreg-ar 51
disgust-ar 1
disid-ir 3
disimil-ar 1
disimul-ar 1

disip-ar 1
dislacer-ar 1
disloc-ar 67
dismembr-ar 53
disminu-ir 42
disoci-ar 1
disolv-er 47,
  except the
  past participle
  is disuelto
dison-ar 25
dispar-ar 1
disparat-ar 1
disparate-ar 1
dispend-er 2
dispens-ar 1
dispers-ar 1
dispert-ar 53
displac-er 48
dispon-er 57
dispuntu-ar 1
disput-ar 1
distanci-ar 1
dist-ar 1
distend-er 39
distermin-ar 1
distil-ar 1
distingu-ir 30
distorsion-ar 1
distra-er 75
distribu-ir 42
disturb-ar 1
disuad-ir 3
disyunc-ir 3,
  with the
  changes in 46
diuque-ar 1
divag-ar 51
divari-ar 1
divaric-ar 1
diverg-ir 3,
  with the
  changes in 23
diversific-ar 67
divert-ir 71
divert-irse 71
divid-ir 3,
  plus the past
  participle
  diviso
divin-ar 1

diviniz-ar 21
divis-ar 1
divorci-ar 1
divulg-ar 51
dobladill-ar 1
dobl-ar 1
dobleg-ar 51
docilit-ar 1
doctor-ar 1
doctore-ar 1
doctrin-ar 1
document-ar 1
dogmatiz-ar 21
dol-ar 25
dol-er 47
dom-ar 1
domell-ar 1
domeñ-ar 1
domestic-ar 67
domicili-ar 1
domific-ar 67
domin-ar 1
don-ar 1
done-ar 1
donjuane-ar 1
doñe-ar 1
dop-ar 1
dor-ar 1
dorm-ir 31
dormit-ar 1
dosific-ar 67
dot-ar 1
dotor-ar 1
dotrin-ar 1
dovel-ar 1
drag-ar 51
dragone-ar 1
dramatiz-ar 21
drans-ar 1
drape-ar 1
dren-ar 1
dribl-ar 1
driz-ar 21
drog-ar 51
dromede-ar 1
dubd-ar 1
duch-ar 1
dud-ar 1
dulcific-ar 67
dulc-ir 3, with
  the changes

in 46
dulzor-ar 1
dulzur-ar 1
duplic-ar 67
dur-ar 1

e

ebanific-ar 1
ebaniz-ar 21
eburnific-ar 1
eccematiz-ar ... 21
ecept-ar 1
eceptu-ar 1
echacorve-ar 1
ech-ar 1
eclesiastiz-ar ... 21
eclips-ar 1
eclosion-ar 1
economiz-ar 21
eczematiz-ar ... 21
edematiz-ar 21
edict-ar 1
edific-ar 67
edit-ar 1
editorializ-ar 21
edr-ar 1
educ-ar 67
educ-ir 58
edulcor-ar 1
efectu-ar 9
efemin-ar 1
efigi-ar 1
eflorec-erse 48
efund-ir 1
egres-ar 1
egris-ar 1
egu-ar 1
eguijarr-ar 1
eguill-ar 1
ejabr-ir 1
ejarr-ar 1
ejecut-ar 1
ejecutori-ar 9
ejempl-ar 1
ejemplariz-ar ... 21
ejemplific-ar 67
ejerc-er 46
ejercit-ar 1
elabor-ar 1

elastific-ar 67
eleboriz-ar 1
electrific-ar 67
electriz-ar 21
electrocut-ar 1
electroliz-ar 21
elegatiz-ar 21
eleg-ir 32, has
  an additional
  past partici-
  ple electo
element-arse ... 80
elev-ar 1
elid-ir 3
elij-ar 1
elimin-ar 1
elips-ar 1
elogi-ar 1
elote-ar 1
elucid-ar 1
elucubr-ar 1
elud-ir 3
eluvi-ar 1
eman-ar 1
emancip-ar 1
emascul-ar 1
embabuc-ar 67
embach-ar 1
embadurn-ar 1
emba-ír 33
embal-ar 1
embaldos-ar 1
emballen-ar 1
emballest-
  arse 80
embalsam-ar 1
embals-ar 1
embalum-ar 1
embanast-ar 1
embanc-ar 67
embanc-arse ... 67
embander-ar 1
embanquet-ar ... 1
embaraz-ar 21
embarb-ar 1
embarbasc-
  ar 67
embarbasc-
  arse 80
embarbec-er 48
embarbill-ar 1

embarc-ar 67
embarcen-ar 1
embarcin-ar 1
embard-ar 1
embarduñ-ar 1
embarg-ar 51
embarnec-er 48
embarniz-ar 21
embarranc-
  ar 67
embarr-ar 1
embarrial-
  arse 80
embarril-ar 1
embarriz-
  arse 21
embarrot-ar 1
embarrull-ar 1
embarrun-ar 1
embarull-ar 1
embas-ar 1
embast-ar 1
embastard-ar 1
embastec-er 48
embasur-ar 1
embat-irse 3
embauc-ar 67
embaul-ar 67
embay-arse 80
embaz-ar 21
embebec-er 48
embeb-er 2
embejuc-ar 67
embelec-ar 67
embeleñ-ar 1
embeles-ar 1
embellac-
  arse 80
embellaquec-
  erse 48
embellec-
  arse 67
embellec-er 48
embeod-ar 1
ember-ar 1
embermej-ar 1
embermejec-
  er 48
embermellon-
  ar 1
emberren-

chin-arse 80
emberrinch-
  arse 80
embest-ir 52
embetun-ar 1
embic-ar 67
embich-arse ... 80
embigot-ar 1
embij-ar 1
embizarr-
  arse 80
embizc-ar 67
emblandec-
  er 48
emblanque-ar ... 1
emblanquec-
  er 48
emblematiz-
  ar 21
embo-ar 1
embob-ar 1
embobec-er 48
embobill-ar 1
embobin-ar 1
emboc-ar 67
embochet-ar 1
embochic-ar 1
embochin-
  arse 80
embochinch-
  ar 1
embocic-
  arse 80
embocin-
  arse 80
embod-arse 80
embodeg-ar 51
emboj-ar 1
embojot-ar 1
embol-ar 1
embolat-ar 1
embolic-ar 67
emboll-ar 1
embols-ar 1
embolsic-ar 67
embolsific-ar 1
embon-ar 1
emboñig-ar 51
emboquill-ar 1
emborn-ar 1

emborrach-ar ... 1
emborr-ar 1
emborrasc-ar ... 67
emborraz-ar 21
emborric-
  arse 67
emborriz-ar 21
emborron-ar 1
emborrull-
  arse 80
emboruc-ar 1
embosc-ar 67
embosquec-
  er 48
embost-ar 1
embot-ar 1
embotell-ar 1
embotic-ar 67
embotic-arse ... 67
embotij-ar 1
embotin-ar 1
emboton-ar 1
emboved-ar 1
embozal-ar 1
emboz-ar 21
embracil-ar 1
embrag-ar 51
embraguet-
  arse 80
embram-ar 1
embras-ar 1
embrav-ar 1
embravec-er ... 48
embrazal-ar 1
embraz-ar 21
embre-ar 1
embreg-arse 51
embreñ-arse ... 80
embret-ar 1
embriag-ar 51
embrib-ar 1
embrid-ar 1
embris-ar 1
embrisc-ar 67
embrocal-ar 1
embroc-
  ar 67
embrochal-ar 1
embroll-ar 1
embrom-ar 1
embroquel-

arse 80
embroquet-ar ... 1
embrosquil-ar ... 1
embrosquill-ar .. 1
embroz-ar 21
embruci-ar 1
embruj-ar 1
embruñ-arse 80
embrut-ar 1
embrutec-er 48
embuchac-
   arse 80
embuch-ar 1
embuci-ar 1
embud-ar 1
embull-ar 1
embullon-ar 1
embuñeg-ar 51
emburr-ar 1
emburri-ar 1
emburuj-ar 1
embuste-ar 1
embustere-ar 1
embust-ir 3
embut-ar 1
embut-ir 3
emend-ar 53
ement-ar 53
emerg-er 23
emetiz-ar 21
emigr-ar 1
emit-ir 3
emocion-ar 1
emol-ir 4
emolument-ar ... 1
empac-ar 67
empac-arse 80
empach-ar 1
empadr-ar 1
empadron-ar 1
empaj-ar 1
empajol-ar 25
empalag-ar 51
empal-ar 1
empali-ar 1
empalic-ar 67
empalidec-er ... 48
empaliz-ar 21
empallet-ar 1
empalm-ar 1
empalmill-ar 1

empalom-ar 1
empalustr-ar 1
empampan-
   arse 80
empamp-
   arse 80
empan-ar 1
empancin-
   arse 80
empand-ar 1
empandill-ar 1
empandorg-
   ar 51
empaner-ar 1
empanet-ar 1
empang-ar 1
empanj-arse 80
empantalon-
   arse 80
empantan-ar 1
empanturr-ar 1
empanz-arse ... 21
empañ-ar 1
empañet-ar 1
empañic-ar 67
empapagay-
   arse 80
empap-ar 1
empapel-ar 1
empapirot-ar 1
empapiz-ar 21
empapuci-ar 1
empapuj-ar 1
empapuz-ar 21
empaquet-ar 1
emparam-
   arse 80
emparament-
   ar 1
empar-ar 1
emparch-ar 1
empard-ar 1
empared-ar 1
emparej-ar 1
emparent-ar 53
emparrand-
   arse 80
emparr-ar 1
emparrill-ar 1
emparv-ar 1
empascu-

arse 80
empast-ar 1
empastel-ar 1
empat-ar 1
empatill-ar 1
empatron-ar 1
empatroniz-
   ar 21
empaturr-
   arse 80
empaut-arse 80
empav-ar 1
empaves-ar 1
empavon-ar 1
empavorec-
   er 48
empec-er 48,
   and used in
   the positions
   in 45
empech-ar 1
empecin-ar 1
empecin-
   arse 80
emped-arse 80
empedec-er 48
empedernec-
   er 48
empedern-ir 4
empedr-ar 53
empeg-ar 51
empegunt-ar 1
empel-ar 1
empelazg-ar 51
empelazg-
   arse 80
empelech-ar 1
empell-ar 1
empellej-ar 1
empell-er 2,
   with the
   changes in 25
empellic-ar 1
empelot-arse ... 80
empenach-ar 1
empendol-ar 1
empenec-
   arse 67
empent-ar 1
empeñ-ar 1
empeñol-

arse 80
empeor-ar 1
empequeñec-
   er 48
emperch-ar 1
empercud-ir 3
emperdig-ar 51
emperduc-irse
   82, with the
   changes in 46
emperejil-ar 1
emperez-ar 21
empergamin-
   ar 1
emperg-ar 51
emperic-arse ... 67
emperifoll-ar 1
emperl-ar 1
empern-ar 1
emperr-ar 1
emperr-arse 80
emperrechin-
   arse 80
emperson-ar 1
empertig-ar 51
empesebr-ar 1
empesg-ar 51
empest-ar 1
empestifer-ar 1
empestill-
   arse 80
empetac-ar 1
empetat-ar 1
empetrenc-
   arse 1
empez-ar 34
empiad-ar 1
empic-ar 67
empic-arse 67
empich-arse 80
empicot-ar 1
empigüel-ar 1
empihuel-ar 1
empil-ar 1
empilch-ar 1
empilch-arse ... 80
empilon-ar 1
empiluch-ar 1
empin-ar 1
empingorot-ar ... 1
empioj-ar 1

empiol-ar 1
empip-ar 1
empip-arse 80
empit-ar 1
empiton-ar 1
empizarr-ar 1
empizc-ar 21
emplantill-ar 1
emplast-ar 1
emplastec-er ... 48
emplaz-ar 21
emplaz-arse 21
emple-ar 1
emplebeyec-
er 48
emplegost-
arse 80
emplom-ar 1
emplumaj-ar 1
emplum-ar 1
emplumec-er ... 48
empobrec-er ... 48
empoch-ar 1
empoder-ar 1
empodrec-er 48
empoj-arse 80
empolin-ar 1
empoll-ar 1
empoller-
arse 80
empoltronec-
erse 48
empolv-ar 1
empolvor-ar 1
empolvoriz-
ar 21
emponch-
arse 80
emponzoñ-ar 1
empop-ar 1
empor-ar 1
emporc-ar 76
emporret-
arse 80
emporrong-
arse 80
empotr-ar 1
empotrer-ar 1
empoz-ar 21
empradiz-ar 21
empr-ar 1

emprend-er 1
emprens-ar 1
emprent-ar 1
empreñ-ar 1
empresent-ar 1
emprest-ar 1
emprestill-ar 1
empretec-er 48
emprim-ar 1
emprimer-ar 1
emprim-ir 3
empring-ar 51
emprision-ar 1
empuch-ar 1
empuj-ar 1
empulg-ar 51
empunt-ar 1
empuñ-ar 1
empuñ-ir 17
empurpur-ar 1
empurr-arse 80
emputec-er 48
empuy-ar 1
emul-ar 1
emulsion-ar 1
enaceit-ar 1
enacer-ar 1
enaciy-ar 1
enaguach-ar 1
enagu-ar 1
enaguaz-ar 21
enajen-ar 1
enalbald-ar 1
enalb-ar 1
enalbard-ar 1
enalfombr-ar 1
enalmagr-ar 1
enalmen-ar 1
enalt-ar 1
enaltec-er 48
enamarillec-
er 48
enamor-ar 1
enamoric-
arse 67
enamorisc-
arse 67
enan-arse 80
enanc-arse 67
enanch-ar 1
enangost-ar 1

enanz-ar 21
enaparej-ar 1
enarbol-ar 1
enarc-ar 67
enardec-er 48
enaren-ar 1
enarmon-ar 1
enarmor-ar 1
enarque-ar 1
enarr-ar 1
enart-ar 1
enasp-ar 1
enast-ar 1
enastil-ar 1
enastill-ar 1
encabalg-ar 51
encaball-ar 1
encab-ar 1
encabell-ar 1
encabellec-
erse 48
encabestr-ar 1
encabez-ar 21
encabezon-ar ... 1
encabill-ar 1
encabrahig-
ar 19
encabrest-ar 1
encabri-ar 9
encabrill-ar 1
encabrit-arse 80
encabron-ar 1
encabruñ-ar 1
encabull-ar 1
encabuy-ar 1
encach-ar 1
encacharr-ar 1
encach-arse 80
encachich-
arse 80
encachil-arse ... 80
encachorr-
arse 80
encad-arse 80
encaden-ar 1
encaec-er 48
encaj-ar 1
encajer-arse 80
encajet-ar 1
encajetill-ar 1
encajon-ar 1

encalabern-
arse 80
encalaboz-ar ... 21
encalabrin-ar 1
encalambr-
arse 80
encalamoc-
ar 67
encalamuc-
ar 67
encal-ar 1
encalat-arse 80
encalc-ar 67
encalet-ar 1
encalill-arse 80
encall-ar 1
encallec-er 48
encallejon-ar 1
encalletr-ar 1
encalm-arse 80
encalom-ar 1
encalostr-
arse 80
encalv-ar 1
encalvec-er 48
encalz-ar 21
encam-ar 1
encamar-ar 1
encamb-ar 1
encambij-ar 1
encambr-ar 1
encambrillon-
ar 1
encambron-ar ... 1
encambuch-ar .. 1
encamin-ar 1
encamis-ar 1
encamon-ar 1
encamorr-
arse 80
encamot-
arse 80
encampan-ar 1
encamp-arse ... 80
encanal-ar 1
encanaliz-ar 21
encanall-ar 1
encan-ar 1
encanast-ar 1
encancel-ar 1
encancer-

arse 80
encanchin-
arse 80
encanchon-ar ... 1
encandec-er 48
encandel-ar 1
encandelill-ar 1
encandell-ar 1
encandil-ar 1
encanec-er 48
encanelon-
arse 80
encanij-ar 1
encanill-ar 1
encant-ar 1
encantar-ar 1
encantus-ar 1
encanut-ar 1
encañam-ar 1
encañ-ar 1
encañiz-ar 21
encañon-ar 1
encañut-ar 1
encapach-ar 1
encap-ar 1
encaparazon-
ar 1
encapaz-ar 21
encaperuz-ar ... 21
encapill-ar 1
encapirot-ar 1
encapot-ar 1,
and for its
use regarding
weather,
see 45
encaprich-
arse 80
encapsul-ar 1
encapuch-ar 1
encapuz-ar 21
encaracol-ar 1
encarajin-
arse 80
encaram-ar 1
encaramillot-
ar 1
encarapit-
arse 80
encar-ar 1
encarcavin-ar ... 1

encarcel-ar 1
encard-arse 80
encarec-er 48
encarg-ar 51
encariñ-ar 1
encar-ir 3
encarn-ar 1
encarnec-er 48
encarniz-ar 21
encarp-ar 1
encarpet-ar 1
encarril-ar 1
encarrill-ar 1
encarroñ-ar 1
encarruj-ar 1
encart-ar 1
encarton-ar 1
encartuch-ar 1
encartul-arse ... 80
encas-ar 1
encascabel-ar ... 1
encasc-ar 67
encascot-ar 1
encasill-ar 1
encasimb-ar 1
encasquet-ar 1
encasquill-ar 1
encast-ar 1
encastill-ar 1
encastr-ar 1
encasull-ar 1
encatalej-ar 1
encativ-ar 1
encatus-ar 1
encauch-ar 1
encaus-ar 1
encaustic-ar 67
encaustific-ar ... 1
encauz-ar 21
encav-arse 80
encebad-ar 1
enceboll-ar 1
enceguec-er 48
encelaj-arse ... 80
encel-ar 1
enceld-ar 1
encell-ar 1
encenag-
arse 51
encencerr-ar 1
encend-er 2,

with the
changes in 53
encendr-ar 1
enceneg-
arse 80
enceniz-ar 21
encens-ar 1
encensu-ar 1
encent-ar 53
encentr-ar 1
encep-ar 1
encer-ar 1
encerc-ar 1
encernad-ar 1
encerot-ar 1
encerr-ar 1
encerriz-ar 21
encert-ar 53
encesped-ar 1
encest-ar 1
encet-ar 1
enchalec-ar 67
enchamarr-ar 1
enchamb-ar 1
enchambran-
ar 1
enchamic-ar 1
enchanclet-ar ... 1
enchap-ar 1
enchaparr-
arse 80
enchapin-
arse 80
enchaquet-
arse 80
encharc-ar 67
encharnel-ar 1
encharral-
arse 80
encharranch-
ar 1
enchat-arse 80
enchauch-
arse 80
enchavet-ar 1
enchepic-ar 1
enchic-ar 67
enchich-arse ... 80
enchil-ar 1
enchilot-arse ... 80
enchin-ar 1

enchinarr-ar 1
enchinch-ar 1
enchip-ar 1
enchiquer-ar 1
enchiron-ar 1
enchism-ar 1
enchisp-ar 1
enchiv-arse 80
enchocor-
arse 80
enchoncl-
arse 80
enchuch-ar 1
enchuec-ar 67
enchuf-ar 1
enchul-arse 80
enchulet-ar 1
enchullec-ar ... 67
enchumb-ar 1
enchut-ar 1
enciel-ar 1
enciguat-
arse 80
encim-ar 1
encinch-ar 1
encing-ar 1
encint-ar 1
encintr-ar 1
encisc-ar 1
encism-ar 1
encit-ar 1
encizañ-ar 1
enclanch-
arse 80
enclar-ar 1,
and for its
use regarding
weather,
see 45
enclaresc-er 1
enclaustr-ar 1
enclav-ar 1
enclavij-ar 1
encloc-ar 76
encloquec-er ... 67
encluc-ar 67
encluec-ar 67
encob-ar 1
encobij-ar 1
encobil-arse 80
encobr-ar 1

encocl-ar 1
encocor-ar 1
encocr-ar 1
encodill-arse 80
encofin-ar 1
encofr-ar 1
encog-er 23
encogoll-
   arse 80
encogull-ar 1
encohet-ar 1
encoj-ar 1
encol-ar 1
encolc-ar 1
encolch-ar 1
encoleriz-ar 21
encoligu-ar 1
encomend-ar ... 53
encomenz-ar ... 21
encomi-ar 1
encompadr-ar ... 1
encompas-ar 1
encon-ar 1
enconch-
   arse 80
enconfit-ar 1
encong-arse 80
enconre-ar 1
encontr-ar 25
encopet-ar 1
encorach-ar 1
encoraj-ar 1
encorajin-ar 1
encorament-ar .. 1
encor-ar 25
encoraz-ar 21
encorch-ar 1
encorchet-ar 1
encorcov-ar 1
encord-ar 25
encordel-ar 1
encordon-ar 1
encorec-er 48
encorm-ar 1
encorn-ar 25
encornud-ar 1
encoroz-ar 21
encorral-ar 1
encorre-ar 1
encorr-er 1
encorsel-ar 1

encorset-ar 1
encort-ar 1
encortin-ar 1
encoruj-arse 80
encorv-ar 1
encostal-ar 1
encost-arse
   80, with the
   changes in 25
encostr-ar 1
encov-ar 25
encovil-arse 80
encras-ar 1
encresp-ar 1
encrest-arse 80
encristal-ar 1
encrudec-er 48
encruelec-er 48
encruquill-
   arse 80
encruz-ar 21
encuadern-ar 1
encuadr-ar 1
encuart-ar 1
encuartel-ar 1
encuat-ar 1
encub-ar 1
encubert-ar 53
encubr-ir 3,
   except the
   past participle
   is encubierto
encuc-ar 67
encucuruch-
   arse 80
encuell-ar 1
encuend-ar 1
encuer-ar 1
encuest-ar 1
encuev-ar 1
encuit-arse 80
encuj-ar 1
encul-arse 80
enculat-ar 1
enculec-arse ... 80
enculill-arse 80
enculp-ar 1
encumbr-ar 1
encun-ar 1
encurd-arse 80
encureñ-ar 1

encurruc-
   arse 67
encurt-ir 3
endam-arse 80
endebl-ar 1
endech-ar 1
endehes-ar 1
endelgadec-
   er 48
endeliñ-ar 1
endemoni-ar 1
endent-ar 53
endentec-er 48
endeñ-arse 80
enderech-ar 1
enderez-ar 21
enderrot-ar 1
endeud-arse 80
endiabl-ar 1
endich-arse 80
endiecioch-
   arse 80
endient-ar 1
endilg-ar 51
endiñ-ar 1
endios-ar 1
endirg-ar 51
endit-arse 80
endobl-ar 1
endoming-ar 51
endoming-
   arse 51
endon-ar 1
endon-arse 80
endorm-ir 31
endors-ar 1
endos-ar 1
endosel-ar 1
endosmos-ar 1
endragon-
   arse 80
endrez-ar 21
endrog-arse 51
endu-ir 42
endulcec-er 48
endulc-ir 3,
   with the
   changes in 23
endulz-ar 21
endulzor-ar 1
endur-ar 1

endurec-er 48
enech-ar 1
enej-ar 1
enemig-ar 1
enemist-ar 1
ener-ar 1
energiz-ar 21
eneriz-ar 21
enert-arse 80
enerv-ar 1
enfad-ar 1
enfaj-ar 1
enfajill-ar 1
enfajin-ar 1
enfald-ar 1
enfaltric-arse ... 80
enfandang-
   arse 80
enfang-ar 51
enfard-ar 1
enfardel-ar 1
enfarusc-
   arse 80
enfasc-ar 1
enfasti-ar 1
enfastidi-ar 1
enfatiz-ar 21
enfatu-ar 1
enfatu-arse 9
enfe-ar 1
enfebrec-er 48
enfelp-ar 1
enferm-ar 1
enfermiz-ar 21
enfermose-ar 1
enferoz-ar 21
enfervorec-er ... 48
enfervoriz-ar 21
enfest-ar 1
enfeud-ar 1
enfi-ar 1
enficion-ar 1
enfiel-ar 1
enfierec-erse ... 48
enfiest-arse 80
enfil-ar 1
enfing-ir 3,
   with the
   changes in 23
enfistol-arse ... 80
enfiuz-ar 21

enflac-ar 67
enflaquec-er 48
enflat-arse 80
enflaut-ar 1
enflech-ar 1
enflor-ar 1
enflorec-er 48
enfoc-ar 67
enfog-ar 1
enfogon-ar 1
enfollin-arse 80
enfollon-ar 1
enforc-ar 67
enform-ar 1
enforn-ar 1
enforr-ar 1
enfortalec-er 48
enfortec-er 48
enfort-ir 3
enfosc-ar 67
enfot-arse 80
enfrail-ar 1
enfranj-ar 1
enfranquec-
    er 48
enfrasc-ar 67
enfrasc-arse 80
enfren-ar 1
enfrenill-ar 1
enfrent-ar 1
enfri-ar 9
enfrijol-arse 80
enfront-ar 1
enfrontil-ar 1
enfrosc-arse 67
enfuci-ar 1
enfuert-arse 80
enfuet-arse 80
enfull-ar 1
enfullin-arse 80
enfunch-ar 1
enfund-ar 1
enfuñ-arse 80
enfuñing-
    arse 80
enfurec-er 48
enfurelec-er 48
enfurgon-ar 1
enfuri-arse 80
enfurruc-
    arse 67

enfurruñ-
    arse 80
enfurrusc-
    arse 67
enfurt-ir 3
enfuruñ-arse 80
enfus-ar 1
enfusc-ar 67
enfus-ir 3
engaendr-ar 1
engaban-ar 1
engaf-ar 1
engafec-er 48
engafet-ar 1
engait-ar 1
engalabern-ar ... 1
engalan-ar 1
engaler-ar 1
engalg-ar 51
engali-ar 9
engalib-ar 1
engall-ar 1
engallet-ar 1
engallol-ar 1
engallot-arse ... 80
enganch-ar 1
enganduj-ar 1
engangoch-ar ... 1
engangren-
    arse 80
engañ-ar 1
engañil-ar 1
engañis-ar 1
engañot-ar 1
engarabat-ar 1
engarabit-ar 1
engaratus-ar 1
engarb-arse 80
engarber-ar 1
engarbull-ar 1
engarf-ar 1
engargant-ar 1
engargol-ar 1
engarigol-ar 1
engaripol-ar 1
engaripol-
    arse 80
engarit-ar 1
engarm-arse 80
engarraf-ar 1
engarr-ar 1

engarri-ar 1
engarron-ar 1
engarrot-ar 1
engarruch-ar 1
engarrull-ar 1
engarruñ-
    arse 80
engarz-ar 21
engasaj-ar 1
engas-ar 1
engasg-arse 51
engast-ar 1
engaston-ar 1
engat-ar 1
engatill-ar 1
engatuñ-arse ... 80
engatus-ar 1
engauch-ar 1
engavi-ar 1
engavilan-ar 1
engavill-ar 1
engayol-ar 1
engaz-ar 21
engaz-arse 80
engazuz-ar 21
engendr-ar 1
engent-arse 80
engeñ-ar 1
enger-ir 71
engib-ar 1
eng-ir 3,
    with the
    changes in 23
englob-ar 1
englut-ir 3
engo-ar 1
engocet-ar 1
engod-ar 1
engol-ar 1
engolf-ar 1
engolill-ar 1
engolill-arse 80
engoll-ar 1
engollet-arse ... 80
engollip-arse ... 80
engolondrin-ar .. 1
engolosin-ar 1
engom-ar 1
engomin-ar 1
engonz-ar 21
engor-ar 25

engord-ar 1
engordec-er 48
engorgon-ar 1
engorgone-
    arse 80
engorgorit-ar 1
engorr-ar 1
engorrin-arse ... 80
engorron-
    arse 80
engot-arse 80
engozgorit-ar 1
engozn-ar 1
engraci-ar 1
engram-ar 1
engrame-ar 1
engramp-ar 1
engran-ar 1
engrand-ar 1
engrandec-er ... 48
engraner-ar 1
engranuj-
    arse 80
engrap-ar 1
engras-ar 1
engrasill-ar 1
engravec-er 48
engred-ar 1
engre-ír 63
engresc-ar 67
engrif-ar 1
engrill-ar 1
engrill-arse 80
engrillet-ar 1
engrinch-
    arse 80
engring-arse 51
engringol-
    arse 80
engrip-arse 80
engros-ar 25
engrosec-er 48
engrud-ar 1
engrues-ar 1
engrumec-
    erse 48
engruñ-ar 1
engrup-ir 3
enguach-
    arse 80
enguachic-ar 1

enguachin-ar 1
enguad-ar 1
engueld-ar 1
engualdrap-ar ... 1
engualich-ar 1
enguanduj-
  arse 80
enguangar-ar 1
enguant-ar 1
enguape-
  arse 80
enguarac-
  arse 80
enguaral-ar 1
enguarap-
  arse 80
enguarapet-
  arse 80
enguaret-
  arse 80
enguasim-ar 1
enguat-ar 1
enguatus-ar 1
enguayab-
  arse 80
engubi-ar 1
enguedej-ar 1
enguer-ar 1
engüer-ar 1
enguerrill-ar 1
enguerrill-
  arse 80
enguijarr-ar 1
enguillot-
  arse 80
enguiñ-arse 80
enguirland-ar 1
enguirnald-ar 1
enguisc-ar 67
enguitarr-
  arse 80
enguizc-ar 67
enguizg-ar 51
engull-ir 17
engurr-ar 1
engurri-ar 1
engurrumin-ar .. 1
engurrum-ir 3
engurruñ-ar 1
engurruñ-ir 3
engusg-arse 51

enhacin-ar 1
enhad-ar 1
enhambrec-
  er 48
enharin-ar 1
enhasti-ar 9
enhastill-ar 1
enhatij-ar 1
enhebill-ar 1
enhebr-ar 1
enhechiz-ar 21
enhen-ar 1
enherbol-ar 1
enhest-ar 53,
  plus the past
  participle
  enhiesto
enhetr-ar 1
enhic-ar 1
enhiel-ar 1
enhil-ar 1
enhoc-ar
  25, with the
  changes in 67
enhollin-ar 1
enhollin-arse ... 80
enhorc-ar 67
enhorn-ar 1
enhorquet-ar 1
enhot-ar 1
enhuec-ar 67
enhuer-ar 1
enhuev-ar 1
enhumedec-
  er 48
enigmatiz-ar 21
enjabeg-arse ... 51
enjabl-ar 1
enjabon-ar 1
enjaez-ar 21
enjagu-ar 7
enjalbeg-ar 51
enjalm-ar 1
enjambr-ar 1
enjamin-ar 1
enjaquim-ar 1
enjaran-arse 80
enjarci-ar 1
enjard-ar 1
enjardin-ar 1
enjaret-ar 1

enjarr-arse 80
enjarret-arse 80
enjaul-ar 1
enjeb-ar 1
enjerg-ar 51
enjer-ir 3
enjerron-ar 1
enjert-ar 1
enjic-ar 67
enjill-arse 80
enjill-irse 82
enjimelg-ar 51
enjiquer-ar 1
enjolon-arse 80
enjordan-ar 1
enjorguin-ar 1
enjorguin-
  arse 80
enjorjet-ar 1
enjorquet-ar 1
enjoy-ar 1
enjoyel-ar 1
enjuag-ar 51
enjuer-ar 1
enjug-ar 51,
  plus the past
  participle
  enjuto
enjugasc-
  arse 67
enjuici-ar 1
enjunc-ar 67
enjunci-ar 1
enjur-ar 1
enjut-ar 1
enlabi-ar 1
enlaci-ar 1
enlacr-ar 1
enladrill-ar 1
enlagun-ar 1
enlaj-ar 1
enlam-ar 1
enlamin-arse ... 80
enlanch-ar 1
enlanguidec-
  er 48
enlard-ar 1
enlat-ar 1
enlaz-ar 21
enlech-ar 1
enlegaj-ar 1

enlegam-ar 1
enleji-ar 9
enlenz-ar 34
enlerd-ar 1
enlig-ar 51
enlij-ar 1
enlis-ar 1
enlist-ar 1
enliston-ar 1
enlitr-arse 80
enliud-ar 1
enliz-ar 21
enllam-ar 1
enllant-ar 1
enllen-ar 1
enllentec-er 48
enlloc-ar 76
enlobreguec-
  er 28
enlod-ar 1
enlodaz-ar 21
enlodocin-
  arse 80
enlom-ar 1
enloquec-er 48
enlos-ar 1
enlozan-arse 80
enlozanec-er ... 48
enloz-ar 21
enlucern-ar 1
enluc-ir 3,
  with the
  changes in 48
enlustrec-er 49
enlut-ar 1
enmabit-ar 1
enmachambr-
  ar 1
enmadej-ar 1
enmader-ar 1
enmadr-arse 80
enmadrastr-ar ... 1
enmaestr-ar 1
enmagrec-er 48
enmalec-er 48
enmalec-
  erse 81
enmalet-ar 1
enmalez-
  arse 21
enmall-ar 1

enmall-arse 80
enmallet-ar 1
enmang-ar 51
enmanigu-
  arse 21
enmanill-ar 1
enmant-ar 1
enm-ar 1
enmarañ-ar 1
enmar-ar 1
enmarc-ar 67
enmarchit-ar 1
enmarid-ar 1
enmarillec-
  erse 48
enmarom-ar 1
enmarques-ar ... 1
enmas-ar 1
enmascar-ar 1
enmasill-ar 1
enmat-arse 80
enmatul-ar 1
enmayen-
  arse 80
enmech-ar 1
enmel-ar 53
enmelot-ar 1
enmend-ar 53
enmenz-ar 21
enmiel-ar 1
enmienz-ar 21
enmocec-er 48
enmochigu-ar ... 1
enmogot-
  arse 80
enmohec-er 48
enmollec-er 48
enmon-arse 80
enmond-ar 1
enmonj-arse 80
enmontañ-
  arse 80
enmont-ar 1
enmont-arse 80
enmonton-
  arse 80
enmoñ-arse 80
enmordaz-ar 21
enmost-ar 1
enmostr-ar 25
enmot-ar 1

enmudec-er 48
enmuesc-ar 67
enmugr-ar 1
enmugrec-er 48
enmur-ar 1
enmusta-ir 3
ennat-ar 1
enneci-arse 80
ennegrec-er 48
ennoblec-er 48
ennudec-er 48
enoc-ar 1
enoj-ar 1
enojot-arse 80
enorgullec-er ... 48
enques-arse 80
enquici-ar 1
enquijot-arse ... 80
enquillotr-ar 1
enquimbr-
  arse 80
enquinch-ar 1
enquiñ-ar 1
enquist-arse 80
enrab-ar 1
enrabi-ar 1
enrabiet-arse ... 80
enrabisc-ar 67
enrac-ar 1
enracim-arse ... 80
enraf-ar 1
enraigon-ar 1
enraiz-ar 35
enrajon-ar 1
enralec-er 48
enram-ar 1
enrambl-ar 1
enranci-ar 1
enrarec-ar 48
enras-ar 1
enrasill-ar 1
enrastr-ar 1
enraton-arse 80
enray-ar 1
enraz-ar 21
enreci-ar 1
enred-ar 1
enrehoj-ar 1
enrejal-ar 1
enrej-ar 1
enrelig-ar 1

enresm-ar 1
enri-ar 9
enrid-ar 1
enriel-ar 1
enriend-ar 1
enrigidec-er 48
enriostr-ar 1
enripi-ar 1
enriquec-er 48
enrisc-ar 67
enristr-ar 1
enriz-ar 21
enrobin-arse 80
enrobustec-
  er 48
enroc-ar 67
enroc-arse 80
enrod-ar 25
enrodel-ar 1
enrodrig-ar 51
enrodrigon-ar ... 1
enroj-ar 1
enrojec-er 48
enrol-ar 1
enroll-ar 1
enrolliz-ar 21
enrom-ar 1
enron-ar 1
enronch-ar 1
enronquec-er ... 48
enroñ-ar 1
enroñec-er 48
enros-ar 1
enrosc-ar 67
enrostr-ar 1
enrubesc-er 2
enrubi-ar 1
enrudec-er 48
enrug-ar 51
enruinec-er 48
enrul-ar 1
enrumb-ar 1
enrun-ar 1
ensaban-ar 1
ensac-ar 67
ensaler-ar 1
ensaliv-ar 1
ensalm-ar 1
ensalmor-ar 25
ensalobr-
  arse 80

ensalvaj-ar 1
ensalvaj-arse ... 80
ensalz-ar 21
ensambenit-ar .. 1
ensambl-ar 1
ensanch-ar 1
ensandec-er 48
ensangost-ar 1
ensangrent-
  ar 53
ensangusti-ar ... 1
ensani-arse 80
ensañ-ar 1
ensarment-ar ... 53
ensarnec-er 48
ensart-ar 1
ensat-ar 1
ensayal-ar 1
ensayal-arse 80
ensay-ar 1
ensay-arse 80
enseb-ar 1
ensec-ar 1
ensed-ar 1
ensell-ar 1
enselv-ar 1
ensen-ar 1
enseñal-ar 1
enseñ-ar 1
enseñore-ar 1
enseñore-
  arse 80
enser-ar 1
enseri-arse 80
enserpent-
  arse 80
ensil-ar 1
ensill-ar 1
ensillar-ar 1
ensilvec-erse ... 48
ensimism-
  arse 80
ensin-ar 1
ensobac-arse ... 80
ensobe-ar 1
ensoberbec-
  er 48
ensobin-arse ... 80
ensobr-ar 1
ensog-ar 51
ensoguill-ar 1

ensoler-ar 1
ensolv-er 47,
  except the
  past participle
  is ensuelto
ensombrec-
  er 48
ensoñ-ar 25
ensop-ar 1
ensord-ar 1
ensordec-er 48
ensort-arse 80
ensortij-ar 1
ensos-ar 1
ensotan-ar 1
ensot-arse 80
ensuavec-er 48
ensuci-ar 1
ensuegr-ar 1
ensug-ar 51
ensunch-ar 1
ensuriz-ar 21
ensuruc-arse ... 80
ensut-arse 80
ensuy-ar 1
entabac-ar 67
entabac-arse ... 67
entaban-arse ... 80
entabic-ar 67
entabl-ar 1
entabler-arse ... 80
entablill-ar 1
entalam-ar 1
entaleg-ar 51
entaling-ar 51
entall-ar 1
entallec-er 48
entalon-ar 1
entamang-
  arse 80
entam-ar 1
entand-ar 1
entang-arse 80
entap-ar 1
entapar-ar 1
entapec-er 48
entapi-ar 1
entapiz-ar 21
entapuj-ar 1
entaquill-ar 21
entarasc-ar 67

entarim-ar 1
entarquin-ar 1
entarr-ar 1
entarug-ar 51
entec-arse 67
entech-ar 1
entej-ar 1
entel-ar 1
entenci-ar 1
entend-er 2,
  with the
  changes in 53
entenebr-ar 1
entenebrec-
  er 48
enter-ar 1
enterc-arse 67
enterci-ar 1
enterciopel-ar ... 1
enternec-er 48
enterr-ar 53
enterreg-ar 1
enterri-ar 1
enterron-ar 1
entes-ar 53
entest-ar 1
entestec-er 48
entib-ar 1
entibi-ar 1
entibiec-er 48
entichel-ar 1
entiemp-arse ... 80
entierr-ar 1
enties-ar 1
entigrec-erse ... 48
entil-ar 1
entin-ar 1
entint-ar 1
entir-ar 1
entirri-arse 80
entirs-ar 1
entis-ar 1
entiz-ar 21
entizn-ar 1
entol-ar 1
entold-ar 1,
  and for its use
  regarding
  weather,
  see 45
entomec-er 48

entomiz-ar 21
entompeat-ar 1
enton-ar 1
entonel-ar 1
entong-ar 51
entononc-ar 1
entont-ar 1
entontec-er 48
entoñ-ar 1
entopet-ar 1
entorc-arse 67
entoril-ar 1
entorn-ar 1
entornill-ar 1
entorpec-er 48
entort-ar 25
entortij-ar 1
entosic-ar 1
entosig-ar 51
entoxic-ar 1
entrab-ar 1
entram-ar 1
entramoj-ar 1
entramp-ar 1
entrampill-ar 1
entrañ-ar 1
entrañiz-ar 21
entrapaj-ar 1
entrap-ar 1
entrapaz-ar 21
entr-ar 1
entreabr-ir 3,
  except the
  past participle
  is entreabierto
entreayud-
  arse 80
entrebol-ar 1
entrecav-ar 1
entrecerr-ar 53
entrechaz-ar 21
entrechoc-ar 67
entreclare-ar 1
entrecog-er 23
entrecom-ar 1
entrecomill-ar ... 1
entrecort-ar 1
entrecri-arse 9
entrecruz-ar 21
entredec-ir 58

entrederram-
  ar 1
entreg-ar 51
entreger-ir 71
entrejer-ir 71
entrejunt-ar 1
entrelaz-ar 21
entreline-ar 1
entrelist-ar 1
entrellev-ar 1
entreluc-ir 3,
  with the
  changes in 48
entremedi-ar 1
entremes-ar 1
entremese-ar ... 1
entremet-er 2
entremezcl-ar ... 1
entremor-ir 31,
  except the
  past participle
  is entremuerto
entremostr-
  ar 25
entren-ar 1
entrenc-ar 67
entrenz-ar 21
entreo-ír 49
entreparec-
  erse 48
entrepel-ar 1
entrepern-ar 53
entrepon-er 57
entrepunz-ar 21
entrerrenglon-
  ar 1
entrerromp-er ... 2
entresac-ar 67
entretall-ar 1
entretej-er 2
entretel-ar 1
entreten-er 74
entretom-ar 1
entreunt-ar 1
entrev-ar 1
entreven-
  arse 80
entreven-ir 77
entrev-er 78
entrever-ar 1
entrevig-ar 51

entrevist-ar 1
entrevolv-er
47, except
the past par-
ticiple is
entrevuelto
entreyac-er 79
entric-ar 67
entrill-ar 1
entrip-ar 1
entriparr-ar 1
entrist-ar 1
entristec-er 48
entriz-ar 21
entroj-ar 1
entromet-er 2
entromp-arse ... 80
entrompet-ar 1
entron-ar 1
entronc-ar 67
entronec-er 48
entroner-ar 1
entroniz-ar 21
entropez-ar 53
entropill-ar 1
entrot-arse 80
entruch-ar 1
entruj-ar 1
entubaj-ar 1
entub-ar 1
entuf-arse 80
entullec-er 48
entumec-er 48
entum-irse 82
entun-ar 1
entun-arse 80
entunic-ar 67
entuñ-arse 80
entup-ir 3
entur-ar 1
enturbi-ar 1
enturron-
arse 80
entus-arse 80
entusiasm-ar 1
entutum-arse ... 80
enucle-ar 1
enumer-ar 1
enunci-ar 1
envac-ar 67
envacun-ar 1

envagar-ar 1
envagon-ar 1
envagr-ar 1
envain-ar 1
envalent-ar 1
envalenton-ar ... 1
envalij-ar 1
envallic-ar 67
envanec-er 48
envar-ar 1
envarbasc-ar ... 67
envareng-ar 1
envaresc-er 2
envarill-ar 1
envaron-ar 1
envas-ar 1
envasij-ar 1
envedij-arse 80
enveg-ar 51
enveg-arse 51
envejec-er 48
envel-ar 1
envellon-ar 1
envend-ar 1
envenen-ar 1
envener-ar 1
enver-ar 1
enverbasc-ar ... 67
enverdec-er 48
enverdin-ar 1
enverd-ir 3
enverdug-ar 1
envered-ar 1
enverg-ar 51
envergonz-ar ... 21
envern-ar 53
enves-ar 1
envest-ir 52
envet-arse 80
enviaj-arse 80
envi-ar 9
envici-ar 1
envicios-arse ... 80
envid-ar 1
envidi-ar 1
envidr-ar 1
enviej-ar 1
envig-ar 51
envigoriz-ar 21
envigot-ar 1
envilec-er 48

envilort-ar 1
envinagr-ar 1
envin-ar 1
envir-ar 1
envisc-ar 67
enviud-ar 1
envolat-ar 1
envolat-arse 80
envolc-arse
80, with the
changes in ... 25
envolv-er 47,
except the
past participle
is envuelto
enyerb-ar 1
enyert-ar 1
enyertec-
erse 48
enyes-ar 1
enyesc-arse 80
enyet-ar 1
enyod-ar 1
enyug-ar 51
enyunt-ar 1
enyuy-arse 80
enzacat-arse ... 80
enzain-arse 9
enzalam-ar 1
enzamarr-ar 1
enzanjon-
arse 80
enzapat-ar 1
enzapat-arse ... 80
enzarz-ar 21
enzocal-ar 1
enzoc-ar 67
enzolv-ar 1
enzoquet-ar 1
enzorr-ar 1
enzulac-ar 1
enzunch-ar 1
enzurdec-er 48
enzuriz-ar 21
enzurron-ar 1
enzurron-
arse 80
epat-ar 1
epigramatiz-
ar 21
epilog-ar 51

epiteliz-ar 1
epitim-ar 1
epitom-ar 1
equidist-ar 1
equilibr-ar 1
equip-ar 1
equipar-ar 1
equiponder-ar ... 1
equival-er 2,
with the
changes in 68
equivoc-ar 67
er-ar 1
ergote-ar 1
ergotiz-ar 21
ergu-ir 36
ergull-ir 17
erig-ir 3, with
the changes
in 23
erisipel-ar 1
eriz-ar 21
erm-ar 1
erog-ar 51
erosion-ar 1
erradic-ar 67
err-ar 37
eruct-ar 1
erut-ar 1
esbagañ-ar 1
esbag-ar 1
esbar-ar 1
esbariz-ar 21
esbatiment-ar ... 1
esbinz-ar 21
esblandec-er 48
esbland-ir 3
esblenc-ar 67
esbog-ar 1
esborreg-ar 51
esboz-ar 21
esbrenc-ar 67
esbrind-arse 80
escabech-ar 1
escabrose-
arse 80
escabuch-ar 1
escabull-ar 1
escabull-ir 17
escach-ar 1
escacharr-ar 1

escachifoll-ar 1
escachifull-ar 1
escaec-er 48
escafil-ar 1
escagarruz-
arse 21
escalabr-ar 1
escal-ar 1
escald-ar 1
escalduf-ar 1
escalec-er 48
escalent-ar 53
escalf-ar 1
escalfec-erse .. 48
escali-ar 1
escalib-ar 1
escalim-arse 80
escalofri-ar 9
escalon-ar 1
escalp-ar 1
escam-ar 1
escamoch-ar 1
escamoche-ar .. 1
escamond-ar 1
escamone-
arse 80
escamot-ar 1
escamote-ar 1
escamp-ar 1,
and for its use
regarding
weather,
see 45
escamuj-ar 1
escanci-ar 1
escandal-ar 1
escandale-ar 1
escandaliz-
ar 21
escandall-ar 1
escandec-er 48
escand-ir 3
escant-ar 1
escantill-ar 1
escañ-arse 80
escap-ar 1
escape-ar 1
escapol-ar 1
escapol-arse 80
escapul-ar 1
escaque-ar 1

escarabaje-ar ... 1
escaramuce-
ar 1
escaramuz-
ar 21
escarapel-ar 1
escarb-ar 1
escarce-ar 1
escarch-ar 1,
and for its
use regarding
weather,
see 45
escarchill-ar 1
escarcuñ-ar 1
escard-ar 1
escardill-ar 1
escare-arse 80
escari-ar 1
escarific-ar 67
escariz-ar 21
escarmen-ar 1
escarment-ar ... 53
escarn-ar 1
escarnec-er 48
escarn-ir 3,
with the
changes in 48
escarol-ar 1
escarp-ar 1
escarpel-ar 1
escarpen-ar 1
escarpi-ar 1
escarram-ar 1
escarranch-
arse 80
escarrañ-ar 1
escarz-ar 21
escase-ar 1
escatim-ar 1
escavan-ar 1
escav-ar 1
escayol-ar 1
escenific-ar 67
escet-ar 1
eschang-ar 1
escharch-ar 1
escib-ar 1
escind-ir 3
escintil-ar 1
esclaf-ar 1

esclar-ar 1
esclarec-er 48
esclavit-ar 1
esclaviz-ar 21
escleros-ar 1
escobaj-ar 1
escob-ar 1
escobaz-ar 21
escobete-ar 1
escobill-ar 1
escobille-ar 1
escoc-ar 67
escoc-er 22
escocher-ar 1
escochifl-ar 1
escochiz-ar 21
escod-ar 1
escofi-ar 1
escofin-ar 1
escog-er 23
escol-ar 25
escolare-ar 1
escolariz-ar 21
escoli-ar 1
escoll-ar 1
escolt-ar 1
escom-ar 1
escombr-ar 1
escome-arse ... 80
escomenz-ar ... 21
escom-erse 81
escond-er 2
esconz-ar 21
escopet-ar 1
escopete-ar 1
escople-ar 1
escor-ar 1
escorch-ar 1
escori-ar 1
escorific-ar 67
escor-ir 3
escorr-er 2
escorromp-er 2
escorrot-arse ... 80
escorz-ar 21
escos-ar 1
escosc-ar 67
escot-ar 1
escotorr-ar 1
escoz-arse 21
escrach-ar 1

escrib-ir 3,
except the
past partici-
ple is escrito
escriptur-ar 1
escritur-ar 1
escrudiñ-ar 1
escrupule-ar 1
escrupuliz-ar ... 21
escrut-ar 1
escuadr-ar 1
escuadron-ar 1
escuadrone-ar .. 1
escuajering-
arse 77
escuch-ar 1
escuchimiz-
ar 21
escud-ar 1
escudere-ar 1
escudill-ar 1
escudriñ-ar 1
escuezn-ar 1
esculc-ar 67
escull-ar 1
escull-ir 3
esculp-ir 3
escultur-ar 1
escup-ir 3
escur-ar 1
escurc-ar 1
escurec-er 48
escurific-ar 1
escurr-ir 3
esdrujuliz-ar 21
esenci-arse 80
esfacel-ar 1
esfarrap-ar 1
esflec-ar 1
esfog-ar 1
esfol-ar 1
esfoll-ar 1
esfornecin-ar ... 1
esforrocin-ar 1
esforz-ar 69
esfoy-ar 1
esfri-ar 1
esfum-ar 1
esfumin-ar 1
esgarabot-ar 1
esgarr-ar 1

esgatiñ-arse 80
esgoard-ar 1
esgoliz-arse 21
esgonz-ar 21
esgrafi-ar 9
esgrim-ir 3
esguardamill-
   ar 1
esguard-ar 1
esguaz-ar 21
esguil-ar 1
esgurrumb-ar ... 1
eslabon-ar 1
eslaviz-ar 21
esle-er 2
esle-ír 3
eslembr-arse ... 80
esling-ar 51
esmalt-ar 1
esmechud-ar 1
esmer-ar 1
esmeril-ar 1
esmirri-arse 80
esmong-ar 1
esmonguill-ar ... 1
esmorec-er 48
esmorus-
   arse 80
esmuci-arse 80
esmu-ir 42
esmuñ-ir 17
espabil-ar 1
espachurr-ar 1
espaci-ar 1
espadañ-ar 1
espad-ar 1
espadill-ar 1
espaladin-ar 1
espal-ar 1
espald-ar 1
espald-arse 80
espalde-ar 1
espaldill-ar 1
espaldon-ar 1
espaldon-
   arse 80
espaletill-ar 1
espalm-ar 1
espanc-irse
   82, with the
   changes in 23

espand-ir 3
espand-irse 82
espant-ar 1
español-ar 1
españole-ar 1
españoliz-ar 21
esparc-ir 3,
   with the
   changes in 23
esparrag-ar 51
esparram-ar 1
esparranc-
   arse 67
esparru-ar 1
espart-ar 1
esparv-ar 1
espasm-ar 1
espatan-arse ... 80
espatarr-arse ... 80
espaturr-ar 1
espavil-ar 1
espavoriz-
   arse 21
espech-ar 1
especializ-ar 21
especi-ar 1
especific-ar 67
espect-ar 1
especul-ar 1
espedaz-ar 21
esped-irse 52
espej-ar 1
espeje-ar 1
espelot-arse 80
espeluc-ar 67
espelusc-ar 1
espeluz-ar 21
espeluzn-ar 1
esperanz-ar 21
esper-ar 1
esperdec-ir 3,
   with the
   changes in 23
esperec-er 48
esperez-arse ... 21
espergur-ar 1
espernanc-
   arse 67
esperri-ar 1
espert-ar 1
espes-ar 1

espet-ar 1
espiant-ar 1
espi-ar 9
espich-ar 1
espiche-ar 1
espig-ar 51
espigue-ar 1
espill-ar 1
espin-ar 1
espinoch-ar 1
espinz-ar 21
espion-ar 1
espir-ar 1
espirit-ar 1
espiritualiz-
   ar 21
espit-ar 1
esplend-er 2
esplendor-ar 1
esplendore-ar ... 1
espole-ar 1
espoli-ar 1
espolin-ar 1
espolone-ar 1
espols-ar 1
espolvor-ar 1
espolvore-ar 1
espolvoriz-ar ... 21
esponj-ar 1
esponje-ar 1
espontane-
   arse 80
esporg-ar 1
esporrondig-
   arse 51
esporronding-
   arse 51
esporte-ar 1
espos-ar 1
espret-ar 1
esprete-ar 1
esprint-ar 1
espuel-ar 1
espuele-ar 1
espulg-ar 51
espul-irse 82
espumaj-ar 1
espumaje-ar 1
espum-ar 1
espumaraje-ar .. 1
espurre-ar 1

espurri-ar 9
espurr-ir 3
esput-ar 1
esquebraj-ar 1
esquej-ar 1
esquelet-ar 1
esqueletiz-ar 21
esquematiz-
   ar 21
esqui-ar 9
esquici-ar 1
esquif-ar 1
esquil-ar 1
esquilm-ar 1
esquin-ar 1
esquinz-ar 21
esquip-ar 1
esquis-ar 1
esquit-ar 1
esquiv-ar 1
estabil-ir 21
estabiliz-ar 21
estable-ar 1
establec-er 48
establ-ir 67
estabul-ar 1
estac-ar 67
estacion-ar 1
estaf-ar 1
estaj-ar 1
estaje-ar 1
estall-ar 1
estambr-ar 1
estamp-ar 1
estampill-ar 1
estanc-ar 67
estandardiz-
   ar 21
estandariz-ar ... 21
estandartiz-
   ar 21
estantal-ar 1
estantill-ar 1
estañ-ar 1
estaque-ar 1
estaquill-ar 1
est-ar 38
estarcicopi-ar ... 1
estarcigrafi-ar ... 1
estarc-ir 3,
   with the

changes in 23
estatific-ar 67
estatiz-ar 21
estatu-ar 9
estatu-ir 42
estay-ar 1
estaz-ar 1
esteb-ar 1
estecl-ar 1
estem-ar 1
estenografi-ar ... 9
estenotipi-ar 1
ester-ar 1
esterc-ar 67
estercol-ar 1
estereotip-ar 1
esterific-ar 67
esteriliz-ar 21
esterill-ar 1
esteriz-ar 1
estez-ar 21
estib-ar 1
estigmatiz-ar ... 21
estil-ar 1
estiliz-ar 21
estill-ar 1
estim-ar 1
estimul-ar 1
estiomen-ar 1
estipendi-ar 1
estiptic-ar 67
estipul-ar 1
estirace-ar 1
estiraj-ar 1
estiraje-ar 1
estir-ar 1
estiraz-ar 21
estirone-ar 1
estiv-ar 1
esto-ar 1
estoc-ar 67
estof-ar 1
estoj-ar 1
estomag-ar 51
estope-ar 1
estoque-ar 1
estorb-ar 1
estorc-er 22
estord-ir 3
estornud-ar 1
estovainiz-ar 21

estov-ar 1
estoz-ar 21
estozol-ar 1
estrag-ar 51
estragol-ar 1
estrall-ar 1
estrangul-ar 1
estrapaj-ar 1
estraperle-ar 1
estrasij-arse 80
estratific-ar 4
estraz-ar 21
estrech-ar 1
estreg-ar 62
estrell-ar 1
estremec-er 48
estren-ar 1
estreñ-ir 64
estrepit-arse ... 80
estri-ar 9
estrib-ar 1
estric-arse 80
estricniz-ar 21
estricul-ar 1
estridul-ar 1
estrig-ar 1
estril-ar 1
estrill-ar 1
estropaje-ar 1
estrope-ar 1
estropez-ar 21
estructur-ar 1
estru-ir 42
estruj-ar 1
estrump-ir 3
estrup-ar 1
estuc-ar 67
estuch-ar 1
estudi-ar 1
estuf-ar 1
estupr-ar 1
estur-ar 1
esturdec-er 48
esturg-ar 51
esturre-ar 1
estus-ar 1
esug-ar 1
esvar-ar 1
etaling-ar 1
eterific-ar 67
eteriz-ar 21

eterniz-ar 21
etic-arse 80
etimologiz-ar ... 21
etiquet-ar 1
eufoniz-ar 21
europeiz-ar 35
evacu-ar 1
evad-ir 3
evalu-ar 9
evangeliz-ar 21
evapor-ar 1
evaporiz-ar 21
even-ir 77
evidenci-ar 1
eviscer-ar 1
evit-ar 1
evoc-ar 67
evol-ar 25
evolucion-ar 1
exacerb-ar 1
exager-ar 1
exalt-ar 1
exalz-ar 21
examin-ar 1
exardec-er 48
exasper-ar 1
exaud-ir 3
excandec-er 1
excarcel-ar 1
excardin-ar 1
excav-ar 1
exced-er 2
excepcion-ar 1
except-ar 1
exceptu-ar 9
excit-ar 1
exclam-ar 1
exclaustr-ar 1
exclu-ir 42,
   plus the
   past participle
   excluso
excogit-ar 1
excomulg-ar 51
excori-ar 1
excorpor-ar 1
excrement-ar 1
excret-ar 1
exculp-ar 1
excursion-ar 1
excus-ar 1

execr-ar 1
exencion-ar 1
exent-ar 1
exfoli-ar 1
exhal-ar 1
exhaust-ar 1
exhered-ar 1
exhib-ir 3
exhort-ar 1
exhum-ar 1
exifore-ar 1
exig-ir 3, with
   the changes
   in 16 and 7
exil-ar 1
exili-ar 1
exim-ir 3, plus
   the past parti-
   ciple exento
ex-ir 3
existim-ar 1
exist-ir 3
exond-ar 1
exoner-ar 1
exor-ar 1
exorciz-ar 21
exordi-ar 1
exord-ir 3
exorn-ar 1
expanc-irse
   82, with the
   changes in 46
expand-ir 3
expansion-
   arse 80
expatri-arse 9
expavec-er 48
expector-ar 1
expedient-ar 1
exped-ir 52
expedit-ar 1
expel-er 2, plus
   the past parti-
   ciple expulso
expend-er 2
expens-ar 1
experiment-ar ... 1
expi-ar 9
expil-ar 1
expir-ar 1
explan-ar 1

explay-ar 1
explic-ar 67
explicote-ar 1
explicote-
  arse 80
explor-ar 1
explosion-ar 1
explot-ar 1
expoli-ar 1
expon-er 57
export-ar 1
exprem-ir 3
expres-ar 1,
  plus the past
  participle
  expreso
exprim-ir 3
expropi-ar 1
expugn-ar 1
expuls-ar 1
expurg-ar 51
exquir-ir 3
exsud-ar 1
extasi-arse 9
extend-er 2,
  with the
  changes in
  53, plus the
  past participle
  extenso
extenu-ar 9
exterioriz-ar 21
extermin-ar 1
extern-ar 1
extingu-ir 30,
  plus the past
  participle
  extinto
extirp-ar 1
extorc-ar 1
extorn-ar 1
extorsion-ar 1
extract-ar 1
extra-er 75
extralimit-ar 1
extralimit-
  arse 80
extranjeriz-ar ... 21
extrañ-ar 1
extrapol-ar 1
extravag-ar 51

extravas-
  arse 80
extraven-ar 1
extravi-ar 9
extrem-ar 1
extrud-ir 3
extub-ar 1
exturb-ar 1
exuber-ar 1
exud-ar 1
exulcer-ar 1
exult-ar 1
exund-ar 1
exvincul-ar 1
eyacul-ar 1
eyect-ar 1
ezquerde-ar 1

f

fabe-ar 1
fabl-ar 1
fablistane-ar 1
fabric-ar 67
fabul-ar 1
fabuliz-ar 21
faccion-ar 1
fac-er 41
facer-ir 71
facet-ar 1
facete-ar 1
fache-ar 1
fachende-ar 1
fachose-ar 1
facilit-ar 1
factoriz-ar 21
factur-ar 1
facult-ar 1
fad-ar 1
fadig-ar 51
faen-ar 1
fafarach-ar 1
fagocit-ar 1
faite-ar 1
faj-ar 1
faje-ar 1
falag-ar 1
fal-ar 1
falcace-ar 1
falc-ar 67

falcaz-ar 1
falde-ar 1
falesc-er 2
fal-ir 3
fall-ar 1
fallec-er 48
fall-ir 3
fals-ar 1
false-ar 1
falsific-ar 67
falt-ar 1
familiariz-ar 21
fanatiz-ar 21
fandangue-ar 1
fanfarre-ar 1
fanfarrone-ar 1
fantase-ar 1
fantastic-ar 1
farabuste-ar 1
farach-ar 1
faradiz-ar 21
faramalle-ar 1
farandule-ar 1
farangue-ar 1
fard-ar 1
farfalle-ar 1
farfull-ar 1
farole-ar 1
farote-ar 1
farre-ar 1
farsante-ar 1
fars-ar 1
farse-ar 1
fart-ar 1
fascin-ar 1
fasqui-ar 1
fastidi-ar 1
fataliz-ar 1
fatig-ar 51
favorec-er 48
fech-ar 1
fecund-ar 1
fecundiz-ar 21
fedeg-ar 51
federaliz-ar 21
feder-ar 1
felicit-ar 1
felp-ar 1
felpe-ar 1
fem-ar 53

femenci-ar 1
feminiz-ar 1
fench-ir 52
fend-er 2, with
  the changes
  in 53
fenec-er 48
fenic-ar 67
fenol-ar 1
feri-ar 1
fer-ir 71
ferm-ar 1
ferment-ar 1
ferr-ar 53
ferret-ar 1
ferric-arse 80
ferroj-ar 1
fertiliz-ar 21
ferv-ir 71
fervor-ar 1
feste-ar 1
festej-ar 1
festin-ar 1
feston-ar 1
feud-ar 1
fiambr-ar 1
fi-ar 9
fic-ar 1
fich-ar 1
fieltr-ar 1
fieste-ar 1
fig-ar 1
figur-ar 1
fij-ar 1, plus
  the past
  participle fijo
fil-ar 1
filete-ar 1
fili-ar 1
filosof-ar 1
filosofe-ar 1
filote-ar 1
filtr-ar 1
finaliz-ar 1
financi-ar 1
fin-ar 1
finc-ar 1
finch-ar 1
fing-ir 3, with
  the changes
  in 23, plus the

past participle
ficto
finiquit-ar 1
fin-ir 3
finte-ar 1
firm-ar 1
fiscale-ar 1
fiscaliz-ar 21
fisg-ar 1
fisgone-ar 1
fision-ar 1
fisique-ar 1
fistol-ar 1
fistul-ar 1
fiuci-ar 1
fiz-ar 21
flage-ar 1
flagel-ar 1
flagr-ar 1
flame-ar 1
flane-ar 1
flanque-ar 1
flaque-ar 1
flaquec-er 48
flaute-ar 1
flebotom-ar 1
flec-ar 1
flech-ar 1
flet-ar 1
flete-ar 1
flexion-ar 1
flirte-ar 1
flocul-ar 1
floje-ar 1
flor-ar 1
flordeliz-ar 21
flore-ar 1
florec-er 48
floresc-er 48
florete-ar 1
florlis-ar 1
flot-ar 1
flote-ar 1
fluctu-ar 9
fluidific-ar 67
flu-ir 42
foc-ar 1
fogare-ar 1
fogariz-ar 21
fogone-ar 1
fogue-ar 1

foguere-ar 1
fo-ir 42
foje-ar 1
folg-ar 25
foli-ar 1
follaje-ar 1
foll-ar 1,
 and alter-
 natively, ... 25
follone-arse 80
foment-ar 1
fonde-ar 1
fonde-arse 80
fond-irse 82
fonografi-ar 1
forad-ar 1
forajit-ar 1
forcate-ar 1
force-ar 1
forcej-ar 1
forceje-ar 1
forci-ar 1
forc-ir 31,
 plus the
 changes in 23
forest-ar 1
forig-ar 51
forj-ar 1
formaliz-ar 21
form-ar 1
formej-ar 1
formid-ar 1
formul-ar 1
fornec-er 48
fornic-ar 67
forn-ir 3
forraje-ar 1
forr-ar 1
fortalec-er 48
fortific-ar 67
fortun-ar 1
forz-ar 39
fos-ar 1
fose-ar 1
fosfat-ar 1
fosfor-ar 1
fosforec-er 48
fosfored-er 48
fosforesc-er 48
fosiliz-arse 21
fotocopi-ar 1

fotograb-ar 1
fotografi-ar 9
fotolitografi-ar ... 9
fotosensibiliz-
 ar 21
fotute-ar 1
fracas-ar 1
fraccion-ar 1
fractur-ar 1
frad-ar 1
fragment-ar 1
fragu-ar 7
frail-ar 1
fraile-ar 1
frair-ar 1
frange-ar 1
frang-ir 3,
 with the
 changes in 23
frangoll-ar 1
franj-ar 1
franje-ar 1
franque-ar 1
frañ-er 2,
 with the
 changes in 17
frase-ar 1
frasqui-ar 1
fratas-ar 1
fraten-ar 1
fraterniz-ar 21
frates-ar 1
fraud-ar 1
frecuent-ar 1
freg-ar 62
fregote-ar 1
freil-ar 1
fre-ír 63, plus
 past partici-
 ple frito that is
 used more
 commonly
 than the
 regular past
 participle
freit-ar 1
fren-ar 1
frenill-ar 1
fres-ar 1
fresque-ar 1
fresz-ar 21

fret-ar 1
frez-ar 21
fric-ar 67
friccion-ar 1
frigorific-ar 67
frigoriz-ar 21
frijole-ar 1
frijoliz-ar 21
fringole-ar 1
fris-ar 1
frit-ar 1
frochigu-ar 1
frog-ar 1
frondose-ar 1
frot-ar 1
fructific-ar 67
fru-ir 42
frunc-ir 3,
 with the
 changes in 23
fruñ-ir 17
frustr-ar 1
frut-ar 1
frute-ar 1
frutec-er 48
frutofic-ar 1
fucil-ar 1, and
 for its use
 regarding
 weather,
 see 45
fuell-ar 1
fuete-ar 1
fuf-ar 1
fug-ar 1
fug-arse 51
fulc-ir 3, with
 the changes
 in 23
fulg-ir 3, with
 the changes
 in 53 and 23
fulgur-ar 1
fulgurec-er 48
fulle-ar 1
fullere-ar 1
fulmin-ar 1
fum-ar 1
fume-ar 1
fumig-ar 51
funcion-ar 1

fundament-ar 1
fund-ar 1
fundibul-ar 1
fund-ir 3
funest-ar 1
fung-ar 51
fung-ir 3, with
  the changes
  in 23
fuñ-ar 1
fuñic-ar 67
furt-ar 1
fusc-ar 1
fusil-ar 1
fusion-ar 1
fustane-ar 1
fustig-ar 51
fute-arse 80
fut-irse 82
futr-arse 80
futr-ir 3
futute-ar 1
futute-arse 80

g

gabane-ar 1
gab-arse 80
gabe-ar 1
gaf-ar 1
gafe-arse 80
gague-ar 1
gaj-ar 1
galante-ar 1
galardon-ar 1
galgu-ar 1
galgue-ar 1
galib-ar 1
galim-ar 1
gall-ar 1
gallarde-ar 1
galle-ar 1
gallete-ar 1
gallof-ar 1
gallofe-ar 1
galone-ar 1
galop-ar 1
galope-ar 1
galuch-ar 1
galvaniz-ar 21

galvanotip-ar 1
gambete-ar 1
gambi-ar 1
gamit-ar 1
gamite-ar 1
gamone-ar 1
ganade-ar 1
gan-ar 1
gand-ir 3
ganduj-ar 1
gandule-ar 1
gangose-ar 1
gangue-ar 1
ganse-ar 1
ganzu-ar 9
gañ-ir 17
gapale-ar 1
garab-ar 1
garabate-ar 1
garafate-ar 1
garafete-ar 1
garand-ar 1
garant-ir 4
garantiz-ar 21
garapiñ-ar 1
gar-ar 1
garate-ar 1
garb-ar 1
garbe-ar 1
garbill-ar 1
garce-ar 1
gard-ar 1
garete-ar 1
garfe-ar 1
garfiñ-ar 1
gargaje-ar 1
gargaliz-ar 21
gargante-ar 1
gargare-ar 1
gargariz-ar 21
garimp-ar 1
garite-ar 1
garl-ar 1
garle-ar 1
garliborle-ar 1
garnache-ar 1
garrafiñ-ar 1
garram-ar 1
garranch-ar 1
garrapate-ar 1

garrapiñ-ar 1
garr-ar 1
garrasp-ar 1
garre-ar 1
garr-ir 3
garroch-ar 1
garroche-ar 1
garrone-ar 1
garrote-ar 1
garruche-ar 1
garrul-ar 1
garsin-ar 1
garu-ar 9, and
  for its use
  regarding
  weather,
  see 45
garub-ar 1
garufe-ar 1
garug-ar 51,
  and used in
  the positions
  in 45
gasaj-ar 1
gasaj-arse 80
gasconiz-ar 21
gase-ar 1
gasific-ar 67
gasnache-ar 1
gaspale-ar 1
gast-ar 1
gate-ar 1
gatuñ-ar 1
gauch-ar 1
gauche-ar 1
gavi-ar 1
gavill-ar 1
gay-ar 1
gazmi-ar 1
gazn-ar 1
gaznate-ar 1
gelatinific-ar 1
gelatiniz-ar 21
gelific-ar 67
gemific-ar 67
gemin-ar 1
gemique-ar 1
gem-ir 52
generaliz-ar 21
gener-ar 1
gentiliz-ar 21

germaniz-ar 21
germific-ar 1
germin-ar 1
gerundi-ar 1
gest-ar 1
geste-ar 1
gesticul-ar 1
gestion-ar 1
get-ar 1
gib-ar 1
gigantiz-ar 21
gigue-ar 1
gilipolle-ar 1
gimoque-ar 1
gimote-ar 1
gimpl-ar 1
gingl-ar 1
gingr-ar 1
gir-ar 1
giron-ar 1
gitane-ar 1
glase-ar 1
glicer-ar 1
glicerin-ar 1
glori-ar 9
glorific-ar 67
glos-ar 1
glotone-ar 1
gluglute-ar 1
glutin-ar 1
gobern-ar 53
gofr-ar 1
golde-ar 1
gole-ar 1
golfe-ar 1
golill-ar 1
gollete-ar 1
golmaje-ar 1
golose-ar 1
golosin-ar 1
golosine-ar 1
golosme-ar 1
golpe-ar 1
golpete-ar 1
golusme-ar 1
gom-ar 1
gomorriz-ar 1
gonce-ar 1
gongoriz-ar 21
goñe-ar 1
gorbete-ar 1

gore-arse 80
gorgoj-arse 80
gorgoje-arse 80
gorgore-ar 1
gorgorite-ar 1
gorgote-ar 1
gorgue-ar 1
gorje-ar 1
gorm-ar 1
gorre-ar 1
gorrone-ar 1
goruchone-ar 1
gote-ar 1, and
  for its use
  regarding
  weather,
  see 45
gotere-ar 1,
  and used in
  the positions
  in 45
goz-ar 21
grab-ar 1
gracej-ar 1
grac-ir 3, with
  the changes
  in 23
grad-ar 1
grade-ar 1
gradec-er 48
gradu-ar 9
grafil-ar 1
graje-ar 1
gram-ar 1
gramatiqu-er 2
granall-ar 1
gran-ar 1
grandec-er 48
grandifac-er 69
grandison-ar 25
grane-ar 1
granel-ar 1
graniz-ar 21,
  and for its use
  regarding
  weather,
  see 45
granje-ar 1
granul-ar 1
grañ-ir 17
grap-ar 1

gras-ar 1
grasin-ar 1
grat-ar 1
gratific-ar 67
gratin-ar 1
gratul-ar 1
grav-ar 1
grave-ar 1
gravit-ar 1
gray-ar 1
grazn-ar 1
grazne-ar 1
grec-ar 67
greciz-ar 21
gregaliz-ar 21
greguiz-ar 21
grete-ar 1
grib-ar 1
grid-ar 1
griet-ar 1
griet-arse 80
griete-arse 80
grif-arse 80
grill-ar 1
grill-arse 80
grillote-ar 1
grip-ar 1
gris-ar 1
grise-ar 1
grit-ar 1
gritone-ar 1
groaj-ar 1
gro-ar 1
groje-ar 1
gru-ar 9
gru-ir 42
gruj-ir 3
gruñ-ir 17
grupe-ar 1
guabine-ar 1
guacale-ar 1
guacamole-ar ... 1
guachache-ar ... 1
guachape-ar 1
guachaque-ar ... 1
guach-ar 1
guache-ar 1
guachi-ar 1
guachific-ar 1
guachine-ar 1
guadañ-ar 1

guadañe-ar 1
guaguare-ar 1
guaguate-ar 1
guaic-ar 1
guaique-ar 1
guait-ar 1
guaje-ar 1
gualambe-ar 1
gualardon-ar 1
gualdrape-ar 1
gualtrape-ar 1
guambi-ar 1
guame-ar 1
guanaque-ar 1
guanchaque-
  ar 1
guane-ar 1
guangue-ar 1
guante-ar 1
guantone-ar 1
guañ-ir 17
guape-ar 1
guaque-ar 1
guarache-ar 1
guarangue-ar 1
guarape-ar 1
guaraque-ar 1
guard-ar 1
guardarray-ar ... 1
guare-ar 1
guare-arse 80
guarec-er 48
guaresc-er 48
guaric-arse 80
guar-ir 3
guarism-ar 1
guarnec-er 48
guarnicion-ar 1
guarn-ir 4
guarre-ar 1
guarrey-ar 1
guase-arse 80
guasque-ar 1
guast-ar 1
guataque-ar 1
guate-ar 1
guate-arse 80
guatele-ar 1
guateque-ar 1
guatrape-ar 1
guayabe-ar 1

guay-ar 1
guayuque-ar 1
gubern-ar 1
guedej-ar 1
güelde-ar 1
guerre-ar 1
guerrile-ar 1
guerrille-ar 1
gui-ar 9
guid-ar 1
guillab-ar 1
guill-arse 80
guillotin-ar 1
guinch-ar 1
guind-ar 1
guiñ-ar 1
guiñe-ar 1
guip-ar 1
guirpiñ-ar 1
guis-ar 1
guisote-ar 1
guit-ar 1
guitarre-ar 1
guitone-ar 1
guizc-ar 67
guizg-ar 51
guizn-ar 1
gulusme-ar 1
gur-ar 1
gurbe-ar 1
gurguci-ar 1
gurr-ar 1
gurrubuce-ar 1
gurruñ-ar 1
gurrupe-ar 1
gusane-ar 1
gust-ar 1
guturaliz-ar 21
guzgue-ar 1

h

hab-ar 1
hab-er 40
habilit-ar 1
habit-ar 1
habitu-ar 9
habl-ar 1
hacend-ar 53
hac-er 41

hacer-ir 71
hach-ar 1
hache-ar 1
hacin-ar 1
had-ar 1
halag-ar 67
hal-ar 1
halcone-ar 1
halde-ar 1
hall-ar 1
hamac-ar 67
hamaque-ar 1
hambre-ar 1
handicap-ar 1
haragane-ar 1
harb-ar 1
harbull-ar 1
hargane-ar 1
harine-ar 1
harisc-arse 67
harmoniz-ar 21
harne-ar 1
harone-ar 1
harp-ar 1
harre-ar 1
hart-ar 1, plus
   the past parti-
   ciple harto
hasti-ar 9
hataj-ar 1
hate-ar 1
hazan-ar 1
hazañ-ar 1
hebet-ar 1
hebill-ar 1
hebraiz-ar 35
hechiz-ar 21
hed-er 2, with
   the changes
   in 53
hedr-ar 1
hel-ar 53, and
   for its use
   regarding
   weather,
   see 45
hele-ar 1
helenistiz-ar 21
heleniz-ar 21
helitransport-
   ar 1

hembre-ar 1
hembrimach-
   ar 1
hemenci-ar 1
hemoliz-ar 21
hench-ir 52
hend-er 2,
   with the
   changes in 53
hend-ir 3,
   with the
   changes in 53
hene-ar 1
henific-ar 67
heñ-ir 64
hepariniz-ar 21
hepatiz-arse 80
herbaj-ar 1
herbaje-ar 1
herbal-ar 1
herb-ar 53
herbec-er 48
herbol-ar 1
herbolec-er 48
herboliz-ar 21
herboriz-ar 21
hered-ar 1
heretic-ar 1
heretiz-ar 21
her-ir 71
herman-ar 1
hermand-
   arse 80
hermane-ar 1
hermanec-er 48
hermose-ar 1
heroific-ar 1
herr-ar 53
herren-ar 1
herrene-ar 1
herrete-ar 1
herrumbr-ar 1
hervent-ar 53
herv-ir 71
hervoriz-arse ... 80
hesit-ar 1
hesp-irse 52
het-ar 1
heterodin-ar 1
hetic-arse 67
hibern-ar 1

hibiern-ar 1
hibometr-ar 1
hidrat-ar 1
hidrofug-ar 1
hidrogen-ar 1
hidroliz-ar 21
hidropic-arse ... 67
hidrosulfur-ar ... 1
hidroxil-ar 1
hidroxiliz-ar 21
hierbe-ar 1
higad-ar 1
higar-ar 1
higieniz-ar 21
hije-ar 1
hijuel-ar 1
hil-ar 1
hilvan-ar 1
himp-ar 1
himpl-ar 1
hinc-ar 67
hinch-ar 1
hinch-ir 52
hinoj-ar 1
hip-ar 1
hipe-ar 1
hiperboliz-ar ... 21
hiperestesi-ar ... 1
hiperovariz-
   ar 21
hipertrofi-ar 9
hipertrofi-
   arse 80
hipnotiz-ar 21
hiposteniz-ar ... 21
hipotec-ar 67
hipovariz-ar 21
hirm-ar 1
hirudiniz-ar 21
hiscal-ar 1
hisop-ar 1
hisope-ar 1
hispaniz-ar 21
hisp-ir 3
histori-ar 1
hit-ar 1
hocic-ar 67
hocique-ar 1
hog-ar 1
hojaldr-ar 1
hoje-ar 1

hojec-er 48
holandiz-ar 21
hole-ar 1
holg-ar 24
holgazane-ar 1
holgaz-ar 21
holl-ar 25
hollin-ar 1
holocaustiz-
   ar 21
hombre-ar 1
homenaje-ar 1
homici-arse 80
homogeneiz-
   ar 21
homogeniz-
   ar 21
homolog-ar 51
hond-ar 1
honde-ar 1
hondi-ar 1
hondon-ar 1
honest-ar 1
honor-ar 1
honorific-ar 67
honr-ar 1
hop-arse 80
hope-ar 1
horac-ar 1
horad-ar 1
horc-ar 67
horm-ar 1
hormej-ar 1
hormigue-ar 1
hormiguill-ar 1
hornague-ar 1
horne-ar 1
hornegue-ar 1
horquete-ar 1
horquill-ar 1
horr-ar 1
horre-ar 1
horrific-ar 67
horripil-ar 1
horroriz-ar 21
hosped-ar 1
hospitaliz-ar 21
hostig-ar 51
hostiliz-ar 21
hoy-ar 1
hoz-ar 21

huachafe-ar 1
huachape-ar 1
huach-ar 1
huaque-ar 1
huarac-ar 1
huaripampe-ar .. 1
huasque-ar 1
huate-ar 1
huate-arse 80
huche-ar 1
huelgue-ar 1
hueric-arse 80
huese-ar 1
hueste-ar 1
huev-ar 1
hueve-ar 1
huevi-ar 1
huilc-ar 1
huinch-arse 80
hu-ir 42
huisach-ar 1
huisache-ar 1
hule-ar 1
hulere-ar 1
human-ar 1
humaniz-ar 21
hum-ar 1
hume-ar 1
humect-ar 1
humed-ar 1
humedec-er 48
humig-ar 1
humili-ar 1
humill-ar 1
hund-ir 3
huracan-arse ... 80
hurg-ar 51
hurgone-ar 1
hurguete-ar 1
hurl-ar 1
hurone-ar 1
hurt-ar 1
husm-ar 1
husme-ar 1

i

idealiz-ar 21
ide-ar 1
identific-ar 67

idiotiz-ar 21
idolatr-ar 1
iet-ar 1
ignifug-ar 51
ignor-ar 1
igual-ar 1
igu-ar 1
ijade-ar 1
ilegitim-ar 1
ilud-ir 3
ilumin-ar 1
ilusion-ar 1
ilustr-ar 1
imagin-ar 1
iman-ar 1
imant-ar 1
imbric-ar 67
imbu-ir 42
imbunch-ar 1
imburs-ar 1
imit-ar 1
impacient-ar 1
impar-ir 3
impart-ir 3
impast-ar 3
imped-ir 52
impel-er 2
impel-ir 3
impend-er 2
imper-ar 1
imperfeccion-
   ar 1
imperi-ar 1
impermeabiliz-
   ar 21
impersonaliz-
   ar 21
impert-ir 71
impetr-ar 1
imping-ar 1
implant-ar 1
impl-ar 1
implic-ar 1,
   and alter-
   natively, ... 67
implor-ar 1
impon-er 57
impopulariz-
   ar 21
importantiz-
   arse 21

import-ar 1
importun-ar 1
imposibilit-ar 1
impost-ar 1
imprec-ar 67
impregn-ar 1
imprem-ir 52
imprent-ar 1
impresion-ar 1
imprim-ar 1
imprim-ir 3,
   except the
   past participle
   is impreso
improb-ar 25
improper-ar 1
impropi-ar 1
improvis-ar 1
impugn-ar 1
impuls-ar 1
impurific-ar 67
imput-ar 1
inaugur-ar 1
incal-er 2
incamer-ar 1
incapacit-ar 1
incardin-ar 1
incaut-arse 80
incendi-ar 1
incens-ar 53
incentiv-ar 1
incer-ar 1
incest-ar 1
incid-ir 3
inciner-ar 1
incit-ar 1
inciviliz-ar 21
inclin-ar 1
inclu-ir 42,
   plus the past
   participle
   incluso
inco-ar 1, and
   used in the
   positions in 45
incomod-ar 1
incomunic-ar ...67
incon-arse 80
incontr-ar 1
incordi-ar 1
incorpor-ar 1

incras-ar 1
increment-ar 1
increp-ar 1
incrimin-ar 1
incrust-ar 1
incuart-ar 1
incub-ar 1
inculc-ar 67
inculp-ar 1
incumb-ir 3,
   and used in
   the positions
   in 45
incumpl-ir 3
incurr-ir 3,
   plus the past
   participle
   incurso
incursion-ar 1
incurv-ar 1
incus-ar 1
indag-ar 51
indemniz-ar 21
independ-
   erse 81
independi-ar 1
independiz-
   ar 21
indianiz-ar 21
indic-ar 67
indici-ar 1
indigest-arse ... 80
indign-ar 1
indilg-ar 51
indin-ar 1
indisciplin-
   arse 80
indispon-er 57
individualiz-
   ar 21
individu-ar 9
induc-ir 59
indulgenci-ar 1
indult-ar 1
indur-ar 1
industrializ-
   ar 21
industri-ar 1
inebri-ar 1
inerv-ar 1
infam-ar 1

infart-ar 1
infatu-ar 9
infeccion-ar 1
infec-ir 52,
  with the
  changes in 46
infect-ar 1
infecund-
  arse 80
infer-ir 71
infern-ar 53
infest-ar 1
infeud-ar 1
infibul-ar 1
inficcion-ar 1
inficion-ar 1
infiltr-ar 1
infing-ir 3,
  with the
  changes in 23
infinit-ar 1
infirm-ar 1
inflam-ar 1
infl-ar 1
inflexion-arse ... 80
inflig-ir 3,
  with the
  changes in 23
infling-ir 3,
  with the
  changes in 23
influenci-ar 1
influ-ir 42
inform-ar 1
infravalor-ar 1
infri-ar 1
infring-ir 3,
  with the
  changes in 23
infund-ir 3,
  plus the past
  participle
  infuso
infurt-ir 3, plus
  the past parti-
  ciple infurto
infus-ar 1
infusc-ar 67
ingeni-ar 1
inger-ir 71,
  plus the past

participle
  ingerto
ingles-ar 1
inglet-ar 1
inglete-ar 1
ingres-ar 1
ingr-ir 3
ingurgit-ar 1
inhabilit-ar 1
inhabit-ar 1
inhal-ar 1
inhest-ar 53
inhi-ar 1
inhib-ir 3
inhonor-ar 1
inhum-ar 1
inici-ar 1
injer-ir 71
injert-ar 1,
  plus the past
  participle
  injerto
injone-ar 1
injum-ar 1
injuri-ar 1
inmaterializ-
  ar 21
inmerg-ir 3,
  with the
  changes in 23
inmigr-ar 1
inmiscu-ir 42
inmol-ar 1
inmortaliz-ar 21
inmoviliz-ar 21
inmuniz-ar 21
inmut-ar 1
innov-ar 1
inobserv-ar 1
inocul-ar 1
inor-ar 1
inquiet-ar 1
inquin-ar 1
inquir-ir 5
insacul-ar 1
insaliv-ar 1
inscrib-ir 3,
  except the
  past partici-
  ples are
  inscrito and

inscripto
insculp-ir 3
insegu-ir 52
insensibiliz-
  ar 21
inser-ir 71
insert-ar 1,
  plus the past
  participle
  inserto
insidi-ar 1
insimul-ar 1
insinu-ar 9
insist-ir 3
insol-ar 1
insolent-ar 1
insolubiliz-ar ... 21
insonoriz-ar 21
inspeccion-ar 1
inspir-ar 1
instal-ar 1
inst-ar 1
instaur-ar 1
instig-ar 51
instil-ar 1
instimul-ar 1
institucionaliz-
  ar 21
institu-ir 42
instru-ir 42
instrument-ar 1
insubordin-ar 1
insud-ar 1
insufl-ar 1
insult-ar 1
insum-ir 3
insurreccion-
  ar 1
integr-ar 1
intelectualiz-
  ar 21
inteligenci-
  arse 80
intencion-ar 1
intens-ar 1
intensific-ar 67
intent-ar 1
intercal-ar 1
intercambi-ar 1
interced-er 2
intercept-ar 1

interclu-ir 42
intercomunic-
  arse 80
interdec-ir 58
interdict-ar 1
interes-ar 1
interfer-ir 71
interfoli-ar 1
interin-ar 1
interior-arse 80
interioriz-ar 21
interline-ar 1
intermedi-ar 1
intermit-ir 3
internacionaliz-
  ar 21
intern-ar 1
interpagin-ar 1
interpel-ar 1
interpol-ar 1
interpon-er 57
interprend-er 2
interpret-ar 1
interrog-ar 51
interrump-ir 3
intersec-arse ... 67
interser-ir 71
interven-ir 77
intervert-ir 71
interview-ar 1
intervist-arse ... 80
interviuv-ar 1
intest-ar 1
intim-ar 1
intimid-ar 1
intitul-ar 1
intoxic-ar 67
intranquiliz-
  ar 21
intrat-ar 1
intribut-ar 1
intric-ar 67
intrig-ar 51
intrinc-ar 67
introduc-ir 59
intromet-erse ... 81
intrus-arse 80
intruse-ar 1
intub-ar 1
intu-ir 42
inund-ar 1

inutiliz-ar 21
invad-ir 3
invagin-ar 1
invalid-ar 1
invectiv-ar 1
inven-ir 77
invent-ar 1
inventari-ar 9
invern-ar 53
invert-ir 71,
   plus the past
   participle
   inverso
investig-ar 51
invest-ir 52
inveter-arse 80
invigil-ar 1
invit-ar 1
invoc-ar 67
involucr-ar 1
inyect-ar 1
inyung-ir 3,
   with the
   changes in 23
inzu-ir 42
ioniz-ar 21
ir 43
ir-arse 80
iridi-ar 1
irire-ar 1
iris-ar 1
ironiz-ar 21
irradi-ar 1
irrespet-ar 1
irreverenci-ar 1
irrig-ar 51
irrit-ar 1
irrog-ar 51
irru-ir 42
irrump-ir 3
islamiz-ar 21
isomeriz-ar 21
ispe-ar 1
ispi-ar 9
istri-ar 9
italianiz-ar 21
iter-ar 1
ivern-ar 52
iz-ar 21
izquierde-ar 1

j

jabalcon-ar 1
jabalcone-ar 1
jabalon-ar 1
jabarde-ar 1
jabe-ar 1
jabel-ar 1
jabelg-ar 1
jabon-ar 1
jabone-ar 1
jabr-ir 3,
   except the
   past participle
   is jabierto
jacale-ar 1
jacare-ar 1
jac-er 79
jacerdan-ar 1
jach-ar 1
jact-ar 1
jact-arse 80
jacul-ar 1
jade-ar 1
jadi-ar 9
jaez-ar 21
jagu-ar 1
jaharr-ar 1
jair-ar 1
jaj-ar 1
jal-ar 1
jalbeg-ar 51
jale-ar 1
jaleiz-ar 21
jall-ar 1
jalon-ar 1
jalone-ar 1
jalpac-ar 67
jamaque-ar 1
jam-ar 1
jam-arse 80
jamb-ar 1
jambr-ar 1
jamerd-ar 53
jamur-ar 1
jane-ar 1
jape-ar 1
japoniz-ar 21
japorc-ar 67
japurc-ar 67
jaque-ar 1

jaqu-ir 3
j-ar 1
jarabe-ar 1
jarane-ar 1
jarapote-ar 1
jarat-ar 1
jarb-ar 1
jarci-ar 1
jarde-ar 1
jare-ar 1
jare-arse 80
jaric-ar 67
jaring-ar 1
jaripe-ar 1
jaroch-ar 1
jarop-ar 1
jarope-ar 1
jarr-ar 1
jarre-ar 1
jarret-ar 1
jart-ar 1
jas-ar 1
jaspe-ar 1
jaspi-ar 1
jate-ar 1
jebr-ar 1
jed-ar 1
jed-er 2, with
   the changes
   in 53
jemique-ar 1
jerarqueriz-
   ar 21
jerarquiz-ar 21
jeremique-ar 1
jericople-ar 1
jerigonce-ar 1
jerigonz-ar 21
jerimique-ar 1
jering-ar 51
jerinque-ar 1
jeroglific-ar 21
jesuse-ar 1
j-ar 1
jete-ar 1
jetend-er 2,
   with the
   changes in 53
jibare-ar 1
jij-ar 1
jije-ar 1

jile-ar 1
jilipolle-ar 1
jilote-ar 1
jimelg-ar 51
jimenz-ar 34
jimique-ar 1
jimpl-ar 1
jinete-ar 1
jinquete-ar 1
jiongl-ar 1
jip-ar 1
jipate-arse 80
jipi-ar 9
jirimique-ar 1
jirpe-ar 1
jit-ar 1
jobe-ar 1
joc-ar 1
joce-ar 1
joch-ar 1
joche-ar 1
joch-er 2
jocote-ar 1
jod-er 2
jom-ar 1
jonde-ar 1
jonjab-ar 1
jonje-ar 1
jonjole-ar 1
jop-ar 1
jop-arse 80
jope-ar 1
jorc-ar 67
jorfe-ar 1
jornal-ar 1
jorob-ar 1
jorope-ar 1
jorr-ar 1
jorre-ar 1
joruche-ar 1
jorung-ar 1
jostr-ar 1
jotr-ar 1
juag-ar 51
juanche-ar 1
juane-ar 1
jubert-ar 1
jubil-ar 1
juch-ar 1
judaiz-ar 21
judg-ar 1

judi-ar 1
judic-ar 1
juergue-arse 80
jug-ar 44
juguete-ar 1
juje-ar 1
julepe-ar 1
jum-arse 80
jumentiz-ar 21
jumetre-ar 1
jun-ar 1
jung-ar 1
junt-ar 1, plus
 the past
 participle
 junto
juñ-ar 1
juñ-ir 17
jupi-ar 1
jupi-arse 80
jurament-ar 1
jur-ar 1
jurg-ar 1
jurguce-ar 1
juriac-ar 21
juri-arse 80
jurung-ar 1
jusmet-erse 81
just-ar 1
justici-ar 1
justific-ar 67
justipreci-ar 1
jutute-ar 1
juvenec-er 48
juzg-ar 51

k

kilometr-ar 1

l

labializ-ar 21
labiose-ar 1
labor-ar 1
labore-ar 1
labr-ar 1
lace-ar 1
lacer-ar 1

lacere-ar 1
lach-ar 1
lache-ar 1
laconiz-ar 21
lacr-ar 1
lacre-ar 1
lacrim-ar 1
lact-ar 1
lade-ar 1
ladr-ar 1
ladre-ar 1
ladrill-ar 1
ladrone-ar 1
lag-ar 1
lagare-arse 80
lagarte-ar 1
lagote-ar 1
lagrimac-er 41
lagrim-ar 1
lagrime-ar 1
laicaliz-ar 21
laiciz-ar 21
laje-ar 1
lal-ar 1
lam-ar 1
lambare-ar 1
lambe-ar 1
lamb-er 2
lambere-ar 1
lambete-ar 1
lambic-ar 1
lambisc-ar 67
lambisque-ar 1
lambruce-ar 1
lambrusque-ar .. 1
lambuce-ar 1
lament-ar 1
lam-er 2
lamin-ar 1
lamisc-ar 67
lampace-ar 1
lamp-ar 1
lampe-ar 1
lampre-ar 1
lanaplen-ar 1
lance-ar 1
lanch-ar 1, and
 used in the
 positions in 45
lancin-ar 1
lande-ar 1

langu-ar 1
languci-ar 1
languidec-er 48
lanz-ar 21
lañ-ar 1
lapach-ar 1
lapid-ar 1
lapidific-ar 67
lapiz-ar 21
laque-ar 1
lard-ar 1
larde-ar 1
larg-ar 51
larraguz-ar 21
lasc-ar 67
last-ar 1
lastim-ar 1
lastr-ar 1
lastre-ar 1
late-ar 1
lateraliz-ar 21
latigue-ar 1
latin-ar 1
latine-ar 1
latiniz-ar 21
lat-ir 3
latit-ar 1
laton-ar 1
latrocin-ar 1
lauc-ar 67
laud-ar 1
laudiniz-ar 21
laure-ar 1
lav-ar 1
lavote-ar 1
lax-ar 1
lay-ar 1
laz-ar 21
lazr-ar 1
le-ar 1
lebreje-ar 1
lech-ar 1
leche-ar 1
lechuce-ar 1
lechug-ar 1
lectit-ar 1
le-er 26
legaj-ar 1
legaliz-ar 21
leg-ar 51
legifer-ar 1

legisl-ar 1
legitim-ar 1
legr-ar 1
leij-ar 1
lej-ar 1
leld-ar 1
lembr-ar 1
lengüe-ar 1
lengüete-ar 1
lenific-ar 67
len-ir 3
leniz-ar 21
lentec-er 48
lentific-ar 67
leñ-ar 1
leñate-ar 1
leñific-ar 21
lep-ar 1
lerde-ar 1
lese-ar 1
lesion-ar 1
leste-ar 1
letific-ar 67
letre-ar 1
leud-ar 1
levant-ar 1
levant-arse 80
lev-ar 1
levig-ar 51
lexicaliz-ar 21
li-ar 9
lib-ar 1
libel-ar 1
liberaliz-ar 21
liber-ar 1
libert-ar 1
libr-ar 1
libre-ar 1
licenci-ar 1
licit-ar 1
licu-ar 9
licuec-er 48
licuefac-er 41,
 except the
 past participle
 is licuefacto
lidi-ar 1
liev-ar 1
lig-ar 51
liger-ar 1
ligere-ar 1

lignific-ar 67
lignific-arse 80
lij-ar 1
lileque-ar 1
lilique-ar 1
lim-ar 1
limit-ar 1
limosn-ar 1
limosne-ar 1
limpi-ar 1
lince-ar 1
linch-ar 1
lind-ar 1
line-ar 1
liofiliz-ar 21
lipid-ar 1
lipidi-ar 1
liquefac-er 41,
  except the
  past participle
  is liquefácido
liquid-ar 1
liquidific-ar 1
lis-ar 1
lisi-ar 1
lisonj-ar 1
lisonje-ar 1
list-ar 1
liste-ar 1
liston-ar 1
lit-ar 1
literate-ar 1
litig-ar 51
litigi-ar 1
litofotografi-ar .. 9
litografi-ar 9
liud-ar 1
lividec-er 48
lixivi-ar 1
liz-ar 21
llag-ar 51
llam-ar 1
llame-ar 1
llante-ar 1
llap-ar 1
llapihu-ar 1
llat-ir 3
llauc-ar 67
llauque-arse 80
lleg-ar 51
llen-ar 1

lleud-ar 1
llev-ar 1
llipihu-ar 1
llor-ar 1
llorique-ar 1
llorisque-ar 1
llorrit-ar 1
llostr-ar 1
llov-er 45
llovizn-ar 1,
  and for its
  use
  regarding
  weather,
  see 45
lo-ar 1
lobe-ar 1
lobregue-ar 1
lobreguec-er
  48, and for
  its use
  regarding
  weather,
  see 45
localiz-ar 21
loc-ar 67
log-ar 51
logiz-ar 21
logr-ar 1
logre-ar 1
lom-ar 1
lombarde-ar 1
lome-ar 1
lonch-ar 1
loncote-ar 1
lonje-ar 1
loque-ar 1
los-ar 1
lote-ar 1
lotific-ar 1
lotiz-ar 21
lov-er 47
lozane-ar 1
lozanec-er 48
lu-ar 1
lubric-ar 67
lubrific-ar 67
luch-ar 1
luci-ar 1
luc-ir 3, with
  the changes

in 48
lucr-ar 1
lucubr-ar 1
ludi-ar 1
lud-ir 3
lueg-ar 51
lu-ir 42
luj-ar 1
lujuri-ar 1
lull-ir 3
lumin-ar 1
lunaniz-ar 21
lunare-ar 1
lupuliz-ar 21
luque-ar 1
lustr-ar 1
lustre-ar 1
lux-ar 1

m

macacine-ar 1
macadamiz-
  ar 21
macane-ar 1
macaque-ar 1
mac-ar 1
mac-arse 67
mace-ar 1
macer-ar 1
macete-ar 1
machac-ar 67
machambr-ar 1
machaque-ar 1
mach-ar 1
mach-arse 80
machasc-
  arse 67
mache-ar 1
machete-ar 1
machiembr-
  arse 80
machihembr-
  ar 1
machimbr-
  arse 80
machin-arse 80
machituc-ar 1
machone-ar 1
machorre-ar 1

machuc-ar 67
maciz-ar 21
macoll-ar 1
macone-ar 1
macoque-ar 1
macuje-ar 1
macul-ar 1
macurc-arse 80
madefact-ar 1
madefic-ar 67
mader-ar 1
madre-ar 1
madre-arse 80
madrug-ar 51
madur-ar 1
madurec-er 48
madurg-ar 51
maestraliz-ar ... 21
maestr-ar 1
maestre-ar 1
magadiz-ar 21
magance-ar 1
maganzone-ar .. 1
magin-ar 1
magnetiz-ar 21
magnific-ar 67
magost-ar 1
magre-ar 1
magrec-er 48
magu-arse 7
magul-ar 1
magull-ar 1
maher-ir 71
mahometiz-
  ar 21
maice-ar 1
maisi-ar 1
majade-ar 1
majadere-ar 1
maj-ar 1
majarete-ar 1
majase-ar 1
majenc-ar 1
majol-ar 25
malacostumbr-
  ar 1
malagor-ar 6
malangrin-ar 1
malanoch-
  arse 80
malañ-ar 1

malax-ar 1
malbarat-ar 1
malcas-ar 1
malcocin-ar 1
malcoloc-ar 1
malcom-er 2
malcorn-ar 25
malcri-ar 9
maldec-ir
  58, plus the
  regular past
  participle
  maldecido
  and the
  irregular past
  participle
  maldito
maleabiliz-ar ... 21
male-ar 1
malefici-ar 1
maleiniz-ar 1
malemple-ar 1
malentend-er
  2, with the
  changes in 53
malete-ar 1
malfac-er 69,
  except the
  past participle
  is malfacido
malfam-ar 1
malgast-ar 1
malhay-ar 21
malher-ir 71
malhumor-ar 1
malici-ar 1
malign-ar 1
malingr-ar 1
mallad-ar 1
mall-ar 1
mallug-ar 1
malmari-ar 1
malmet-er 2
malmodi-ar 1
malogr-ar 1
maloje-ar 1
malone-ar 1
maloque-ar 1
malpar-ar 1
malpar-ir 3
malpas-ar 1

malple-ar 1
malquer-er 60,
  plus the past
  participle
  malquisto
malquist-ar 1
malrot-ar 1
malsin-ar 1
malson-ar 25
malt-ar 1
malte-ar 1
maltra-er 75
maltrat-ar 1
malv-ar 1
malvend-er 2
malvers-ar 1
malvez-ar 21
malviv-ir 3
mamante-ar 1
mam-ar 1
mamarrach-ar .. 1
mamone-ar 1
mamoniz-ar 21
mampar-ar 1
mamposte-ar 1
mampres-ar 1
mamuj-ar 1
mamull-ar 1
mamuse-ar 1
man-ar 1
manc-ar 67
mancell-ar 1
manch-ar 1
mancill-ar 1
mancip-ar 1
mancomun-ar ... 1
mancorn-ar 25
mancorne-ar 1
mand-ar 1
mandil-ar 1
mandril-ar 1
manduc-ar 67
mane-ar 1
manej-ar 1
mangane-ar 1
manganzone-
  ar 1
mang-ar 51
mang-arse 80
mangone-ar 1
mangrull-ar 1

manguare-ar 1
mangue-ar 1
maniat-ar 1
manifest-ar 53,
  plus the past
  participle
  manifiesto
manij-ar 1
maniobr-ar 1
manipul-ar 1
manipule-ar 1
man-ir 4
manjol-ar 1
manlev-ar 1
manobr-ar 1
manobri-ar 1
manoj-ar 1
manoje-ar 1
manose-ar 1
manote-ar 1
manque-ar 1
mansalvi-ar 1
mante-ar 1
manteca-er 20
manten-er 74
manteque-ar 1
mantorn-ar 1
manualiz-
  arse 80
manufactur-ar ... 1
manumit-ir 3,
  plus the past
  participle
  manumiso
manuscrib-ir
  3, except the
  past participle
  is manuscrito
manuten-er 74
many-ar 1
manzane-ar 1
mañan-ar 1
mañane-ar 1
mañe-ar 1
mañere-ar 1
mañose-ar 1
mapole-ar 1
maque-ar 1
maquete-ar 1
maquil-ar 1
maquile-ar 1

maquill-ar 1
maquin-ar 1
maquiniz-ar 21
marañ-ar 1
maraque-ar 1
maravill-ar 1
marc-ar 67
marce-ar 1,
  and used in
  the positions
  in 45
marcen-ar 1
marcham-ar 1
march-ar 1
marchit-ar 1,
  plus the past
  participle
  marchito
mare-ar 1
marg-ar 51
margen-ar 1
margin-ar 1
margom-ar 1
margull-ar 1
marid-ar 1
marimbe-ar 1
marin-ar 1
marine-ar 1
maripose-ar 1
marisc-ar 67
mariz-ar 21
mariz-arse 80
marlot-ar 1
marmitone-ar ... 1
marmote-ar 1
marmull-ar 1
marome-ar 1
marque-ar 1
marquet-ar 1
marramiz-ar 21
marrane-ar 1
marr-ar 1
marre-ar 1
marroj-ar 1
marrull-ar 1
marsupializ-
  ar 21
martaj-ar 1
martigu-ar 1
martill-ar 1
martille-ar 1

martiriz-ar 21	mazon-ar 1	meneque-ar 1	metodiz-ar 21
marulle-ar 1	mazone-ar 1	mengu-ar 7	metrall-ar 1
masacr-ar 1	mazorc-ar 67	menor-ar 1	metre-ar 1
masaje-ar 1	me-ar 1	menore-ar 1	metrific-ar 67
mas-ar 1	mecaniz-ar 21	menorg-ar 1	meuc-ar 67
masc-ar 67	mecanografi-	menoscab-ar 1	mexicaniz-ar ...21
mascar-ar 1	ar 9	menospreci-ar ..1	mezcl-ar 1
mascuj-ar 1	mecate-ar 1	menstru-ar 9	mezquin-ar 1
masculiniz-ar ...21	mec-er 46	mensualiz-ar ...21	mezuque-ar 1
mascull-ar 1	mech-ar 1	mensur-ar 1	miag-ar 51
mase-ar 1	mechific-ar 67	mentaliz-ar 21	miañ-ar 1
masill-ar 1	mechone-ar 1	ment-ar 53	mi-ar 9
maste-ar 1	med-ar 1	ment-ir 71	microcopi-ar 1
mastic-ar 67	medianiz-ar 21	menude-ar 1	microfilm-ar 1
mastig-ar 1	medi-ar 1	menuz-ar 21	microfiltr-ar 1
masturb-ar 1	mediatiz-ar 21	mer-ar 1	microniz-ar 21
masturb-arse ...80	medicament-	mercade-ar 1	mig-ar 51
mataperre-ar 1	ar 1	mercance-ar 1	migr-ar 1
mat-ar 1	medic-ar 1	mercantiliz-	miguele-ar 1
matasell-ar 1	medicin-ar 1	ar 21	milagre-ar 1
mate-ar 1	med-ir 52	merc-ar 67	milimetr-ar 1
materializ-ar 21	medit-ar 1	merce-ar 1	milit-ar 1
materniz-ar 1	medr-ar 1	merced-ar 1	militariz-ar 21
matiz-ar 21	meduc-ar 1	mercende-ar 1	millone-ar 1
matone-ar 1	mej-er 2	merceriz-ar 21	milongue-ar 1
matrac-ar 1	mejicaniz-ar 21	mercurializ-	milpe-ar 1
matraque-ar 1	mejor-ar 1	ar 21	mim-ar 1
matratuc-ar 1	melancoliz-	merec-er 48	mimbr-ar 1
matrere-ar 1	ar 21	merend-ar 53	mimbre-ar 1
matricul-ar 1	mel-ar 53	merendill-ar 1	mimeografi-ar ...9
matrimoni-ar 1	melcoch-ar 1	mereng-ar 51	mimose-ar 1
matriz-ar 21	meld-ar 1	meretric-ar 1	min-ar 1
matufi-ar 1	mele-ar 1	merit-ar 1	minch-ar 1
maturrangue-	melecin-ar 1	merm-ar 1	mindangue-ar ...1
ar 1	melen-ar 1	merode-ar 1	mine-ar 1
matute-ar 1	melg-ar 51	mes-ar 1	mineraliz-ar 21
mauc-ar 1	melific-ar 67	mescab-ar 1	ming-ar 51
maul-ar 9	melindre-ar 1	mescl-ar 1	mingone-ar 1
maule-ar 1	melindriz-ar 21	mestiz-ar 21	mingu-ar 1
maull-ar 9	mell-ar 1	mestur-ar 1	mini-ar 1
maximiz-ar 21	mellor-ar 1	mesur-ar 1	miniaturiz-ar 21
may-ar 1	membr-ar 1	metafisique-ar ..1	minific-ar 67
maye-ar 1,	memor-ar 1	metaforiz-ar 21	minimiz-ar 21
and used in	memoriz-ar 21	metal-ar 1	ministr-ar 1
the positions	men-ar 1	metaliz-ar 21	minor-ar 1
in 45	menaz-ar 21	metamorfose-	minut-ar 1
mayor-ar 1	mencion-ar 1	ar 1	miñ-arse 80
mayordome-ar ..1	mendig-ar 51	metatiz-ar 1	miñoque-ar 1
mazamorre-ar ...1	mendigue-ar 1	meteoriz-ar 21	mique-ar 1
maz-ar 21	mending-ar 51	met-er 2	mir-ar 1
mazn-ar 1	mene-ar 1	metil-ar 1	mirific-ar 67

miristic-arse 80
mirl-ar 1
mirl-arse 80
mis-ar 1
miseñore-ar 1
misere-ar 1
mision-ar 1
mist-ar 1
mistific-ar 67
mistur-ar 1
mitay-ar 1
mitig-ar 51
mitisar-ar 1
mitote-ar 1
mitr-ar 1
mitridatiz-ar 21
mixte-ar 1
mixtific-ar 67
mixtur-ar 1
mobl-ar 25
moc-ar 67
moce-ar 1
moch-ar 1
mocion-ar 1
model-ar 1
moder-ar 1
moderniz-ar 21
modest-ar 1
modific-ar 67
modorr-ar 1
modul-ar 1
mof-ar 1
mofe-ar 1
mofle-ar 1
mofle-arse 80
mofl-ir 3
mogoll-ar 1
mogolle-ar 1
mogosi-ar 1
mohatr-ar 1
mohec-er 48
mohose-arse ... 80
moj-ar 1
mojon-ar 1
mojose-arse 80
molcajete-ar 1
mold-ar 1
molde-ar 1
moldur-ar 1
mole-ar 1
mol-er 47

molest-ar 1
molete-ar 1
molific-ar 67
molle-ar 1
mollent-ar 1
mollesc-er 2
mollic-ar 1
mollific-ar 67
molline-ar 1,
  and used in
  the positions
  in 45
moll-ir 17
mollizn-ar 1,
  and for its
  use regarding
  weather,
  see 45
mollizne-ar 1,
  and for its
  use regard-
  ing weather,
  see 45
molonque-ar 1
moltur-ar 1
mome-ar 1
momific-ar 67
mond-ar 1
mone-ar 1
moned-ar 1
monede-ar 1
monetiz-ar 21
mongue-ar 1
monolog-ar 51
monopoliz-ar ... 21
monoptong-
  ar 51
montadg-ar 51
montane-ar 1
montante-ar 1
mont-ar 1
montazg-ar 51
monte-ar 1
monumentaliz-
  ar 21
moque-ar 1
moquete-ar 1
moquite-ar 1
moralzi-ar 21
mor-ar 1
morc-ar 67

mordent-ar 1
mord-er 47
mordic-ar 67
mordisc-ar 67
mordisque-ar ... 1
morete-ar 1
morf-ar 1
morfiniz-ar 21
morige-ar 1
moriger-ar 1
mor-ir 31,
  except the
  past participle
  is muerto
mormorote-ar ... 1
mormull-ar 1
mormur-ar 1
moron-ar 1
morr-ar 1
morre-ar 1
morrongue-ar 1
mortaj-ar 1
mortific-ar 67
mortigu-ar 1
mosc-ar 67
moscarde-ar 1
moscone-ar 1
mosque-ar 1
mosquete-ar 1
moste-ar 1
mostr-ar 25
mostre-ar 1
mot-ar 1
mote-ar 1
motej-ar 1
motil-ar 1
motiv-ar 1
motoriz-ar 21
mov-er 47
moviliz-ar 21
mozone-ar 1
muchache-ar 1
muchigu-ar 1
mud-ar 1
muebl-ar 1
muelle-ar 1
mueque-ar 1
muergane-
  arse 80
muerganiz-
  arse 21

muesc-ar 67
mufl-ir 3
mug-ar 51
mug-ir 3,
  with the
  changes in 23
mugron-ar 1
mu-ir 42
muj-ar 1
mujere-ar 1
mulab-ar 1
mulate-ar 1
mulatiz-ar 21
mulc-ar 1
mulete-ar 1
mullic-ar 67
mull-ir 17
mult-ar 1
multicopi-ar 1
multiplic-ar 67
mundane-ar 1
munde-ar 1
mundializ-ar 21
mundific-ar 67
municion-ar 1
municipaliz-
  ar 21
mun-ir 3
muñeque-ar 1
muñ-ir 17
muque-ar 1
muqu-ir 3
mur-ar 1
murci-ar 1
murmuje-ar 1
murmull-ar 1
murmur-ar 1
murmure-ar 1
mus-ar 1
music-ar 67
mus-irse 82
musit-ar 1
musti-arse 80
mutil-ar 1

n

nacar-ar 1
nac-er 48 has
  a past partici-

ple nato
nacionaliz-ar 21
nad-ar 1
nafr-ar 1
naguale-ar 1
nagualiz-ar 21
naj-ar 1
nalgue-ar 1
namor-ar 1
nance-ar 1
nane-ar 1
nant-ar 1
naquer-ar 1
narcotiz-ar 21
narigone-ar 1
narr-ar 1
nasaliz-ar 21
nast-ar 1
naturaliz-ar 21
naufrag-ar 51
naur-ar 1
nause-ar 1
navaje-ar 1
naveg-ar 51
navig-ar 1
nazare-ar 1
nebline-ar 1,
   and for its use
   regarding
   weather,
   see 45
nebuliz-ar 21
nece-ar 1
necesit-ar 1
necrosific-ar 67
neg-ar 62
negoci-ar 1
negre-ar 1
negrec-er 48
negreg-ar 51
negregue-ar 1
nej-ar 1
nembr-ar 1
neni-ar 1
nervi-ar 1
nesg-ar 51
neurotiz-ar 21
neutraliz-ar 21
neutrodin-ar 1
nev-ar 53,
   and for its

use regarding
   weather,
   see 45
nevisc-ar
   67, and for
   its use
   regarding
   weather,
   see 45
nidific-ar 67
niel-ar 1
nimb-ar 1
niñe-ar 1
niquel-ar 1
niqueliz-ar 21
nitraf-ar 1
nitr-ar 1
nitrific-ar 67
nitrogen-ar 1
nivel-ar 1
nixques-ar 1
nixquez-ar 21
noblec-er 48
noc-er 48
noc-ir 59
noctambul-ar 1
nombr-ar 1
nomin-ar 1
noque-ar 1
nordeste-ar 1
nordoveste-ar ... 1
normaliz-ar 21
normaniz-ar 1
norm-ar 1
noroeste-ar 1
norte-ar 1
norueste-ar 1
not-ar 1
notici-ar 1
notific-ar 67
nov-ar 1
novel-ar 1
novele-ar 1
noveliz-ar 21
novi-ar 1
nubl-ar 1, and
   for its use
   regarding
   weather,
   see 45
nuc-ir 59

nudr-ir 56
nulific-ar 1
numer-ar 1
nunci-ar 1
nutr-ir 3

ñ

ñafi-ar 1
ñafite-ar 1
ñafr-ar 1
ñam-ar 1
ñang-ar 1
ñangot-arse 80
ñangue-ar 1
ñap-ar 1
ñape-ar 1
ñarre-ar 1
ñate-ar 1
ñau-ar 1
ñeque-ar 1
ñip-ar 1
ñong-arse 80
ñongot-arse 80
ñongue-ar 1
ñoñ-ar 1
ñoñe-ar 1
ñubl-ar 1
ñusc-ar 67
ñut-ir 3

o

obcec-ar 67
obceg-ar 51
obedec-er 48
obel-ar 1
obenqui-ar 1
obisp-ar 1
obispe-ar 1
objet-ar 1
objetiv-ar 1
obl-ar 1
oblicu-ar 1
oblig-ar 51
obliter-ar 1
obnubil-ar 1
obr-ar 1
obscur-ar 1

obscurec-er
   48, and for
   its use
   regarding
   weather,
   see 45
obsecr-ar 1
obsed-er 2
obsedi-ar 1
obsequi-ar 1
observ-ar 1
obsesion-ar 1
obstaculiz-ar 21
obst-ar 1
obstin-arse 80
obstruccion-ar .. 1
obstru-ir 42
obtemper-ar 1
obten-er 2
obtur-ar 1
obvi-ar 1
ocale-ar 1
ocasion-ar 1
occidentaliz-
   ar 21
ocel-ar 1
och-ar 1
ochav-ar 1
ochave-ar 1
oci-ar 1
ociose-ar 1
oclu-ir 42
octav-ar 1
octave-ar 1
octuplic-ar 67
ocult-ar 1
ocup-ar 1
ocurr-ir 3
odi-ar 1
odiose-ar 1
ofend-er 2
ofens-ar 1
ofert-ar 1
oficializ-ar 21
ofici-ar 1
ofrec-er 48
ofrend-ar 1
ofusc-ar 67
o-ír 49
ojal-ar 1
oj-ar 1

oje-ar 1
ojete-ar 1
ojetill-ar 1
ojot-arse 80
ole-ar 1
ol-er 50
olete-ar 1
olfate-ar 1
oligarquiz-ar ... 21
olisc-ar 67
olisme-ar 1
olisque-ar 1
oliv-ar 1
oliv-arse 80
oloriz-ar 21
oloros-ar 1
olvid-ar 1
omblig-ar 1
omin-ar 1
omit-ir 3,
  plus the past
  participle
  omiso
once-ar 1
onde-ar 1
ondison-ar 1
ondr-ar 1
ondul-ar 1
onec-er 48
onot-ar 1
opac-ar 67
opacific-ar 1
opaliz-ar 21
ope-ar 1
oper-ar 1
opil-ar 1
opil-arse 80
opin-ar 1
opon-er 57
oposit-ar 1
opres-ar 1
oprim-ir 3,
  plus the past
  participle
  opreso
oprobi-ar 1
opsonific-ar 1
opsoniz-ar 21
opt-ar 1
optim-ar 1
optimiz-ar 21

opugn-ar 1
or-ar 1
orbay-ar 1
orden-ar 1
ordeñ-ar 1
ordin-ar 1
ore-ar 1
orec-er 48
orej-ar 1
oreje-ar 1
orfanec-er 48
orf-ar 1
organ-ar 1
organiz-ar 21
orgullec-er 48
ori-ar 1
orientaliz-ar 21
orient-ar 1
orific-ar 67
originaliz-
  arse 21
origin-ar 1
orill-ar 1
orille-ar 1
orin-ar 1
orinc-ar 67
orinec-er 48
orinque-ar 1
orl-ar 1
ormej-ar 1
ornament-ar 1
orn-ar 1
orne-ar 1
oronde-ar 1
oropel-ar 1
orquest-ar 1
ortig-ar 1
ortografi-ar 9
orvall-ar 1,
  and for its
  use regarding
  weather,
  see 45
orvay-ar 1,
  and for its
  use regarding
  weather,
  see 45
orz-ar 21
os-ar 1
oscil-ar 1

oscurec-er
  48, and for
  its use
  regarding
  weather,
  see 45
ose-ar 1
osific-ar 67
osl-ar 1
ostent-ar 1
ostiñ-ar 1
ot-ar 1
ote-ar 1
otil-ar 1
otoñ-ar 1
otorg-ar 51
ovacion-ar 1
oval-ar 1
ov-ar 1
overe-ar 1
ovill-ar 1
oviposit-ar 1
oxe-ar 1
oxid-ar 1
oxigen-ar 1
oxim-ar 1
ozon-ar 1
ozonific-ar 67
ozoniz-ar 21

p

pabl-ar 1
paccion-ar 1
pacent-ar 53
pac-er 48
pachamangue-
  ar 1
pachorre-ar 1
pachote-ar 1
pachurr-ar 1
pacific-ar 67
pact-ar 1
padec-er 48
padre-ar 1
padrine-ar 1
padrote-ar 1
paganiz-ar 21
pag-ar 51
pagin-ar 1

pair-ar 1
paire-ar 1
pait-ar 1
pajar-ar 1
pajare-ar 1
pajarole-ar 1
pajarote-ar 1
paje-ar 1
palabre-ar 1
palade-ar 1
paladin-ar 1
palangane-ar 1
palanque-ar 1
palanque-
  arse 80
pal-ar 1
palataliz-ar 21
palatiz-ar 21
pale-ar 1
palenque-ar 1
palete-ar 1
pali-ar 1
palidec-er 48
palique-ar 1
pallap-ar 1
pallaque-ar 1
pall-ar 1
palm-ar 1
palme-ar 1
palmete-ar 1
palmote-ar 1
palome-ar 1
palone-ar 1
palote-ar 1
palp-ar 1
palpit-ar 1
palpote-ar 1
paluche-ar 1
pampane-ar 1
pampe-ar 1
pampone-ar 1
panade-ar 1
pancreatiz-ar ... 21
pand-ar 1
pande-ar 1
panderete-ar 1
pandorgue-ar 1
pane-ar 1
panegiriz-ar 21
panele-ar 1
pang-ar 51

pangare-ar 1
pangue-àr 1
panific-ar 67
panigu-arse 80
panoj-ar 1
panque-ar 1
pantalle-ar 1
pantoc-ar 1
panuc-ar 67
papach-ar 1
papale-ar 1
papalote-ar 1
pap-ar 1
paparre-ar 1
pape-ar 1
papele-ar 1
papelete-ar 1
papeletiz-ar 21
papelone-ar 1
paporre-ar 1
papuj-arse 80
paque-ar 1
paquete-ar 1
paraboliz-ar 21
parachut-ar 1
parafin-ar 1
parafrase-ar 1
paragon-ar 1
parahus-ar 9
paralel-ar 1
paralitic-arse ... 67
paraliz-ar 21
paralogiz-ar 21
param-ar 1,
    and used in
    the positions
    in 45
parame-ar 1,
    and used in
    the positions
    in 45
parament-ar 1
parangon-ar 1
parapet-ar 1
parapet-arse 80
par-ar 1
paraus-ar 9
parcel-ar 1
parcemic-ar 1
parch-ar 1
parche-ar 1

parcializ-ar 21
parc-ir 3, with
    the changes
    in 23
parde-ar 1
pare-ar 1
parec-er 48
pareje-ar 1
parific-ar 67
par-ir 3
parkeriz-ar 21
parkesiz-ar 21
parlament-ar 1
parlamente-ar ... 1
parl-ar 1
parlote-ar 1
parodi-ar 1
parol-ar 1
parpade-ar 1
parp-ar 1
parque-ar 1
parrafe-ar 1
parrande-ar 1
parr-ar 1
parte-ar 1
particip-ar 1
particulariz-
    ar 21
parve-ar 1
parvific-ar 67
pasaman-ar 1
pasaport-ar 1
pasaporte-ar 1
pas-ar 1, plus
    the past par-
    ticiple paso,
    and for its use
    regarding
    weather,
    see 45
pasc-ar 67
pascone-ar 1
pase-ar 1
pasigrafi-ar 1
pasm-ar 1
pasp-ar 1
pasp-arse 80
pasquin-ar 1
past-ar 1
paste-ar 1

pastele-ar 1
pasteriz-ar 21
pasteuriz-ar 21
pastore-ar 1
pastoriz-ar 21
pastur-ar 1
patale-ar 1
patalete-ar 1
patane-ar 1
patate-arse 80
pate-ar 1
patent-ar 1
patentiz-ar 21
patin-ar 1
patiquebr-ar 53
patoche-ar 1
patoje-ar 1
patole-ar 1
patraque-ar 1
patri-ar 1
patrocin-ar 1
patrone-ar 1
patrull-ar 1
patuleque-ar 1
patull-ar 1
paul-ar 1
paus-ar 1
paut-ar 1
pave-ar 1
paviment-ar 1
pavon-ar 1
pavone-ar 1
pavorde-ar 1
payan-ar 1
payane-ar 1
pay-ar 1
payase-ar 1
peal-ar 1
pebrin-ar 1
pecane-ar 1
pec-ar 67
pechac-ar 67
pech-ar 1
peche-ar 1
pecilg-ar 51
pecore-ar 1
pect-ar 1
pedace-ar 1
pedale-ar 1
pedante-ar 1
pedaz-ar 21

ped-ir 52
pedorre-ar 1
pe-er 2
peg-ar 51
pegoste-ar 1
pegostr-ar 1
pegote-ar 1
pegunt-ar 1
pein-ar 1
peindr-ar 1
pelambr-ar 1
pel-ar 1
pele-ar 1
pelech-ar 1
peliche-ar 1
peligr-ar 1
pelizc-ar 67
pellizc-ar 67
pelote-ar 1
pelude-ar 1
peluque-ar 1
penaliz-ar 21
pen-ar 1
penc-ar 67
pendeje-ar 1
pendenci-ar 1
pend-er 2
pendone-ar 1
pendr-ar 1
penej-ar 1
peneje-ar 1
penetr-ar 1
penitenci-ar 1
pens-ar 53
pension-ar 1
pension-arse ...70
peñ-arse 80
peñasque-ar 1
peñer-ar 1
peñisc-ar 67
peñor-ar 1
peon-ar 1
peor-ar 1
pepe-ar 1
pepen-ar 1
peptonific-ar 67
peptoniz-ar 21
peragr-ar 1
peralt-ar 1
percanz-ar 21
percat-ar 1

perch-ar	1	ar	53
perche-ar	1	pernoch-ar	1
perchon-ar	1	pernoct-ar	1
perchuf-ar	1	pernot-ar	1
percib-ir	3	perogrulle-ar	1
percol-ar	1	peror-ar	1
percoll-ar	25	peroxid-ar	1
perconte-ar	1	perpas-ar	1
percud-ir	3	perpen-ar	1
percut-ir	3	perpetr-ar	1
perd-er 2,		perpetu-ar	9
with the		perpul-ir	3
changes in	53	perquir-ir	5
perdig-ar	51	perscrut-ar	1
perdon-ar	1	persegu-ir	70
perdur-ar	1	persever-ar	1
perece-ar	1	persianiz-ar	1
perec-er	48	persign-ar	1
peregrin-ar	1	persist-ir	3
perenniz-ar	21	persog-ar	51
perfeccion-ar	1	personaliz-ar	21
perfectiv-ar	1	person-arse	80
perfil-ar	1	personific-ar	67
perfor-ar	1	perspir-ar	1
perfum-ar	1	persuad-ir	3
perfume-ar	1	pertenec-er	48
pergeni-ar	1	pertigue-ar	1
pergeñ-ar	1	pertrech-ar	1
perhinch-ir	3	pertugue-ar	1
periclit-ar	1	perturb-ar	1
pericote-ar	1	peruaniz-ar	21
perifoll-ar	1	pervert-ir	71
perifone-ar	1	perviv-ir	3
perifrase-ar	1	pervulg-ar	51
perige-ar	1	pes-ar 1, and	
periodique-ar	1	used in the	
peripon-erse	57	positions in	45
perique-ar	1	pesc-ar	67
perjudic-ar	67	pescoce-ar	1
perjur-ar	1	pescud-ar	1
perlific-ar	67	pescuece-ar	1
perlong-ar	51	pesete-ar	1
permanec-er	48	pesg-ar	51
permit-ir	3	peshac-ar	67
permut-ar	1	pesi-ar	1
perne-ar	1	pespite-ar	1
perniabr-ir 3,		pespunt-ar	1
except the		pespunte-ar	1
past participle		pesquer-ir	71
is perniabierto		pesquir-ir	39
perniquebr-		pesquis-ar	1
pestañ-ar	1	pimpollec-er	48
pestañe-ar	1	pin-ar	1
pestiñ-ar	1	pincel-ar	1
petaque-ar	1	pinch-ar	1
pet-ar	1	pinchule-ar	1
petarde-ar	1	pindariz-ar	21
peticion-ar	1	pindongue-ar	1
petrarquiz-ar	21	pinene-ar	1
petrenc-arse	67	ping-ar	51
petrific-ar	67	pingone-ar	1
petrole-ar	1	pingorote-ar	1
peyor-ar	1	pingote-ar	1
piaf-ar	1	pinguete-ar	1
pial-ar	1	pinguij-ar	1
pi-ar	9	pinj-ar	1
picane-ar	1	pint-ar	1
pic-ar	67	pintarraj-ar	1
picarde-ar	1	pintarraje-ar	1
picariz-ar	21	pinte-ar 1,	
picaz-ar	21	and used in	
pich-arse	80	the positions	
pichinch-ar	1	in	45
pichinche-ar	1	pintigu-ar	1
pichipar-arse	80	pintipar-ar	1
pichise-ar	1	pintone-ar	1
pichisebe-ar	1	pintore-ar	1
pichiside-ar	1	pintorete-ar	1
pichole-ar	1	pintorre-ar	1
pichone-ar	1	pintorrete-ar	1
pichule-ar	1	pinture-ar	1
picote-ar	1	pinz-ar	21
picure-arse	80	piñ-arse	80
pif-ar	1	piñe-ar	1
pifi-ar	1	piñisc-ar	67
pigment-ar	1	piñizc-ar	67
pignor-ar	1	piñone-ar	1
pijote-ar	1	piñongue-ar	1
pil-ar	1	piñor-ar	1
pilc-ar	1	piol-ar	1
pilf-arse	80	pionc-arse	80
pilgu-arse	80	pip-ar	1
pill-ar	1	pipet-ar	1
pille-ar	1	pipete-ar	1
pillunte-ar	1	pipi-ar	9
pilon-ar	1	pique-ar	1
pilot-ar	1	piquichone-ar	1
pilote-ar	1	piquine-ar	1
piltrafe-ar	1	pir-ar	1
piment-ar	1	pir-arse	80
pimpl-ar	1	pirate-ar	1
pimpolle-ar	1	pirc-ar	67

pirl-arse 80
pirogen-ar 1
pirograb-ar 1
pirope-ar 1
pirquine-ar 1
pirr-arse 80
pirroniz-ar 21
piruete-ar 1
pis-ar 1
pisc-ar 67
pisht-ar 1
pisone-ar 1
pisote-ar 1
pisp-ar 1
pist-ar 1
pistole-ar 1
pitagoriz-ar 21
pit-ar 1
pitarrase-ar 1
pite-ar 1
pitirre-ar 1
pitoje-ar 1
pitorre-arse 80
piul-ar 1
pivote-ar 1
pizc-ar 67
plac-ar 67
place-ar 1
placente-
  arse 80
plac-er 54
plag-ar 51
plagi-ar 1
plaje-ar 1
planch-ar 1
planche-ar 1
plane-ar 1
planific-ar 67
plant-ar 1
plante-ar 1
plantific-ar 67
plantill-ar 1
plañ-ir 17
plaque-ar 1
plasm-ar 1
plaste-ar 1
plastec-er 48
plastific-ar 67
plate-ar 1
platic-ar 67
platin-ar 1

platoniz-ar 21
playe-ar 1
plebiscit-ar 1
pleg-ar 62
pleite-ar 1
plis-ar 1
plom-ar 1
plome-ar 1
plor-ar 1
plumaje-ar 1
plume-ar 1
pluraliz-ar 21
pobl-ar 25
pobrete-ar 1
poce-ar 1
pod-ar 1
podenque-ar 1
pod-er 55
podrec-er 48
podr-ir 56
poet-ar 1
poetiz-ar 21
poic-ar 67
poj-ar 1
polariz-ar 21
polc-ar 67
polemiz-ar 21
policopi-ar 1
polimeriz-ar 21
polimeriz-
  arse 21
poliniz-ar 21
pol-ir 4
politip-ar 1
politique-ar 1
politiz-ar 21
polle-ar 1
polole-ar 1
poltrone-ar 1
poltroniz-
  arse 21
polve-ar 1
polvific-ar 67
polvore-ar 1
polvoriz-ar 21
pomp-ar 1
pompe-ar 1
pompone-
  arse 80
ponch-ar 1
ponch-arse 80

ponche-ar 1
ponder-ar 1
pon-er 57
pontazgue-ar 1
ponte-ar 1
pontific-ar 67
ponzoñ-ar 1
pop-ar 1
popore-ar 1
popul-ar 1
populariz-ar 21
porc-ar 21
pordiose-ar 1
porfi-ar 9
porfidiz-ar 1
porfij-ar 1
porfiriz-ar 21
porg-ar 51
porhij-ar 1
pormenoriz-
  ar 21
porome-ar 1
porrace-ar 1
porre-ar 1
port-ar 1
portazg-ar 51
porte-ar 1
portill-ar 1
poruñe-ar 1
porvid-ar 1
pos-ar 1
posdat-ar 1
pose-er 26,
  plus the past
  participle
  poseso
posesion-ar 1
posfech-ar 1
posibilit-ar 1
positiv-ar 1
pospon-er 57
post-ar 25
poste-ar 1
posterg-ar 51
postil-ar 1
postine-ar 1
postr-ar 1
postsincroniz-
  ar 21
postul-ar 1
potabiliz-ar 21

pot-ar 1
potenci-ar 1
potinc-arse 80
potre-ar 1
poy-ar 1
poz-ar 21
practic-ar 67
pre-ar 1
prebend-ar 1
precaucion-
  arse 80
precautel-ar 1
precav-er 2
preced-er 2
precept-ar 1
preceptu-ar 9
preci-ar 1
precing-ir 3,
  with the
  changes in 23
precint-ar 1
precipit-ar 1
precis-ar 1
precit-ar 1
preconceb-ir 52
preconiz-ar 21
preconoc-er 48
pred-ar 1
predec-ir 58
predefin-ir 3
predestin-ar 1
predetermin-
  ar 1
predic-ar 67
predispon-er 57
predomin-ar 1
preeleg-ir 32,
  plus the past
  participle
  preelecto
preenton-ar 1
preestablec-
  er 48
preexist-ir 3
prefabric-ar 67
prefer-ir 71
prefigur-ar 1
prefij-ar 1
prefin-ir 3
preflame-ar 1
preform-ar 1

preg-ar 1
pregon-ar 1
pregunt-ar 1
pregust-ar 1
prejuzg-ar 51
preluc-ir 3,
  with the
  changes in 48
preludi-ar 1
premedit-ar 1
premi-ar 1
premit-ir 3
premor-ir 31,
  except the
  past participle
  is premuerto
premostr-ar 25
premun-ir 3
prend-ar 1
prend-er 2,
  plus past
  participle
  preso that is
  used more
  commonly
  than the
  regular past
  participle
prenot-ar 1
prenunci-ar 1
preñ-ar 1
preocup-ar 1
preopin-ar 1
preordin-ar 1
prepar-ar 1
preponder-ar 1
prepon-er 57
preposter-ar 1
presagi-ar 1
pres-ar 1
prescind-ir 3
prescrib-ir 3,
  except the
  past partici-
  ples are
  prescrito and
  prescripto
presenci-ar 1
present-ar 1
present-ir 71
preserv-ar 1

presidi-ar 1
presid-ir 3
presion-ar 1
prest-ar 1
prestidigit-ar 1
prestigi-ar 1
prest-ir 3
presum-ir 3,
  plus the past
  participle
  presunto
presupon-er 57
presupuest-ar ... 1
presuriz-ar 21
prete-ar 1
pretend-er 2,
  with the
  changes in
  21, plus the
  past participle
  pretenso
pretens-ar 1
preter-ir 4
pretermit-ir 1
preternaturaliz-
  ar 21
pretext-ar 1
pretin-ar 1
prevalec-er 48
preval-er 2,
  with the
  changes in 68
prevaric-ar 67
prevelic-ar 67
preven-ir 77
prev-er 78
previlej-ar 1
pri-ar 1
pri-arse 80
prim-ar 1
prime-arse 80
primeri-ar 1
primore-ar 1
princip-ar 1
principi-ar 1
pring-ar 51,
  and used in
  the positions
  in 45
pris-ar 1
prisc-ar 67

prismatiz-ar 21
priv-ar 1
privilegi-ar 1
privillej-ar 1
prob-ar 25
proced-er 2
proces-ar 1
proclam-ar 1
procrastin-ar 1
procre-ar 1
procur-ar 1
prodig-ar 51
produc-ir 59
proej-ar 1
proeje-ar 1
profan-ar 1
profaniz-ar 21
profaz-ar 21
profer-ir 71,
  plus an
  antiquated
  past partici-
  ple proferto
profes-ar 1
profesionaliz-
  ar 21
profet-ar 1
profetiz-ar 21
profij-ar 1
proflig-ar 51
profund-ar 1
profundiz-ar 21
program-ar 1
progres-ar 1
prohib-ir 3,
  with the
  changes in 9
prohij-ar 9
prolaps-arse 80
proletariz-ar 21
prolifer-ar 1
prolije-ar 1
prolog-ar 51
prologuiz-ar 21
prolong-ar 51
proman-ar 1
promedi-ar 1
promet-er 2
promiscu-ar 9
promocion-ar 1
promov-er 47

promulg-ar 51
pronostic-ar 67
prontuari-ar 1
pronunci-ar 1
propag-ar 51
propal-ar 1
propas-ar 1
propend-er 2,
  plus the past
  participle
  propenso
propici-ar 1
propin-ar 1
propon-er 57
proporcion-ar 1
proposit-ar 1
propugn-ar 1
propuls-ar 1
prorrate-ar 1
prorrog-ar 51
prorrump-ir 3
prosaiz-ar 21
proscrib-ir 3,
  except the
  past partici-
  ples are
  proscrito and
  proscripto
prose-ar 1
prosegu-ir 70
prosific-ar 67
prospect-ar 1
prosper-ar 1
prostern-arse ...80
prostitu-ir 42,
  plus the past
  participle
  prostituto
prostr-ar 1
prosupon-er 57
protagoniz-ar ...21
proteg-er 23
protest-ar 1
protocol-ar 1
protocoliz-ar 21
provag-ar 1
provec-er 48
provech-ar 1
prove-er 22,
  plus past par-
  ticiple provisto

that is used
more com-
monly than the
regular past
participle
proven-ir 77
provenzaliz-
  ar 21
proverbi-ar 1
providenci-ar 1
provist-ar 1
provoc-ar 67
proyect-ar 1
prudenci-ar 1
prudenci-
  arse 80
pu-ar 9
pubesc-er 2
public-ar 67
puch-ar 1
puchere-ar 1
pudel-ar 1
pudibundiz-
  arse 80
pudr-ir 56
puente-ar 1
puertafere-ar 1
puerte-ar 1
puertere-ar 1
pueste-ar 1
pugn-ar 1
puj-ar 1
pulgone-ar 1
puliment-ar 1
pul-ir 4
pulp-ar 1
pulpi-ar 1
puls-ar 1
pulse-ar 1
pulul-ar 1
pulveriz-ar 21
pun-ar 1
punch-ar 1
puncion-ar 1
pung-ir 3,
  with the
  changes in 23
pun-ir 3
punn-ar 1
punque-ar 1
puntale-ar 1

punt-ar 1
punte-ar 1
puntill-ar 1
puntille-ar 1
puntualiz-ar 21
puntu-ar 9
punz-ar 21
punzon-ar 1
puñale-ar 1
pur-ar 1
pure-ar 1
purg-ar 51
purific-ar 67
purisc-ar 1
purpur-ar 1
purpure-ar 1
pusuque-ar 1
putañe-ar 1
pute-ar 1
puy-ar 1

q

quebraj-ar 1
quebraje-ar 1
quebrant-ar 1
quebr-ar 53
quebraz-arse ... 21
qued-ar 1
quej-ar 1
quejumbr-ar 1
quellotr-ar 1
quem-ar 1
quencharche-
  ar 1
quer-ar 1
queratiniz-ar 21
querell-arse 80
quer-er 60,
  plus an anti-
  quated past
  participle
  quisto
queroch-ar 1
quese-ar 1
quess-ar 1
quichuiz-ar 21
quiet-ar 1
quijote-ar 1
quilat-ar 1

quilde-ar 1
quilific-ar 67
quill-ar 1
quillotr-ar 1
quilombe-ar 1
quilp-ar 1
quiltre-ar 1
quimbe-ar 1
quimbre-ar 1
quimere-ar 1
quimeriz-ar 21
quimific-ar 67
quin-ar 1
quinch-ar 1
quinchone-ar 1
quine-ar 1
quingue-ar 1
quinole-ar 2
quintaesenci-
  ar 1
quint-ar 1
quintuplic-ar 67
quiñ-ar 1
quirquinch-ar 1
quisne-ar 1
quisquill-ar 1
quisqu-irse 82
quist-arse 80
quit-ar 1
quiz-ar 21

r

rabe-ar 1
rabere-ar 1
rabi-ar 1
rabiat-ar 1
rabil-ar 1
rabiz-ar 21
rabon-ar 1
rabone-ar 1
rabose-ar 1
rabot-ar 1
rabote-ar 1
racane-ar 1
rach-ar 1
rachiz-ar 1
racim-ar 1
raciocin-ar 1
racionaliz-ar 21

racion-ar 1
radi-ar 1
radicaliz-ar 21
radic-ar 67
radioautografi-
  ar 1
radiobaliz-ar 21
radiodifund-ir 3
radiodirig-ir 3,
  with the
  changes in 23
radiografi-ar 9
radiogui-ar 9
radiolocaliz-
  ar 21
radiotelefone-
  ar 1
radiotelegrafi-
  ar 9
ra-er 61
rafe-ar 1
rafez-ar 21
ragu-ar 1
rahez-ar 21
raice-ar 1
raig-ar 1
raim-ar 1
raiz-ar 35
raj-ar 1
rajete-ar 1
rajuñ-ar 1
ralb-ar 1
rale-ar 1
rall-ar 1
ramaje-ar 1
ramale-ar 1
rame-ar 1
ramific-ar 67
ramone-ar 1
ranc-ar 67
rance-ar 1
ranch-ar 1
ranche-ar 1
ranci-ar 1
rancl-arse 80
rane-ar 1
ranfuñ-ar 1
rap-ar 1
rapel-ar 1
rapiñ-ar 1
rapiz-ar 21

rapose-ar 1
rapt-ar 1
rapuz-ar 21
raque-ar 1
raquiocoainiz-
ar 21
raquistovainiz-
ar 21
rarefac-er 41,
except the
past participle
is rarefacto
rarific-ar 67
ras-ar 1
ras-arse 80
rascabuch-ar ... 1
rascabuche-ar .. 1
rascadill-ar 1
rasc-ar 67
rascol-ar 1
rascuñ-ar 1
rasg-ar 51
rasgue-ar 1
rasguñ-ar 1
rasmill-ar 1
raspahil-ar 9
rasp-ar 1
raspe-ar 1
raspone-ar 1
rasquete-ar 1
rast-ar 1
rastill-ar 1
rastrall-ar 1
rastr-ar 1
rastre-ar 1
rastrill-ar 1
rastrille-ar 1
rastroj-ar 1
rastrill-ar 1
rastrille-ar 1
rastroj-ar 1
rastroje-ar 1
rasur-ar 1
rate-ar 1
ratific-ar 67
ratig-ar 51
raton-ar 1
raume-ar 1
ray-ar 1
raz-ar 1
raz-arse 80

razi-ar 1
razon-ar 1
reabr-ir 3,
except the
past participle
is reabierto
reabsorb-er 2
reaccion-ar 1
reactiv-ar 1
reacuñ-ar 1
readapt-ar 1
readmit-ir 3
reafirm-ar 1
reagradec-er ... 48
reagrav-ar 1
reagrup-ar 1
reajust-ar 1
realegr-arse 80
realiz-ar 21
realquil-ar 1
realz-ar 21
ream-ar 1
reanim-ar 1
reanud-ar 1
reaparec-er 48
reaplic-ar 67
reapret-ar 53
rear-ar 1
reargü-ir 42
rearm-ar 1
reasegur-ar 1
reasent-ar 1
reasign-ar 1
reasum-ir 3
reat-ar 1
reavent-ar 53
reaviv-ar 1
rebab-arse 80
rebaj-ar 1
rebalg-ar 51
reball-ar 1
rebals-ar 1
reban-ar 1
rebane-ar 1
rebañ-ar 1
rebaque-ar 1
rebas-ar 1
rebat-ar 1
rebat-ir 3
rebautiz-ar 21
rebeb-er 2

rebel-arse 80
rebenque-ar 1
reber-ar 1
rebez-ar 21
rebin-ar 1
rebit-ar 1
reblandec-er ... 48
rebl-ar 1
rebobin-ar 1
reboc-ar 1
rebole-ar 1
rebomb-ar 1
reboñ-ar 1
rebord-ar 1
reborde-ar 1
reboruj-ar 1
rebos-ar 1
rebot-ar 1
reboz-ar 21
rebram-ar 1
rebrill-ar 1
rebrinc-ar 67
rebrot-ar 1
rebruñ-ir 17
rebudi-ar 1
rebuf-ar 1
rebuj-ar 1
rebull-ir 17
rebumb-ar 1
reburde-ar 1
reburuj-ar 1
rebusc-ar 67
rebut-ir 3
rebuzn-ar 1
recab-ar 1
recabd-ar 1
recache-ar 1
recad-ar 1
reca-er 20
recair-ar 1
recal-ar 1
recalc-ar 67
recalcitr-ar 1
recalent-ar 53
recalz-ar 21
recam-ar 1
recambi-ar 1
recant-ar 1
recapacit-ar 1
recapitul-ar 1
recarg-ar 51

recat-ar 1
recate-ar 1
recatone-ar 1
recauch-ar 1
recauchut-ar 1
recaud-ar 1
recav-ar 1
recaz-ar 21
receb-ar 1
receboj-ar 1
receboll-ar 1
recech-ar 1
recej-ar 1
recel-ar 1
recent-ar 53
receñ-ir 64
recept-ar 1
recerc-ar 67
reces-ar 1
recet-ar 1
rechaz-ar 21
rechifl-ar 1
rechin-ar 1
rechispe-ar 1
rechist-ar 1
rechiz-ar 21
rechup-ar 1
recib-ir 3
recicl-ar 1
recidiv-ar 1
recinch-ar 1
reciproc-ar 67
recit-ar 1
reclam-ar 1
reclav-ar 1
reclin-ar 1
reclu-ir 42,
plus the past
participle
recluso
reclut-ar 1
recobr-ar 1
recoc-er 22
recochine-
arse 80
recod-ar 1
recod-ir 3
recog-er 23
recol-ar 25
recolect-ar 1
recoleg-ir 32

recolet-ar 1
recomend-ar 53
recomenz-ar 34
recom-erse 81
recompart-ir 3
recompens-ar ... 1
recompon-er 57
reconcentr-ar ... 1
reconcili-ar 1
reconcom-
erse 81
reconden-ar 1
reconduc-ir 59
reconect-ar 1
reconfirm-ar 1
reconfort-ar 1
reconoc-er 48
reconquist-ar ... 1
reconsider-ar ... 1
reconstitu-ir 42
reconstru-ir 42
recont-ar 25
reconvalec-
er 48
reconvenc-er ... 2
reconven-ir 77
reconvert-ir 71
recopil-ar 1
recoque-arse ...80
record-ar 25
recorr-er 2
recort-ar 1
recorv-ar 1
recos-er 2
recost-ar 25
recov-ar 1
recre-ar 1
recrec-er 48
recri-ar 9
recrimin-ar 1
recrudec-er 48
recruj-ir 3
recruz-ar 21
rect-ar 1
rectific-ar 67
rector-ar 1
recuadr-ar 1
recubr-ir 3,
except the
past participle
is recubierto

recud-ir 3
recuest-ar 1
recul-ar 1
recuñ-ar 1
recuper-ar 1
recur-ar 1
recurr-ir 3
recurv-ar 1
recus-ar 1
redact-ar 1
redam-ar 1
red-ar 1
redargu-ir 42
redargü-ir 42
rede-ar 1
redec-ir 58
redescubr-ir
3, except the
past partici-
ple is
redescubierto
redhib-ir 3
rediezm-ar 1
redil-ar 1
redile-ar 1
redim-ir 3
redistribu-ir 42
reditu-ar 9
redobl-ar 1
redobleg-ar 51
redol-ar 1
redol-er 50
redomone-ar 1
redonde-ar 1
redor-ar 1
redr-ar 1
redroj-ar 1
reduc-ir 59
redund-ar 1
redund-ir 3
reduplic-ar 67
reedific-ar 67
reedit-ar 1
reeduc-ar 67
reeleg-ir 32,
plus the past
participle
reelecto
reelig-ir 3,
with the
changes in 23

reembarc-ar 67
reembarg-ar 51
reembols-ar 1
reemplaz-ar 21
reemprend-er ... 2
reencarn-ar 1
reencauch-ar ... 1
reencuadern-
ar 1
reenganch-ar ... 1
reengendr-ar 1
reenroll-ar 1
reensay-ar 1
reentr-ar 1
reenvi-ar 9
reenvid-ar 1
reescrib-ir 3,
except the past
participle
is reescrito
reestren-ar 1
reestructur-ar ... 1
reexamin-ar 1
reexped-ir 52
reexport-ar 1
refaccion-ar 1
refac-er 69,
except the
past participle
is refacido
refal-ar 1
refeccion-ar 1
refer-ir 71
refert-ar 1
refez-ar 21
refigur-ar 1
refil-ar 1
refin-ar 1
refirm-ar 1
refistole-ar 1
refitole-ar 1
reflect-ar 1
reflej-ar 1
reflexion-ar 1
reflorec-er 48
reflu-ir 42
refocil-ar 1,
and used in
the positions
in 45
reforest-ar 1

reforj-ar 1
reform-ar 1
reforz-ar 39
refract-ar 1
refreg-ar 62
refre-ír 63,
plus the
past partici-
ple refrito
refren-ar 1
refrend-ar 1
refrent-ar 1
refresc-ar 67
refri-ar 1
refri-arse 9
refriger-ar 1
refring-ir 3,
with the
changes in 23
refucil-ar 1
refugi-ar 1
refulg-ir 3,
with the
changes in 23
refund-ir 3
refunfuñ-ar 1
refut-ar 1
regace-ar 1
regal-ar 1
regalone-ar 1
regañ-ar 1
regañ-ir 17
reg-ar 62
regat-ar 1
regate-ar 1
regatone-ar 1
regaz-ar 21
regener-ar 1
regent-ar 1
regente-ar 1
regiment-ar 53
regimpl-ar 1
regionaliz-ar ...21
reg-ir ....3?
registr-ar ....
reglament-ar ....
regl-ar ....
reglete-ar ....
regocij-ar ....
regode-ar ....
regode-arse .....

regoetr-ar 1
regold-ar 25
regolf-ar 1
regorj-arse 80
regost-arse 80
regotr-ar 1
regraci-ar 1
regres-ar 1
regros-ar 25
regruñ-ir 17
reguard-ar 1
reguard-arse 80
reguarnec-er ... 48
reguc-ir 59
reguerete-ar 1
reguil-ar 1
regul-ar 1
regulariz-ar 21
regurgit-ar 1
rehabilit-ar 1
rehac-er 41
rehall-ar 1
rehart-ar 1
rehele-ar 1
rehench-ir 52
rehend-er 2,
  with the
  changes in 53
reher-ir 71
reherr-ar 53
reherv-ir 71
rehil-ar 9
rehinch-ir 52
rehog-ar 51
reholl-ar 25
rehoy-ar 1
rehug-ar 1
rehu-ir 42
rehumect-ar 1
rehumedec-
  er 48
rehund-ir 3
rehurt-arse 80
rehus-ar 1
reil-ar 9
reimpatri-ar 1
reimplant-ar 1
reimport-ar 1
reimprim-ir 3,
  plus the past
  participle

reimpreso
rein-ar 1
reincid-ir 3
reincorpor-ar 1
reingres-ar 1
reinscrib-ir 3,
  except the
  past partici-
  ples are
  reinscrito and
  reinscripto
reinstal-ar 1
reintegr-ar 1
reintub-ar 1
reinvert-ir 71
re-ír 63
reiter-ar 1
reivindic-ar 67
rejac-ar 67
rejit-ar 1
rejone-ar 1
rejund-ir 3
rejunt-ar 1
rejuvenec-er 48
relabr-ar 1
relacion-ar 1
relaj-ar 1
relaje-ar 1
relam-er 2
relampague-ar
  1, and for its
  use regarding
  weather,
  see 45
relanz-ar 21
relat-ar 1
relauch-ar 1
relauche-ar 1
relav-ar 1
relax-ar 1
relaz-ar 21
rele-er 26
releg-ar 51
relej-ar 1
relentec-er 48
relev-ar 1
reli-ar 1
relig-ar 51
relim-ar 1
relimpi-ar 1
relinch-ar 1

reling-ar 51
rellan-ar 1
rellen-ar 1
reluch-ar 1
reluc-ir 3,
  with the
  changes in 48
reluj-ar 1
relumbr-ar 1
relv-ar 1
remach-ar 1
remall-ar 1
reman-ar 1
remand-ar 1
remanec-er 48
remang-ar 51
reman-ir 4
remans-arse 80
rem-ar 1
remarc-ar 67
remat-ar 1
rembols-ar 1
remec-er 23
remed-ar 1
remedi-ar 1
remed-ir 52
remej-er 2
remell-ar 1
remembr-ar 53
rememor-ar 1
remend-ar 53
remene-ar 1
remes-ar 1
remet-er 2
remilg-arse 51
remilitariz-ar ... 21
remir-ar 1
remit-ir 3
remoj-ar 1
remol-ar 25
remolc-ar 67
remold-ar 1
remol-er 47
remolin-ar 1
remoline-ar 1
remoll-ar 25
remolone-ar 1
remond-ar 1
remont-ar 1
remor-ar 1
remord-er 47

remosque-
  arse 80
remost-ar 1
remostec-
  erse 48
remov-er 48
remoz-ar 21
remplaz-ar 21
rempuj-ar 1
remud-ar 1
remudi-ar 1
remug-ar 51
remull-ir 17
remuner-ar 1
remusg-ar 51
renac-er 48
rencion-ar 1
rencur-arse 80
rend-ar 1
rend-ir 52
reneg-ar 62
renegre-ar 1
reng-ar 51
rengue-ar 1
reniñ-ir 1
renombr-ar 1
renov-ar 25
renque-ar 1
rentabiliz-ar 21
rent-ar 1
renunci-ar 1
renvals-ar 1
renvid-ar 1
reñ-ir 64
reoctav-ar 1
reorden-ar 1
reorganiz-ar 21
repac-er 48
repag-ar 51
repanchig-
  arse 51
repantig-arse ... 51
repapil-arse 80
repar-ar 1
repart-ir 3
repas-ar 1
repast-ar 1
repatri-ar 9
repech-ar 1
repein-ar 1
repel-ar 1

repel-er 2
repell-ar 1
repens-ar 53
repent-irse 71
repentiz-ar 21
repepen-ar 1
repercud-ir 3
repercut-ir 3
reperiquete-ar ... 1
repes-ar 1
repesc-ar 67
repet-ir 52
repic-ar 67
repicote-ar 1
repin-arse 80
repint-ar 1
repiquete-ar 1
repis-ar 1
repispe-ar 1
repizc-ar 67
replan-ar 1
replant-ar 1
replante-ar 1
replantig-
    arse 80
repleg-ar 62
replet-ar 1
replic-ar 67
repobl-ar 25
repod-ar 1
repodr-ir 56
repoll-ar 1
repon-er 57
report-ar 1
reporte-ar 1
repos-ar 1
repost-ar 1
repoy-ar 1
repregunt-ar 1
reprehend-er 2
reprend-er 2
repres-ar 1
represent-ar 1
reprim-ir 3
repris-ar 1
reprob-ar 25
reproch-ar 1
reproduc-ir 59
repropi-arse 80
rept-ar 1
republicaniz-

ar 21
repuch-ar 1
repudi-ar 1
repudr-ir 56
repugn-ar 1
repuj-ar 1
repulg-ar 51
repul-ir 3
repuls-ar 1
repulul-ar 1
repunt-ar 1
repurg-ar 51
reput-ar 1
requebr-ar 53
requem-ar 1
requer-er 60
requer-ir 71
request-ar 1
requint-ar 1
requinte-ar 1
requis-ar 1
requisicion-ar ... 1
resab-er 66
resabi-ar 1
resac-ar 67
resal-ar 1
resalg-arse 80
resal-ir 68
resall-ar 1
resalt-ar 1
resalud-ar 1
resan-ar 1
resarc-ir 3,
    with the
    changes in 23
resbal-ar 1
rescald-ar 1
rescat-ar 1
rescind-ir 3
rescold-ar 1
rescolde-
    arse 80
rescontr-ar 25
rescrib-ir 3,
    except the
    past partici-
    ples are
    rescrito and
    rescripto
resec-ar 67
reseg-ar 62

resegu-ir 52
resell-ar 1
resembr-ar 53
resent-irse 71
reseñ-ar 1
reserv-ar 1
resfal-ar 1
resfri-ar 9
resgat-ar 1
resguard-ar 1
residenci-ar 1
resid-ir 3
resieg-ar 51
resign-ar 1
resill-ar 1
resin-ar 1
resis-ar 1
resist-ir 3
resob-ar 1
resobr-ar 1
resolg-ar 25
resoll-ar 25
resolt-arse
    80, with the
    changes in 25
resolv-er 47,
    except the
    past participle
    is resuelto
reson-ar 25
resondr-ar 1
resopl-ar 1
resorb-er 2
respagil-ar 1
respahil-ar 9
respail-ar 1
respald-ar 1
respect-ar 1
respeluz-ar 21
respet-ar 1
respig-ar 51
resping-ar 51
respir-ar 1
resplandec-
    er 48
respond-er 2
responsabiliz-
    ar 21
responsa-
    biliz-arse 21
respons-ar 1

response-ar 1
resquebraj-ar 1
resquebr-ar 53
resquem-ar 1
resquil-ar 1
resquit-ar 1
restablec-er 48
restall-ar 1
restamp-ar 1
restañ-ar 1
rest-ar 1
restaur-ar 1
restell-ar 1
resting-ar 51
restir-arse 80
restitu-ir 42
restreg-ar 62
restrell-ar 1
restrib-ar 1
restrill-ar 1
restring-ir 3,
    with the
    changes in 23
restriñ-ir 17
resucit-ar 1
resud-ar 1
result-ar 1,
    and used in
    the positions
    in 45
resum-ir 3
resurg-ir 3,
    with the
    changes in 23
resurt-ir 3
retac-ar 67
retace-ar 1
retach-ar 1
retaj-ar 1
retall-ar 1
retallec-er 48
retaque-ar 1
ret-ar 1
retard-ar 1
retas-ar 1
retaz-ar 21
retej-ar 1
retej-er 2
retembl-ar 53
retempl-ar 1
reten-er 74

retent-ar 53
reteñ-ir 64,
  plus the past
  participle
  retinto
retes-ar 1
retestin-ar 1
retestiñ-ar 1
retijerete-ar 1
retin-ar 1
retingl-ar 1
retintine-ar 1
retiñ-ir 17
ret-ir 52
retir-ar 1
retob-ar 1
retobe-ar 1
retoc-ar 67
retom-ar 1
retoñ-ar 1
retoñec-er 48
retoplic-ar 1
retorc-er 2,
  plus the
  past partici-
  ple retuerto
retorcij-ar 1
retoric-ar 67
retorn-ar 1
retortij-ar 1
retost-ar 25
retoz-ar 21
retrab-ar 1
retract-ar 1
retraduc-ir 59
retra-er 75
retranc-ar 67
retranque-ar 1
retras-ar 1
retrat-ar 1
retrech-ar 1
retrep-arse 80
retribu-ir 42
retrill-ar 1
retrob-ar 1
retroc-ar 25,
  with the
  changes in 67
retroced-er 2
retrograd-ar 1

retron-ar 25,
  and for its
  use regarding
  weather,
  see 45
retrotra-er 75
retrovacun-ar 1
retrovend-er 2
retruc-ar 67
retumb-ar 1
retund-ir 3
reunific-ar 67
reun-ir 9
reunt-ar 1
revacun-ar 1
revalid-ar 1
revalor-ar 1
revaloriz-ar 21
revalu-ar 9
reveget-ar 1
revejec-er 41
revel-ar 1
revel-er 2
reven-ar 1
revenc-er 2
revend-er 2
reven-ir 77
revent-ar 53
rev-er 78
rever-ar 1
reverber-ar 1
reverbere-ar 1
reverdec-er 48
reverenci-ar 1
revers-ar 1
revert-er 39
revert-ir 71
reves-ar 1
revest-ir 52
revez-ar 21
revid-ar 1
revigoriz-ar 21
revin-ar 1
revindic-ar 67
revir-ar 1
revis-ar 1
revist-ar 1
revitaliz-ar 21
revit-ar 1
reviv-ar 1
revivific-ar 67

reviv-ir 3
revoc-ar 67
revol-ar 25
revolc-ar 76
revole-ar 1
revolisque-ar 1
revolote-ar 1
revolte-ar 1
revolucion-ar 1
revolv-er 47,
  except the
  past participle
  is revuelto
revot-arse 80
revuelc-ar 67
revuls-ar 1
rey-ar 1
reyert-ar 1
reyun-ar 1
rezag-ar 51
rez-ar 21
rezondr-ar 1
rezong-ar 51
rezongl-ar 1
rezum-ar 1
rezumb-ar 1
rezurc-ir 3,
  with the
  changes in 23
ribete-ar 1
ridiculiz-ar 21
riel-ar 1, and
  for its use
  regarding
  weather,
  see 45
rif-ar 1
ril-ar 1
rim-ar 1
rimbomb-ar 1
ring-ar 51
ringlete-ar 1
ringuelete-ar 1
rinz-ar 21
riostr-ar 1
ripe-ar 1
ripi-ar 1
risc-ar 67
risote-ar 1
risp-ar 1
rispi-ar 1

ritm-ar 1
rivaliz-ar 21
riz-ar 21
rob-ar 1
robl-ar 1
roblon-ar 1
robor-ar 1
robr-ar 1
robustec-er 48
rocambore-ar ... 1
roch-ar 1
rochele-ar 1
roci-ar 9, and
  used in the
  positions in 45
rodaje-ar 1
rod-ar 25
rode-ar 1
rodrig-ar 51
ro-er 65
rog-ar 24
roguete-ar 1
roje-ar 1
rol-ar 1
rold-ar 1
role-ar 1
roll-ar 1
romadiz-arse ... 21
roman-ar 1
romance-ar 1
romane-ar 1
romaniz-ar 21
romanz-ar 21
rome-ar 1
romp-er 1,
  plus the past
  participle roto
  that is used
  more com-
  monly than
  the regular
  past
  participle
ronc-ar 67
ronce-ar 1
ronch-ar 1
rond-ar 1
ronque-ar 1
ronrone-ar 1
ronz-ar 21
roñ-ar 1

ror-ar 1
rorre-ar 1
ros-ar 1, and
   used in the
   positions in 45
ros-arse 80
rosc-ar 67
rose-ar 1
roseg-ar 1
rosig-ar 51
rosm-ar 1
rosn-ar 1
rosque-ar 1
rost-ir 3
rot-ar 1
rote-ar 1
rotul-ar 1
rotur-ar 1
roy-arse 80
roz-ar 21
rozn-ar 1
ru-ar 9
rubific-ar 67
ruboriz-ar 21
rubric-ar 67
rucane-ar 1
ruc-ar 67
ruce-ar 1
ruch-ar 1
ruci-ar 1
rufiane-ar 1
rug-ar 51
rug-ir 3, with
   the changes
   in 23, and
   used in the
   conjugations
   in 45
ruin-ar 1
ruji-ar 1
rul-ar 1
rumaje-ar 1
rumbanche-ar ... 1
rumb-ar 1
rumbe-ar 1
rumi-ar 1
rumor-ar 1
rumor-arse 80
rumore-ar 1
rumore-arse 80
rund-ir 3

runfi-ar 1
runfl-ar 1
runrune-ar 1
runrune-arse 80
ruñ-ar 1
ruñ-ir 3
rusent-ar 53
rusific-ar 67
rustic-ar 67
rust-ir 3
rustr-ir 3
rut-ar 1
rute-ar 1
ruti-ar 1
rutil-ar 1, and
   for its use
   regarding
   weather,
   see 45
rutr-ir 3

S

sabane-ar 1
sabatiz-ar 21
sab-er 66
sable-ar 1
sabore-ar 1
saborg-ar 51
sabote-ar 1
sabrose-ar 1
saburr-ar 1
sac-ar 67
sacarific-ar 67
sach-ar 1
saci-ar 1
sacraliz-ar 21
sacrament-ar 1
sacrific-ar 67
sacud-ir 3
saet-ar 1
saete-ar 1
saf-ar 1
sagr-ar 1
sahorn-arse 80
sahum-ar 9
sain-ar 9
sainete-ar 1
saj-ar 1
sajel-ar 1

salabarde-ar 1
sal-ar 1
salari-ar 1
salcoch-ar 1
salcochon-ar 1
sald-ar 1
sale-arse 80
saleg-ar 51
salg-ar 51
salific-ar 67
sal-ir 68
saliv-ar 1
sall-ar 1
salm-ar 1
salme-ar 1
salmodi-ar 1
salmore-ar 1
salmuer-arse ... 80
salom-ar 1
salpic-ar 67
salpiment-ar 53
salpique-ar 1
salpres-ar 1,
   plus the past
   participle
   salpreso
salpull-ir 17
salse-ar 1
salt-ar 1
salte-ar 1
salteri-ar 1
saltic-ar 1
salud-ar 1
salvaguard-ar ... 1
salvaguardi-ar .. 1
salv-ar 1, plus
   the past
   participle
   salvo
samaque-ar 1
sam-ar 1
sambenit-ar 1
sambut-ir 3
samure-ar 1
samurr-ar 1
san-ar 1
sancion-ar 1
sancoch-ar 1
sandungue-ar ... 1
sane-ar 1
sanforiz-ar 21

sangarete-ar 1
sangr-ar 1
sangrent-ar 53
sanguific-ar 67
sanguiform-ar ... 1
sanj-ar 1
sanjuane-ar 1
santific-ar 67
santigu-ar 7
sape-ar 1
saponific-ar 67
sapote-ar 1
saque-ar 1
sarate-arse 80
sargente-ar 1
sarj-ar 1
sarment-ar 53
sarpull-ir 17
sarrapi-ar 1
sateliz-ar 21
satin-ar 1
satiriz-ar 21
satisfac-er 69
satur-ar 1
sazon-ar 1
sebe-ar 1
sebose-ar 1
sec-ar 67
seccion-ar 1
secrest-ar 1
secret-ar 1
secrete-ar 1
secuestr-ar 1
seculariz-ar 21
secund-ar 1
secut-ar 1
sed-ar 1
sede-ar 1
sediment-ar 1
seduc-ir 59
se-er 2
seg-ar 61
segment-ar 1
segreg-ar 51
segud-ar 1
seguete-ar 1
segu-ir 70
segund-ar 1
segunde-ar 1
segur-ar 1
seisav-ar 1

sele-ar 1
seleccion-ar 1
seleniz-ar 1
sell-ar 1
semblante-ar 1
sembl-ar 1
sembr-ar 53
semej-ar 1
sement-ar 53
semiarrodill-
  arse 80
semiaturd-
  irse 82
semill-ar 1
semin-ar 1
sender-ar 1
sendere-ar 1
sensibiliz-ar 21
sensitiz-ar 21
sent-ar 53
sentenci-ar 1
sent-ir 71
señal-ar 1
señaliz-ar 21
señ-ar 1
señole-ar 1
señore-ar 1
separ-ar 1
sepel-ir 3,
  plus the past
  participle
  sepulto
septuplic-ar 67
sepult-ar 1,
  plus the past
  participle
  sepulto
sequi-ar 1
s-er 72
serane-ar 1
seren-ar 1
seri-ar 1
sermon-ar 1
sermone-ar 1
serpe-ar 1
serpente-ar 1
serpoll-ar 1
serranj-ar 1
serr-ar 53
serruch-ar 1
serv-ar 1

servici-ar 1
serv-ir 52
sese-ar 1
sesg-ar 51
sesgue-ar 1
sesion-ar 1
sest-ar 1
seste-ar 1
seten-ar 1
sextaferi-ar 1
sextav-ar 1
sextuplic-ar 67
shugu-ar 1
shunt-ar 1
sigil-ar 1
sign-ar 1
signific-ar 67
siguete-ar 1
silab-ar 1
silabe-ar 1
silabiz-ar 1
silb-ar 1
silbote-ar 1
silenci-ar 1
silg-ar 51
silicatiz-ar 21
silogiz-ar 21
siluete-ar 1
sim-ar 1
simbel-ar 1
simboliz-ar 21
simenz-ar 34
simetriz-ar 21
simoniz-ar 21
simp-ar 1
simpatiz-ar 21
simplific-ar 67
simul-ar 1
simultane-ar 1
sinalef-ar 1
sinastr-ar 1
sincer-ar 1
sincop-ar 1
sincopiz-ar 21
sincroniz-ar 21
sindic-ar 67
sing-ar 51
singl-ar 1
singulariz-ar 21
sinteriz-ar 21
sintetiz-ar 21

sintoniz-ar 21
sirc-ar 1
sirg-ar 51
sis-ar 1
sise-ar 1
sism-ar 1
sistem-ar 1
sistematiz-ar ... 21
sit-ar 1
siti-ar 1
situ-ar 9
ski-ar 1
soalz-ar 21
soas-ar 1
sobaj-ar 1
sobaje-ar 1
sob-ar 1
sobarc-ar 67
soberane-ar 1
soberbi-ar 1
sobord-ar 1
soborn-ar 1
sobrad-ar 1
sobr-ar 1
sobras-ar 1
sobraz-ar 21
sobreabund-ar .. 1
sobreagu-ar 7
sobrealiment-
  ar 1
sobrealz-ar 21
sobreañad-ir 3
sobrear-ar 1
sobreas-ar 1
sobrebarr-er 2
sobrebeb-er 2
sobrecalent-
  ar 53
sobrecarg-ar 51
sobrecart-ar 1
sobrecen-ar 1
sobrecog-er 23
sobrecomprim-
  ir 3
sobrecos-er 2
sobrecrec-er 48
sobrecur-ar 1
sobred-ar 27
sobredor-ar 1
sobreedific-
  ar 67

sobreentend-
  er 2, with the
  changes in 53
sobreentren-ar .. 1
sobreest-ar 38
sobreestim-ar ... 1
sobreexager-
  ar 1
sobreexced-er .. 2
sobreexcit-ar 1
sobreexpon-
  er 57
sobrefund-ir 3
sobregan-ar 1
sobregir-ar 1
sobreher-ir 71
sobrehil-ar 9
sobrelev-ar 1
sobrellav-ar 1
sobrellen-ar 1
sobrellev-ar 1
sobrenad-ar 1
sobrenaturaliz-
  ar 21
sobrenombr-ar .. 1
sobrentend-er
  2, with the
  changes in 53
sobreostent-ar .. 1
sobrepag-ar 1
sobrepas-ar 1
sobrepint-
  arse 80
sobrepon-er 57
sobrepuj-ar 1
sobresal-ir 68
sobresalt-ar 1
sobresalte-ar 1
sobresan-ar 1
sobresatur-ar ... 1
sobrescrib-ir
  3, except the
  past partici-
  ples are
  sobrescrito
  and
  sobrescripto
sobrese-er 26
sobresell-ar 1
sobresembr-
  ar 53

sobresol-ar 25
sobrest-ar 38
sobrestim-ar 1
sobretej-er 2
sobreven-ir 77
sobrevert-erse
  81, with the
  changes in 53
sobrevest-ir 52
sobreviv-ir 3
sobrevol-ar 25
sobrexced-er 2
sobrexcit-ar 1
socal-ar 1
socaliñ-ar 1
socalz-ar 21
socap-ar 1
soc-ar 67
socarr-ar 1
socav-ar 1
sociabiliz-ar 21
socializ-ar 21
sococh-ar 1
socol-ar 25
socollone-ar 1
socorr-er 2
sofald-ar 1
sofistic-ar 67
soflam-ar 1
sofoc-ar 67
sofreg-ar 53
sofre-ír 63,
  plus the past
  participle
  sofrito
sofren-ar 1
sogue-ar 1
sojuzg-ar 51
solace-ar 1
solap-ar 1
solape-ar 1
solaque-ar 1
sol-ar 25
solariz-arse 21
solaz-ar 21
sold-ar 25
sole-ar 1
solej-ar 1
solemniz-ar 21
sol-er 73
solet-ar 1

solete-ar 1
solevant-ar 1
solev-ar 1
solfe-ar 1
solicit-ar 1
solid-ar 1
solidariz-ar 21
solidific-ar 21
soliloqui-ar 1
soliviant-ar 1
solivi-ar 1
sollam-ar 1
soll-ar 1
sollisp-arse 80
solloz-ar 21
solmen-ar 1
solmis-ar 1
solmiz-ar 21
solt-ar 25,
  plus the past
  participle
  suelto
soltere-ar 1
solubiliz-ar 21
solucion-ar 1
solvent-ar 1
solv-er 2
somant-ar 1
somarr-ar 1
somat-ar 1
sombr-ar 1
sombre-ar 1
somet-er 2
somorguj-ar 1
somormuj-ar 1
sompes-ar 1
sonaje-ar 1
son-ar 25
sond-ar 1
sonde-ar 1
sonete-ar 1
sonetiz-ar 21
songue-ar 1
sonoch-ar 1
sonoriz-ar 21
sonre-ír 63
sonris-ar 1
sonrod-arse
  80, with the
  changes in 25
sonroj-ar 1

sonroje-ar 1
sonros-ar 1
sonrose-ar 1
sonrostr-arse ... 80
sonrug-irse
  82, with the
  changes in 23
sonsac-ar 67
sonsañ-ar 1
sonse-ar 1
sonsonete-ar 1
sonsonich-ar 1
soñ-ar 25
sopalanc-ar 67
sopape-ar 1
sopapi-ar 1
sop-ar 1
sope-ar 1
sopes-ar 1
sopete-ar 1
sopl-ar 1
soplone-ar 1
soploniz-ar 21
soport-ar 1
sopunt-ar 1
soque-ar 1
soquete-ar 1
sorb-er 2
sordec-er 48
soreraj-ar 1
sormigr-ar 1
sorn-ar 2
soroch-arse 80
sororiz-ar 21
sorprend-er 2
sorrab-ar 1
sorraj-ar 1
sorrape-ar 1
sorrasc-ar 1
sorrase-ar 1
sorreg-ar 62
sorrong-ar 51
sorrostr-ar 1
sorrostric-ar 1
sorte-ar 1
sosac-ar 67
sosañ-ar 1
soseg-ar 62
soslay-ar 1
sospech-ar 1
sospes-ar 1

sosquin-ar 1
sosten-er 74
sostitu-ir 42
sotane-ar 1
sot-ar 1
sotavent-
  arse 80
sotavente-
  arse 80
soterr-ar 53
sotil-arse 80
sotiliz-ar 21
sovietiz-ar 21
standardiz-ar ... 21
suavec-er 48
suavific-ar 67
suaviz-ar 21
subaliment-ar ... 1
subalquil-ar 1
subaltern-ar 1
subarrend-ar 53
subast-ar 1
subdeleg-ar 51
subdiacron-ar ... 1
subdistingu-
  ir 30
subdivid-ir 3
subentend-er
  2, with the
  changes in 53
subestim-ar 1
subexpon-er 57
subflet-ar 1
subfund-ir 3
subintr-ar 1
sub-ir 3
subject-ar 1
subjetiv-ar 1
subjug-ar 1
subjuzg-ar 51
sublev-ar 1
sublim-ar 1
sublimiz-ar 21
subministr-ar 1
subordin-ar 1
subray-ar 1
subripu-ir 42
subrog-ar 51
subsan-ar 1
subscrib-ir
  3, except

the past
participles
are subscrito
and
subscripto
subsegu-ir 59
subsist-ir 3
subsol-ar 25
substanci-ar 1
substantiv-ar 1
substitu-ir
42, plus the
past participle
substituto
substra-er 75
subtend-er
2, with the
changes in
53, plus the
past participle
substituto
subtiliz-ar 21
subtitul-ar 1
subtra-er 75
subvencion-ar ... 1
subven-ir 77
subvert-ir 71
subyug-ar 51
succed-er 2
succion-ar 1
suced-er 2,
and for its
use regarding
weather,
see 45
sucint-arse 80
sucuche-ar 1
sucumb-ir 3
sud-ar 1
suele-ar 1
suest-ar 1
sufl-ar 1
sufoc-ar 67
sufrag-ar 51
sufr-ir 3
suger-ir 71
sugestion-ar 1
suicid-arse 80
sujet-ar 1,
plus the past
participle

sujeto
sujunc-ar 1
sulc-ar 1
sulfat-ar 1
sulfil-ar 1
sulfit-ar 1
sulfur-ar 1
sulfuriz-ar 21
sum-ar 1
sumari-ar 1
sumerg-ir 3,
with the
changes in 23
suministr-ar 1
sum-ir 3
sunch-ar 1
sunsuni-ar 1
sunt-ar 1
supedit-ar 1
superabund-ar .. 1
superaliment-
ar 1
super-ar 1
supercapitaliz-
ar 21
supercomprim-
ir 3
superentend-er
2, with the
changes in 53
superit-ar 1
superoxid-ar 1
superpon-er 57
supersatur-ar 1
supervalor-ar 1
superven-ir 77
supervis-ar 1
superviv-ir 3
supin-ar 1
supirit-ar 1
suplant-ar 1
suplic-ar 67
suplici-ar 1
supl-ir 3
supon-er 57
suport-ar 1
suposit-ar 1
suprim-ir 3,
plus the past
participle
supreso

supur-ar 1
suput-ar 1
surc-ar 67
surd-ir 3
surg-ir 3,
with the
changes in 23
surmont-ar 1
surque-arse 80
surrungue-ar 1
surt-ir 3
suscit-ar 1
suscrib-ir 3,
except the
past participle
is suscrito
suspend-er 2,
plus the past
participle
suspenso
suspir-ar 1
susquine-ar 1
sustanci-ar 1
sustantiv-ar 1
sustent-ar 1
sustitu-ir 42,
plus the past
participle
sustituto
sustra-er 75
susungue-ar 1
susurr-ar 1
sutiliz-ar 21
sutur-ar 1
suvert-ir 71

t

tabale-ar 1
tabaque-ar 1
tabe-ar 1
tabell-ar 1
taberniz-ar 21
tabic-ar 67
table-ar 1
tablete-ar 1
tabul-ar 1
tacane-ar 1
tacañe-ar 1
tac-ar 67

tach-ar 1
tachon-ar 1
tacone-ar 1
tafe-ar 1
tafilete-ar 1
tagarote-ar 1
tagu-ar 1
tahure-ar 1
tailoriz-ar 21
taim-arse 9
taj-ar 1
taje-ar 1
tajone-ar 1
tajure-ar 1
talac-ar 1
taladr-ar 1
tal-ar 1
talion-ar 1
tall-ar 1
tallec-er 48
talon-ar 1
talone-ar 1
talud-ar 1
tamale-ar 67
tambale-ar 1
tamb-ar 1
tambore-ar 1
tamborile-ar 1
tamborite-ar 1
tamille-ar 1
tamiz-ar 21
tampon-ar 1
tangale-ar 1
tangane-ar 1
tang-ir 3,
with the
changes in 23
tangue-ar 1
tante-ar 1
tañ-ar 1
tañ-er 2,
with the
changes in 17
tap-ar 1
tapare-ar 1
tapeque-arse ... 80
taperuj-arse 80
tapet-ar 1
tapial-ar 1
tapi-ar 1
tapiñ-ar 1

tapiruj-arse 80
tapisc-ar 67
tapiz-ar 21
tapizc-ar 67
tapon-ar 1
tapuj-arse 80
taque-ar 1
taquigrafi-ar 9
tarace-ar 1
tarantine-ar 1
tar-ar 1
tarare-ar 1
tarasc-ar 67
taraz-ar 21
tard-ar 1
tarde-ar 1
tardec-er 48,
   and for its use
   regarding
   weather,
   see 45
tarif-ar 1
tarific-ar 1
tarj-ar 1
tarje-ar 1
tarjet-arse 80
tarjete-arse 80
tarrasc-ar 67
tarre-ar 1
tartaje-ar 1
tartale-ar 1
tartamude-ar 1
tartariz-ar 21
tasaje-ar 1
tas-ar 1
tasc-ar 67
tasque-ar 1
tast-ar 1
tatarate-ar 1
tatarati-ar 9
tatare-ar 1
tatarete-ar 1
tatem-ar 1
tatole-ar 1
tatu-ar 9
tauque-ar 1
tayloriz-ar 21
taz-ar 21
tchelac-arse 80
teatraliz-ar 21
tech-ar 1

tecle-ar 1
tedi-ar 1
tej-ar 1
tej-er 1
tel-ar 1
telautografi-ar ... 1
telecompon-
   er 57
telecomunic-
   ar 67
teledirig-ir
   3, with the
   changes in 23
telefer-ar 1
telefon-ar 1
telefone-ar 1
telegrafi-ar 9
telegui-ar 9
telepatiz-ar 21
teleproces-ar 1
televis-ar 1
tem-ar 1
tembl-ar 53
tembleque-ar 1
temblete-ar 1
tem-er 2
temoriz-ar 21
tempan-ar 1
temper-ar 1
tempest-ar 1
tempeste-ar 1,
   and for its use
   regarding
   weather,
   see 45
templ-ar 1
temporale-ar 1
temporaliz-ar ... 21
temporej-ar 1
temporiz-ar 21
tenace-ar 1
tende-ar 1
tend-er 2, with
   the changes
   in 53
tenel-ar 1
ten-er 74
tenoriz-ar 21
tens-ar 1
tentale-ar 1
tent-ar 53

teñ-ir 64,
   plus the past
   participle
   tinto
teologiz-ar 21
teoriz-ar 21
tequi-ar 1
tercere-ar 1
terci-ar 1
terebr-ar 1
tergivers-ar 1
termin-ar 1
terque-ar 1
terraplen-ar 1
terre-ar 1
terrec-er 48
ters-ar 1
tertuli-ar 1
terutere-ar 1
tes-ar 1
tesauriz-ar 21
tesoriz-ar 21
testament-ar 1
test-ar 1
testare-ar 1
testere-ar 1
testific-ar 67
testigu-ar 1
testimoni-ar 1
tetaniz-ar 21
tet-ar 1
tez-ar 21
tibi-ar 1
tich-ar 1
tifi-ar 1
tigici-ar 1
tijerete-ar 1
tild-ar 1
tilingue-ar 1
tilint-ar 1
tilinte-ar 1
till-ar 1
tim-ar 1
timb-ar 1
timbe-ar 1
timbr-ar 1
timone-ar 1
timpaniz-
   arse 21
tinc-ar 67
tindaliz-ar 21

ting-ar 1
tingl-ar 1
tinque-ar 1
tint-ar 1
tinterill-ar 1
tintin-ar 1
tintine-ar 1
tintur-ar 1
tipi-ar 1
tipific-ar 67
tiple-ar 1
tipografi-ar 9
tique-ar 1
tiramoll-ar 1
tiraniz-ar 21
tirante-ar 1
tir-ar 1
tirit-ar 1
tirone-ar 1
tirote-ar 1
tisch-ar 1
tit-ar 1
tite-ar 1
titil-ar 1
titile-ar 1
titirit-ar 1
titub-ar 1
titube-ar 1
titul-ar 1
titulariz-ar 21
tiz-ar 21
tizn-ar 1
tizone-ar 1
tlach-ar 1
to-ar 1
tob-ar 1
toc-ar 67
toch-ar 1
tocolote-ar 1
told-ar 1
toler-ar 1
tolete-ar 1
tollec-er 48
toll-er 1
toll-ir 3
tom-ar 1
ton-ar 25, and
   for its use
   regarding
   weather,
   see 45

tonc-arse 80
tongone-arse ... 80
tonific-ar 67
tononc-ar 1
tononque-ar 1
tonsur-ar 1
tonte-ar 1
tontole-ar 1
top-ar 1
tope-ar 1
topet-ar 1
topete-ar 1
topone-ar 1
toquete-ar 1
toquine-ar 1
toquite-ar 1
torc-er 22,
 plus past
 participle
 tuerto
tore-ar 1
torment-ar 1
torn-ar 1
tornasol-ar 1
torne-ar 1
torpe-ar 1
torpec-er 48
torped-ar 1
torpede-ar 1
torr-ar 1
torre-ar 1
torrefact-ar 1,
 plus the past
 participle
 torrefacto
tortole-ar 1
tortor-ar 1
tortur-ar 1
tosej-ar 1
tos-er 2
tosig-ar 51
tosique-ar 1
tost-ar 25
tostone-ar 1
totaliz-ar 21
tote-ar 1
totole-ar 1
totume-ar 1
toxic-ar 67
toz-ar 21
trabai-arse 80

trabaj-ar 1
trab-ar 1
trabuc-ar 67
tracamude-ar 1
tract-ar 1
traduc-ir 59
tra-er 75
trafag-ar 51
trafic-ar 67
trafil-ar 1
trafulc-ar 67
trag-ar 51
tragel-ar 1
tragone-ar 1
trague-ar 1
traguete-arse ... 80
traicion-ar 1
traill-ar 9
traje-ar 1
trajel-ar 1
trajin-ar 1
tralac-arse 80
tram-ar 1
trambuc-ar 67
trambuluque-
 arse 80
tramit-ar 1
tramont-ar 1
tramoy-ar 1
trampe-ar 1
trampill-ar 1
tranc-ar 67
tranque-ar 1
tranquil-ar 1
tranquiliz-ar 21
trans-ar 1
transbard-ar 1
transbord-ar 1
transcend-er
 2, with the
 changes in 53
transcrib-ir
 3, except the
 past participles
 are transcrito
 and transcripto
transcurr-ir 3
transelement-
 ar 1
transfer-ir 71
transfigur-ar 1

transflor-ar 1
transflore-ar 1
transform-ar 1
transfreg-ar 62
transfret-ar 1
transfund-ir 3
transgred-ir 4
transig-ir 3,
 with the
 changes in 23
trans-ir 3
transistoriz-
 ar 21
transit-ar 1
translimit-ar 1
transline-ar 1
transluc-irse
 82, with the
 changes in 48
transmigr-ar 1
transmit-ir 3
transmont-ar 1
transmud-ar 1
transmut-ar 1
transparent-
 arse 80
transpir-ar 1
transplant-ar 1
transpon-er 57
transport-ar 1
transtermin-ar .. 1
transubstanci-
 ar 1
transustanci-
 ar 1
transvas-ar 1
transverber-ar ... 1
transvert-ir 71
tranz-ar 21
trapace-ar 1
trapalc-arse 80
trapale-ar 1
trapalone-ar 1
trapaz-ar 21
trape-ar 1, and
 used in the
 positions in 45
trapic-ar 1
trapich-ar 1
trapiche-ar 1
trapilc-ar 1

trapisonde-ar 1
trapuje-ar 1
traque-ar 1
traqueotomiz-
 ar 21
traquete-ar 1
traquin-ar 1
trasanej-ar 1
trasañej-ar 1
trasboc-ar 67
trasbord-ar 1
trasbuc-ar 67
trascart-arse 80
trascend-er
 2, with the
 changes in 5
trascol-ar 25
trasconej-
 arse 80
trascord-arse
 80, with the
 changes in 47
trascorr-er 2
trascrib-ir 3,
 except the
 past participle
 is trascrito
trascuñ-ar 1
trascurr-ir 3
trasdobl-ar 1
trasdos-ar 1
trasdose-ar 1
trasech-ar 1
traseg-ar 62
traseñal-ar 1
trasfer-ir 71
trasfigur-ar 1
trasflor-ar 1
trasflore-ar 1
trasfoj-ar 1
trasform-ar 1
trasfreg-ar 62
trasfret-ar 1
trasfund-ir 3
trasgred-ir 4
trasgue-ar 1
trashoj-ar 1
trashum-ar 1
trasig-ar 51
traslad-ar 1
traslap-ar 1

trasline-ar 1
traslo-ar 1
trasluch-ar 1
trasluc-ir 3,
  with the
  changes in 48
trasluc-irse
  82, with the
  changes in 48
traslumbr-ar 1
trasmand-
  arse 80
trasmañan-ar 1
trasmaravill-ar .. 1
trasmat-ar 1
trasmigr-ar 1
trasmin-ar 1
trasmit-ir 3
trasmoch-ar 1
trasmont-ar 1
trasmud-ar 1
trasmut-ar 1
trasnoch-ar 1
trasnombr-ar 1
traso-ír 49
trasoñ-ar 25
trasorce-ar 1
traspal-ar 1
traspale-ar 1
traspapel-ar 1
traspapel-
  arse 80
trasparec-er 48
trasparent-
  arse 80
traspas-ar 1
traspein-ar 1
traspell-ar 1
traspill-ar 1
traspint-ar 1
traspint-arse 80
traspir-ar 1
trasplant-ar 1
traspon-er 57
trasport-ar 1
trasquil-ar 1
trasrosc-arse 67
trastab-arse 80
trastabill-ar 1
traste-ar 1
trastej-ar 1

trastel-ar 1
trastermin-ar 1
trastes-ar 1
trastig-ar 1
trastoc-ar 67
trastorn-ar 1
trastrab-arse 80
trastrabill-ar 1
trastroc-ar 76
trastumb-ar 1
trasud-ar 1
trasunt-ar 1
trasvas-ar 1
trasvasij-ar 1
trasven-arse 80
trasv-er 78
trasvert-er 2,
  with the
  changes in 53
trasvin-arse 80
trasvol-ar 25
trat-ar 1
traumatiz-ar 21
traves-ar 53
travese-ar 1
travest-ir 52
travolc-ar 25,
  with the
  changes in 67
traz-ar 21
trazum-arse 80
trebej-ar 1
treche-ar 1
trefil-ar 1
tregu-ar 1
trelac-arse 80
trem-ar 1
trem-er 2
tremol-ar 1
trencill-ar 1
trenz-ar 21
trepan-ar 1
trep-ar 1
trepic-arse 80
trepid-ar 1
tresañej-ar 1
tresdobl-ar 1
tresn-ar 1
tresquil-ar 1
trezn-ar 1
triangul-ar 1

tri-ar 9
tribu-ir 42
tribul-ar 1
tribut-ar 1
tric-ar 1
tricot-ar 1
trifurc-ar 1
trifurc-arse 67
triguer-ar 1
tril-ar 1
trill-ar 1
trim-ar 1
trin-ar 1
trincafi-ar 1
trinc-ar 67
trinch-ar 1
trinche-ar 1
trintrique-ar 1
tripart-ir 3
triplic-ar 67
triptong-ar 51
tripudi-ar 1
tripul-ar 1
triquine-ar 1
tris-ar 1
tris-arse 80
trisc-ar 67
trisec-ar 67
triseccion-ar 1
tritric-ar 67
tritur-ar 1
triunf-ar 1
triz-ar 21
trobell-ar 1
troc-ar 76
troce-ar 1
troch-ar 1
troc-ir 59
trocisc-ar 67
tromp-ar 1
trompe-ar 1
trompete-ar 1
trompez-ar 34
trompic-ar 67
trompill-ar 1
tron-ar 25,
  and for its
  use regarding
  weather,
  see 45
tronc-ar 67

tronch-ar 1
troner-ar 1
tronic-ar 1
tronque-ar 1
tronz-ar 21
trope-ar 1
tropell-ar 1
tropez-ar 34
tropic-ar 1
troquel-ar 1
trot-ar 1
trote-ar 1
trotin-ar 1
trov-ar 1
troz-ar 21
truc-ar 67
truchimane-ar ... 1
trucid-ar 1
truf-ar 1
truhane-ar 1
trujamane-ar 1
truj-ar 1
trull-ar 1
trunc-ar 67
truntune-ar 1
trunuc-ar 67
trununc-ar 67
trunuque-ar 1
truque-ar 1
truquiñ-ar 1
tuberculiniz-
  ar 21
tuberculiz-ar 21
tubuliz-ar 21
tuert-ar 1
tuerte-ar 1
tuf-ar 1
tug-ar 1
tullec-er 48
tull-ir 17
tumb-ar 1
tumbe-ar 1
tumbone-ar 1
tumefac-er
  41, except
  the past
  participles
  are
  tumefecho
  and
  tumefacto

tumultu-ar 9
tunante-ar 1
tun-ar 1
tun-arse 80
tunde-ar 1
tund-ir 3
tune-ar 1
tupi-ar 1
tup-ir 3
tuqui-ar 1
tur-ar 1
turb-ar 1
turbi-ar 1
turere-ar 1
turibul-ar 1
turific-ar 67
turn-ar 1
turne-ar 1
turque-arse 80
turr-ar 1
tus-ar 1
tusturr-ar 1
tute-ar 1
tutel-ar 1
tutque-ar 1
tutube-ar 1
tutubi-ar 1
tuz-ar 21

U

ubic-ar 67
uce-ar 1
ufan-arse 80
ufane-arse 80
uf-ar 1
ulcer-ar 1
ulere-ar 1
ulpe-ar 1
ultim-ar 1
ultraj-ar 1
ultralimit-ar 1
ultrapas-ar 1
ulul-ar 1
umbral-ar 1
unc-ir 3,
  with the
  changes in 23
undul-ar 1
ung-ir 3, with

the changes
  in 23
unific-ar 67
uniform-ar 1
uniformiz-ar 21
unimism-ar 1
un-ir 3
unison-ar 25
universaliz-ar ... 21
univoc-arse 67
unt-ar 1
uñ-ar 1
uñate-ar 1
uñete-ar 1
uñ-ir 17
up-ar 1
uraje-ar 1
urbaje-ar 1
urbaniz-ar 21
urd-ir 3
urg-ir 3, with
  the changes
  in 23, and
  used in the
  positions in 45
urraque-ar 1
us-ar 1
usucap-ir 3,
  and used in
  the positions
  in 45
usufructu-ar 9
usur-ar 1
usure-ar 1
usurp-ar 1
utiliz-ar 21
uvi-ar 1
uvioliz-ar 21
uze-ar 1

V

vac-ar 67
vaccin-ar 1
vaci-ar 9
vacil-ar 1
vacun-ar 1
vade-ar 1
vafe-ar 1
vagabunde-ar ... 1

vagamunde-ar .. 1
vag-ar 51
vague-ar 1
vah-ar 1
vahe-ar 1
vainill-ar 1
vaivene-ar 1
vaje-ar 1
val-er 2, with
  the changes
  in 68
valid-ar 1
vallade-ar 1
vall-ar 1
valon-ar 1
valone-arse 80
valor-ar 1
valore-ar 1
valoriz-ar 21
vals-ar 1
valu-ar 9
valum-ar 1
vanaglori-
  arse 80
van-arse 80
vane-ar 1
vaneg-ar 1
vapor-ar 1
vapore-ar 1
vaporiz-ar 21
vapul-ar 1
vapule-ar 1
vaque-ar 1
vaquere-ar 1
var-ar 1
vare-ar 1
varete-ar 1
vari-ar 9
varill-ar 1
varraque-ar 1
vast-ar 1
vaticin-ar 1
vecind-ar 1
ved-ar 1
veget-ar 1
vej-ar 1
veje-ar 1
vejec-er 48
vel-ar 1
velariz-ar 21
velej-ar 1

veleje-ar 1
velic-ar 67
venade-ar 1
ven-ar 1
venc-er 23
vend-ar 1
vend-er 2
vendimi-ar 1
venefici-ar 1
venen-ar 1
vener-ar 1
veng-ar 51
ven-ir 77
ventaj-ar 1
ventaje-ar 1
ventane-ar 1
vent-ar 53, and
  for its use
  regarding
  weather,
  see 45
vente-ar 1, and
  for its use
  regarding
  weather,
  see 45
ventil-ar 1
ventisc-ar 67,
  and for its use
  regarding
  weather,
  see 45
ventisque-ar 1,
  and for its use
  regarding
  weather,
  see 45
ventose-ar 1
v-er 78
veragu-arse 80
veran-ar 1
verane-ar 1
verbene-ar 1
verber-ar 1,
  and for its
  use regard-
  ing weather,
  see 45
verbose-ar 1
verde-ar 1
verdec-er 48

verdeg-ar 1
verdegue-ar 1
vergue-ar 1
verific-ar 67
verile-ar 1
veringue-
arse 80
vermene-ar 1
vernaliz-ar 21
veronique-ar 1
verraque-ar 1
verrec-er 48
verruguet-ar 1
verruguete-ar ... 1
vers-ar 1
verse-ar 1
versific-ar 67
vertebr-ar 1
vert-er 2, with
the changes
in 5
vesqu-ir 52
vest-ir 52
vet-ar 1
vete-ar 1
vez-ar 21
viaj-ar 1
vi-ar 1
viatic-ar 67
vibore-ar 1
vibr-ar 1
vicariz-ar 21
vich-ar 1
viche-ar 1
vici-ar 1
victim-ar 1
victore-ar 1
vidri-ar 1
vigi-ar 9
vigil-ar 1
vigor-ar 1
vigoriz-ar 21
vilec-er 48
vilipend-er 2
vilipendi-ar 1
viltrote-ar 1
vinagr-ar 1
vincul-ar 1
vindic-ar 67
vinteni-ar 1

viol-ar 1
violent-ar 1
vir-ar 1
virgul-ar 1
viriliz-ar 21
virute-ar 1
vis-ar 1
vise-ar 1
visibiliz-ar 21
vision-ar 1
visit-ar 1
vislumbr-ar 1
visor-ar 1
visore-ar 1
visualiz-ar 21
vitaliz-ar 21
vitaminiz-ar 21
vit-ar 1
vitogue-ar 1
vitore-ar 1
vitrific-ar 67
vitriol-ar 1
vituall-ar 1
vituper-ar 1
vivaque-ar 1
viv-ar 1
vivific-ar 67
viv-ir 3
vocaliz-ar 21
voce-ar 1
vocifer-ar 1
vocingle-ar 1
volande-ar 1
vol-ar 25
volatiliz-ar 21
volatine-ar 1
volatiz-ar 21
volcaniz-ar 21
volc-ar 25,
with the
changes in 67
vole-ar 1
volit-ar 1
volote-ar 1
volque-arse 80
volte-ar 1
voltej-ar 1
volteje-ar 1
volunt-ar 1
volv-er 47,
except the

past partici-
ple is vuelto
vomit-ar 1
vorace-ar 1
vose-ar 1
vot-ar 1
vozn-ar 1
vulcaniz-ar 21
vulg-ar 1
vulgariz-ar 21
vulner-ar 1

X

xam-ar 1
xaporc-ar 1
xapurc-ar 1
xeg-ar 1
xerocopa-ir 3
xerografi-ar 9
xilograb-ar 1
ximielg-ar 51

Y

yac-er 79
yaconiz-ar 21
yant-ar 1
yap-ar 1
yeld-ar 1
yerb-ar 1
yerbe-ar 1
yerm-ar 1
yod-ar 1
yodur-ar 1
yog-ar 1
yug-ar 51
yugul-ar 1
yunt-ar 1, plus
the past parti-
ciple yunto
yuque-ar 1
yute-ar 1
yuxtapon-er 57
yuyusc-ar 67

Z

zabord-ar 1
zaboy-ar 1
zabuc-ar 67
zabu-ir 17
zabull-ir 17
zabuque-ar 1
zacate-ar 1
zace-ar 1
zafan-arse 80
zaf-ar 1
zagual-ar 1
zaher-ir 71
zaheriz-ar 1
zahond-ar 1
zahor-ar 1
zahori-ar 1
zahum-ar 1
zajarr-ar 1
zale-ar 1
zalenque-ar 1
zall-ar 1
zalom-ar 1
zamarre-ar 1
zamarrone-ar 1
zambe-ar 1
zambuc-ar 67
zambu-ir 3
zambull-ir 17
zambut-ir 3
zambut-irse 82
zamin-ar 1
zamp-ar 1
zampe-ar 1
zampuz-ar 21
zamurg-ir 3
zancadille-ar 1
zancaje-ar 1
zangane-ar 1
zang-ar 1
zangarre-ar 1
zangolote-ar 1
zangorre-ar 1
zangote-ar 1
zanj-ar 1
zanje-ar 1
zanque-ar 1
zanquete-ar 1
zap-ar 1
zaparrastr-ar 1

What the Pattern Verbs Illustrate

Outline

Group	Page
A. Regular verbs	183
B. Verbs containing spelling changes that retain pronunciation	183
C. Irregular verbs	183
1 Vowels change	183
2 Vowels change, plus spelling changes that retain pronunciation	184
3 Consonants change	185
4 Vowels and consonants change	185
5 Vowels and consonants change, plus spelling changes that retain pronunciation	187
D. Accent mark	187
1 Accent mark is on a stressed weak vowel	187
2 Accent mark is on a stressed weak vowel, plus changes that retain pronunciation	187
E. Verbs having more than one root	187
F. Verbs customarily not used in some conjugations	189
G.Other categories of verb conjugations	189
Reflexive verbs	189
Compound verbs	189
Progressive tense	189
Passive voice	189

Description

A. Regular verbs

Category	Description	Pattern Verb #
Verbs ending in ar	No example stem. Add any stem.	1
Verbs ending in er	No example stem. Add any stem.	2
Verbs ending in ir	No example stem. Add any stem.	3

B. Verbs containing spelling changes that retain pronunciation (These are sometimes called orthographic-changing verbs.)

The change	When	Retained Sound	Pattern Verb	Translation	Pattern Verb #
c ➡ qu	before e	k	sacar	to take out	67
c ➡ z	before a, o	s or th	mecer	to rock, to swing	46
g ➡ gu	before e	hard g	pagar	to pay	51
g ➡ j	before a, o	ha	coger	to catch, to pick	23
gu ➡ g	before a, o	hard g	distinguir	to distinguish	30
gu ➡ gü	before e	gw	aguar	to dilute, to water	7
qu ➡ c	before a, o	k	delinquir	to be delinquent	29
z ➡ c	before e	s or th	cazar	to hunt	21

C. Irregular verbs

C.1 Vowels change

a ➡ i or ie, á ➡ a, e ➡ é, é ➡ e or í, ó ➡ io, y (a vowel sound) is added.
  Dar (27) (to give) is the pattern verb.

e ➡ i.
  Pedir (52) (to ask) is the pattern verb.

e ➡ i, i is deleted.
  Reñir (64) (to fight) is the pattern verb.

e ➡ i or í, e is deleted, i ➡ í.
  Reír (63) (to laugh) is the pattern verb.

e in stem ➡ ie when stressed.
  Pensar (53) (to think) is the pattern verb.

e ➡ ie when stressed, e ➡ i.
  Sentir (71) (to feel) is the pattern verb.

e is added, é ➡ e, í ➡ i, ó ➡ o, irregular past participle.
  Ver (78) (to see) is the pattern verb.

e is deleted, é ➡ e, o ➡ u or ue, ó ➡ o.
  Poder (55) (to be able) is the pattern verb.

i in stem ➠ ie when stressed.
Adquirir (5) (to acquire) is the pattern verb.

i ➠ y between two vowels, and i ➠ í when the weak vowel i is in the same syllable as a strong vowel and the weak vowel receives the stress.
Creer (26) (to believe) is the pattern verb.

i ➠ y between vowels in some instances, y is added between vowels in other instances.
Huir (42) (to flee) is the pattern verb.

i ➠ y between two vowels in some instances, y is added between vowels in other instances, as in huir (42) (to flee), and ü ➠ u before y.
Argüir (12) (to imply, to argue) is the pattern verb.

i is deleted before e or o.
Bruñir (17) (to polish) is the pattern verb.

o ➠ hue when stressed.
Oler (50) (to smell) is the pattern verb.

o ➠ ue when stressed.
Contar (25) (to count) is the pattern verb ending in ar.
Mover (47) (to move) is the pattern verb ending in er.

o ➠ ue when stressed, o ➠ u when unstressed and the following syllable contains stressed a, ie, or ió.
Dormir (31) (to sleep) is the pattern verb.

o ➠ üe when stressed. The result is a change in pronunciation from a hard g to gw.
Agorar (6) (to predict) is the pattern verb.

y (a vowel sound) is added before e in stem when e is stressed.
Errar (37) (to be mistaken) is the pattern verb.

C.2 Vowels change, plus spelling changes that retain pronunciation

e ➠ i, gu ➠ g before a or o. Seguir, the pattern verb, is conjugated like pedir (52) (to ask), plus distinguir (30) (to distinguish).
Seguir (70) (to follow) is the pattern verb.

e ➠ ie when stressed, g ➠ gu before e. Regar, the pattern verb, conjugates like pensar (53) (to think), plus pagar (51) (to pay).
Regar (62) (to water, to irrigate) is the pattern verb.

e in stem ➠ ie when stressed, z ➠ c before e. Empezar, the pattern verb, conjugates like pensar (53) (to think), plus cazar (21) (to hunt).
Empezar (34) (to begin) is the pattern verb.

o ➠ ue when stressed, c ➠ qu before e. Trocar, the pattern verb, is conjugated like mover (47) (to move), plus sacar (67) (to take out).
Trocar (76) (to exchange) is the pattern verb.

o ⟶ ue when stressed, c ⟶ z before a or o. Cocer, the pattern verb, is conjugated like mover (47) (to move), plus mecer (46) (to rock, to swing).
    Cocer (22) (to cook, to boil) is the pattern verb.

o ⟶ ue when stressed, g ⟶ gu before e. Colgar, the pattern verb, is conjugated like contar (25) (to count), plus pagar (51) (to pay).
    Colgar (24) (to hang, as a curtain) is the pattern verb.

o ⟶ ue when stressed, z ⟶ c before e. Forzar, the pattern verb, is conjugated like contar (25) (to count), plus cazar (21) (to hunt).
    Forzar (39) (to force) is the pattern verb.

o ⟶ üe when stressed, z ⟶ c before e. Avergonzar, the pattern verb, conjugates like agorar (6) (to foretell), plus cazar (21) (to hunt).
    Avergonzar (15) (to shame) is the pattern verb.

u ⟶ ue when stressed, g ⟶ gu before e.
    Jugar (44) (to play, gamble, risk) is the pattern verb.

C.3 Consonants change

c ⟶ zc before a or o.
    Nacer (48) (to be born, to bud) is the pattern verb.

c ⟶ zc or j, i is deleted.
    Producir (59) (to produce, to yield, to beat) is the pattern verb.

g is added.
    Asir (13) (to grasp) is the pattern verb.

C.4 Vowels and consonants change

a ⟶ e or u, e is deleted, b ⟶ p. The following conjugations are irregular: yo in the present tense, and yo and usted in the past (pretérito) tense.
    Saber (66) (to know, to find out) is the pattern verb.

a ⟶ e or u, e ⟶ a, o ⟶ e, b ⟶ y, delete a, e and b. Hay is the impersonal usted form. Haber, the pattern verb, like estar, ser, and tener (all called auxiliary verbs), is used with other verbs (e.g., hablar) to make compound verbs.
    Haber (40) (to have) is the pattern verb.

a ⟶ i, c ⟶ g or z, delete c or e, irregular past participle.
    Hacer (41) (to make, to do) is the pattern verb.

a ⟶ i, c ⟶ g or z, delete c or e, irregular past participle, as in hacer (41) (to make, to do), plus a regular form of the tú imperative as an alternative.
    Satisfacer (69) (to satisfy) is the pattern verb.

a ⟶ i or ie, é ⟶ e, ó ⟶ o, uv is added. Andar, the pattern verb, has some similarities to estar (38) (to be, to stand, to look).
    Andar (10) (to walk, to move, to go) is the pattern verb.

a ➡ i or ie, é ➡ e, ó ➡ o, add uv or y, accents are added in the imperative mood. Estar, the pattern verb, has some similarities to andar (10) (to walk, to move, to go). Estar, the pattern verb, like haber, ser, and tener (all called auxiliary verbs) is used with other verbs (e.g., hablar with haber) to make compound verbs.

    Estar (38) (to be) is the pattern verb.

e ➡ i, delete ec, delete i, c ➡ g or j, irregular final letter in the past (pretérito) tense of yo and usted. Decir, the pattern verb, has some similarities to predecir (58) (to predict). Decir and predecir have unusual past participles.

    Decir (28) (to say, to tell, to talk) is the pattern verb.

e ➡ i, delete i, c ➡ g or j, irregular final letter in the past (pretérito) tense of yo and usted. Predecir, the pattern verb, has some similarities to decir (28) (to say, to tell). Decir and predecir have unusual past participles.

    Predecir (58) (to predict) is the pattern verb.

e ➡ i, g ➡ j, plus an additional past participle electo.

    Elegir (32) (to elect, to choose, to select) is the pattern verb.

e ➡ ie or i, delete, i, add d or g, delete the final vowel in the tú form of the verb in the imperative mood.

    Venir (77) (to come) is the pattern verb.

e ➡ ie or i, delete e, r ➡ s, irregular ending in the yo and usted conjugations of the past (pretérito) tense.

    Querer (60) (to want, to need, to love) is the pattern verb.

e ➡ ie or u, delete e, add d or g, n ➡ v, irregular ending in the yo and usted conjugations of the past (pretérito) tense. Tener, like haber, estar, and ser (all called auxiliary verbs) is used with other verbs (e.g., hablar with haber) to make compound tenses.

    Tener (74) (to have, to own, to hold) is the pattern verb.

e is deleted, o ➡ u, add d or g, n ➡ s, irregular ending in yo and usted past (pretérito) conjugation, irregular past participle.

    Poner (57) (to put, to set, to lay, to place) is the pattern verb.

i is deleted, add d or g. Salir, the pattern verb, has some similarities to asir (13) (to grasp).

    Salir (68) (to leave, to go out) is the pattern verb.

ig or j is added, i in the ending is deleted, irregular ending in the yo and usted past (pretérito) conjugation. The present and past participles are irregular.

    Traer (75) (to bring, to carry, to wear) is the pattern verb.

ig is added, i ➡ í or y. Caer, the pattern verb, has some similarities to oír (49) (to hear).

    Caer (20) (to fall, to decline) is the pattern verb.

ig or y is added, i ➡ í or y. Oír, the pattern verb, has some similarities to caer (20) (to fall).

    Oír (49) (to hear) is the pattern verb.

C.5 Vowels and consonants change, plus spelling changes that retain pronunciation

a ⟶ u or e, b ⟶ p, c ⟶ qu before e (because of a change in the stem from "a" to "e"), e is deleted.

Caber (18) (to fit, to fit into) is the pattern verb.

D. Accent mark   An accent mark is used when a weak vowel (i or u) appears in the same syllable with a strong vowel (a, e or o) and the weak vowel is stressed, or when h (a silent letter) separates a stressed weak vowel from a strong vowel.

D.1 Accent mark is on a stressed weak vowel

i ⟶ í (or u ⟶ ú in verbs that follow the pattern of the verb actuar [to act]) when the weak vowel i (or the weak vowel u) and a strong vowel appear in the same syllable and the weak vowel is stressed.

Airar (9) (to anger, to irritate) is the pattern verb for i ⟶ í.

Actuar is not shown as a separate pattern verb. The u ⟶ ú occurs in the verb actuar in the same conjugations as the i ⟶ í occurs in the verb airar.

D.2 Accent mark is on a stressed weak vowel, plus changes that retain pronunciation

i ⟶ í when stressed, c ⟶ qu before e to retain the k sound. Ahincar, the pattern verb, conjugates like airar (9) (to anger, to irritate), plus sacar (67) (to take out).

Ahincar (8) (to urge) is the pattern verb.

i ⟶ í when stressed, g ⟶ gu before e. Cabrahigar, the pattern verb, conjugates like airar (9) (to anger, to irritate), plus pagar (51) (to pay).

Cabrahigar (19) (to pollinate, such as fruit trees by bees) is the pattern verb.

i ⟶ í when stressed, z ⟶ c before e. Enraizar, the pattern verb, conjugates like airar (9) (to anger, to irritate), plus cazar (21) (to hunt).

Enraizar (35) (to grow roots, to take root) is the pattern verb.

E. Verbs having more than one root

Pattern Verb	Other Roots	Explanation
erguir	irg (e ⟶ i)	+ gu ⟶ g before a or o.
	yerg (add y)	Erguir (36) (to become erect, to straighten up) is the pattern verb.

187

Pattern Verb	Other Roots	Explanation
ir	v, va, vay, ib, fu	+ e or i → a, i → y, í → i, ie → e, delete i or í. The verb ir has no stem; the infinitive form of the verb is a verb ending only. So roots are added in some conjugations, but not in all, in order to have a stem plus an ending. Ir has only one root in each conjugation. Ir (43) (to go) is the pattern verb.
placer	pleg (a → e, c → g) plug (a → u, c → g)	+ c → zc before a or o, g → gu before e or i to retain the hard g sound. Placer (54) (to please) is the pattern verb.
podrir and pudrir	podr and pudr	+ o → u. Podrir (56) (to rot) is the pattern verb.
raer	raig (add ig) ray (add y)	+ i → í or y. Except for the additional roots, raer is like caer (20) (to fall, to decline) and the verb roer (65) (to gnaw). Raer (61) (to scrape, to scratch, to become worn or frayed) is the pattern verb.
roer	roig (add ig) roy (add y)	+ i → í or y. Roer is conjugated like raer (61) (to scrape) except for keeping more regular roots as alternatives. Roer (65) (to gnaw) is the pattern verb.
ser	er (delete s, add er) fu (s → fu) se (add e)	+ e → é or o, plus other changes. Ser, like estar, haber, and tener (all called auxiliary verbs) is used with other verbs (e.g., hablar with haber) to make compound verbs. Ser (72) (to be) is the pattern verb.
yacer	yag (c → g) yaz (c → z) yazc (c → zc before a or o) yazg (c → zg)	Yacer (79) (to lie somewhere, to rest, e.g., cattle at night) is the pattern verb.

F. Verbs customarily not used in some conjugations

abolir (4) (to abolish, to annul) is the pattern verb.

aplacer (11) (to please, to satisfy) is the pattern verb.

atañer (14) (to concern) is the pattern verb.

balbucir (16) (to stammer) is the pattern verb.

embaír (33) (to deceive) is the pattern verb. Embaír is usually used in the same positions as abolir (4) (to abolish), plus i ➡ y between two vowels, and i ➡ í, as in creer (26) (to believe).

llover (45) (to rain) is the pattern verb. o ➡ ue. Llover, and other "impersonal verbs," some of which refer to atmospheric phenomena, typically are used only in the third person singular as shown by llover.

soler (73) (to be accustomed to [followed by a verb in the infinitive form]) is the pattern verb. o ➡ ue when stressed, as in mover (47) (to move).

G. Other categories of verb conjugations

Reflexive verbs (80, 81, 82) (sometimes called pronominal verbs). They always require use of a reflexive pronoun. The subject of the verb receives the action of the verb. In the list of 15,000 Spanish verbs, these verbs, (because they are listed in their infinitive form) end in "arse", "erse", or "irse".

Compound verbs (non-reflexive verbs follow pattern 83, reflexive verbs follow pattern 84). Compound verbs are formed by using two verbs, one of which is haber, estar, ser, or tener.

Progressive tense (non-reflexive verbs follow pattern 85, reflexive verbs follow pattern 86).

Passive voice (87). The passive voice does not have an explicit subject of the verb. The passive voice is formed by adding ser or estar to the participle of the main verb.

Pattern Verbs Contained Here
That Are Not in
Other Verb Books

Pattern Verbs Contained Here
That Are Not in
Other Verb Books

501 Spanish Verbs
abolir 4	argüir 12	balbucir 16	embaír 33	roer 65
agorar 6	atañer 14	cabrahigar ... 19	enraizar 35	trocar 76
aplacer 11	avergonzar ... 15	cocer 22	podrir 56	

Bescherelle. *El Arte de Conjugar en Español*
aplacer 11	argüir 12	atañer 14	balbucir 16	llover 45

Das Spanische Verb
agorar 6	avergonzar ... 15	embaír 33	raer 61	seguir 70
aguar 7	balbucir 16	empezar 34	regar 62	soler 73
ahincar 8	cabrahigar ... 19	enraizar 35	reír 63	trocar 76
aplacer 11	cocer 22	forzar 39	roer 65	
argüir 12	colgar 24	llover 45	sacar 67	
atañer 14	elegir 32	predecir 58	satisfacer ... 69	

Langenscheidts Verb-Tabellen Spanisch
ahincar 8	balbucir 16	empezar 34	predecir 58	seguir 70
aplacer 11	cabrahigar ... 19	enraizar 35	raer 61	trocar 76
argüir 12	cocer 22	forzar 39	regar 62	
asir 13	colgar 24	llover 45	reñir 64	
atañer 14	elegir 32	mecer 46	roer 65	
avergonzar ... 15	embaír 33	podrir 56	satisfacer ... 69	

Larousse da la Conjugación and *Larousse Verbformen Spanisch*
aplacer 11	atañer 14	creer 26	llover 45
argüir 12	balbucir 16	huir 42	soler 73

Los Quince Mil Verbos Españoles
adquirir 5	argüir 12	coger 23	empezar 34	regar 62
agorar 6	avergonzar ... 15	colgar 24	enraizar 35	sacar 67
aguar 7	cabrahigar ... 19	delinquir 29	mecer 46	seguir 70
ahincar 8	cazar 21	distinguir 30	pagar 51	trocar 76
airar 9	cocer 22	elegir 32	querer 60	

VerbiCard: Todos los Verbos Catellanos Conjugados
agorar 6	ahincar 8	cabrahigar 19	enraizar 35	trocar 76
aguar 7	aplacer 11	embaír 33	mecer 46	